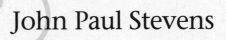

John Paul Stevens

JOHN PAUL STEVENS

An Independent Life

BILL BARNHART *and* GENE SCHLICKMAN

NORTHERN ILLINOIS

UNIVERSITY

PRESS

DeKalb

Library of Congress Cataloging-in-Publication Data

Barnhart, Bill, 1946–

John Paul Stevens : an independent life / Bill Barnhart and Gene Schlickman.

    p.   cm.

Includes bibliographical references and index.

ISBN 978-0-87580-419-4 (clothbound : alk. paper)

1. Stevens, John Paul, 1920– . 2. United States. Supreme Court—Biography. 3. Judges—United States—Biography. I. Schlickman, Eugene F., 1929– . II. Title.

KF8745.S78B37 2010

347.73'2634—dc22

[B]   2009048462

Permission has been granted on a worldwide basis by Al Franken to quote the lyrics that appear in Chapter 11 of this work.

FRONTISPIECE PHOTO: Justice John Paul Stevens outside the Supreme Court building, 1988. Photo by Abe Frajndlich © 2009.

To our wives,

Kate and Sherry,

for their contributions

measurable and immeasurable.

"Learning on the job is essential to the process of judging."

—JUSTICE JOHN PAUL STEVENS

"At the very least, these details will humanize the judge for you, so that you will be arguing to a human being instead of a chair."

—JUSTICE ANTONIN SCALIA AND BRYAN A. GARNER

Contents

Acknowledgments

Compared to the political branches of the U.S. government—Congress and the presidency—few journalists, academics, and concerned individuals study the third branch—the federal courts. Indeed, we discovered that it can't be done without a great deal of help. Many people contributed their time and talents to this book.

We are especially grateful to two people who were our unofficial Library of Congress researchers, Vicki Fredrichs and Eric Romsted. Their incredible diligence over many days in the library's public reading room in Washington, D.C., allowed us, in the comfort of our homes, to tap into the rich veins of knowledge available in the papers left by Supreme Court justices of the past. As Justice John Paul Stevens notes in this book, the record of the Court and its activities is abundant. But digging up and sorting the documents is no easy task.

As outsiders to the relatively small cohort of journalists and scholars who track the Court, early in our work we benefitted from critiques and encouragement from two individuals who know Justice Stevens well: law professors Kenneth A. Manaster of Santa Clara University School of Law and Joseph T. Thai of the University of Oklahoma College of Law. Professor Manaster was a member of the unpaid staff who investigated wrongdoing by members of the Illinois Supreme Court in 1969. His book *Illinois Justice: The Scandal of 1969 and the Rise of John Paul Stevens* is a fascinating account of a critical episode in Stevens's professional life. Professor Thai's scholarly paper "The Law Clerk Who Wrote *Rasul v. Bush*: John Paul Stevens's Influence from World War II to the War on Terror" gave us the type of link between past and present that biographers love.

Justice Stevens remained impartial—one might even say independent—throughout the process of our research and writing of this book. While he did not sit for extensive interviews, he provided anecdotes, made himself available when questions arose, and was, throughout, a gracious and interested spectator. Nellie A. Pitts and Janice Harley of the Justice Stevens chambers assisted us in every way we asked, as did the staff of the Supreme Court of the United States, especially Kathleen L. Arberg in the public information office and Lauren Morrell in the curator's office. Dozens of former Stevens law clerks granted us on-the-record interviews.

We are grateful to Justice Stevens's daughters, Kathryn S. Jedlicka, Elizabeth J. Sesemann, and Susan R. Mullen, for their insights into their father. Unfortunately, William K. Stevens, Justice Stevens's only surviving brother when we undertook this project, did not live to see the result. Bill Stevens was a supportive and helpful source.

Several members of the legal community came to our aid. In particular, Judge John M. Ferren of the District of Columbia Court of Appeals in Washington, D.C., was an enthusiastic supporter and source. His 2004 biography of Justice Wiley B. Rutledge, *Salt of the Earth, Conscience of the Court,* demonstrates the enormous value of biographical inquiry into even lesser-known individuals who put on the robes of a U.S. Supreme Court justice. When he was a young man, Collins T. Fitzpatrick, circuit executive for the U.S. Court of Appeals for the Seventh Circuit in Chicago, caddied for golfer John Paul Stevens. At present he's a busy administrator who found time to assist us with recollections and documents. Seventh Circuit Judge William J. Bauer grounded us, as only he can, in the reality of politics and culture of the Illinois judicial system. Terrence M. Murphy, executive director of the Chicago Bar Association (CBA), opened the association's archive and explained CBA governance. Richard Cardelli, of the Administrative Office of the United States Courts in Washington, D.C., gave us his recollections as a former Supreme Court reporter for The Associated Press.

We developed a great fondness for archives and archivists. At the Chicago History Museum, we were granted exclusive access to the voluminous collection of former U.S. Senator Charles H. Percy's papers. The museum also holds papers and photographs left by Justice Stevens's father. Our benefactors at the museum included Gary T. Johnson, Russell Lewis, M. Alison Eisendrath, Jennifer J. Fowle, Benn P. Joseph, Elizabeth E. Reilly, Christine S. McNulty, Leslie Martin, AnneMarie Chase, Debbie Vaughan, and Erin Tikovitsch. At the National Archives and Records Administration in College Park, Maryland, and Washington, D.C., we were assisted by Lee A. Gladwin, Barry Zerby, Fred J. Romanski, John E. Taylor, Sam Rushay, and Tom Eisinger. At other important public resources, we were aided by Daun van Ee at the Library of Congress in Washington, D.C.; David A. Hatch, historian at the National Security Agency, Fort George G. Meade, Maryland; Rowena Clough, librarian of the National Cryptologic Museum and Library at Fort Meade; Helmi Raaska and Nancy Mirshah of the Gerald R. Ford Presidential Library in Ann Arbor, Michigan; Frank H. Mackaman of the Dirksen Congressional Center in Pekin, Illinois; and Cheryl Schnirring of the Abraham Lincoln Presidential Library in Springfield, Illinois. A great resource available to the public in downtown Chicago in the Daley Center is the Cook County Law Library, which is administered by Montell Davenport and his staff.

We called on the faculties and staffs of numerous academic institutions for research materials and guidance. At the University of Chicago, where Justice Stevens was educated from kindergarten through his senior year of college, we thank Alice Schreyer, Daniel Meyer, Julia Gardner, and Christine Colburn of the Special Collections Research Center at the Regenstein Library; Abner J. Mikva, Dennis J. Hutchinson, and Judith Wright of the University of Chicago Law School; David Pervin of the University of Chicago Press; and William Harms of the University of Chicago news department. At Northwestern University in Evanston and Chicago, where Justice Stevens attended law school, we were aided by Professors Dawn Clark Netsch and Robert W. Bennett of the law school; Kevin B. Leonard and Patrick M. Quinn of the university's library; and Pat Vaughan Tremmel of the media relations office. A 2005 seminar on Justice Stevens at the Fordham University School of Law in New York City was a gold mine for us. We thank Dean William Michael Treanor, Professor Abner S. Greene, and Reference Librarian Janice E. Greer of the law school library. Hemant Kumar Sharma of the University of Tennessee Political Science Department conducted a swift and useful analysis of the Spaeth Supreme Court Database on our behalf. Anne S.K. Turkos, archivist for the University of Maryland Library, provided background on one of Justice Stevens's mentors, Leon P. Smith, Jr. Nona Kay Watt, associate librarian at the Law Library of Indiana University Maurer School of Law, opened to

XII   *Acknowledgments*

us the document and photo collection of Judge Wilbur F. Pell, Jr. Sarah I. Hartwell of the Rauner Special Collections Library at Dartmouth College unearthed an oral history by Chicago lawyer Justin A. Stanley. John Jacob at the Washington and Lee School of Law Library gave us ready access to the papers of Justice Lewis F. Powell, Jr. We also thank Adrienne Sonder of Tarlton Law Library of the University of Texas in Austin, Texas; Erin McAdams of Saint Mary's College, Notre Dame, Indiana; Steven R. Probst and Mandy Shell of the Valparaiso University School of Law, Valparaiso, Indiana; Professor John E. Hallwas of Western Illinois University, Macomb, Illinois; and Gordon Hogg of the Special Collections Library at the University of Kentucky, Lexington, Kentucky.

Reporters and officials of several media organizations rallied to our call: at the *Chicago Tribune,* Randall A. Weissman, Debra Bade, Margaret J. Walker, Denise R. Praught-Kale, and Glen Elsasser; Kristen Davis and Sharon E. Dennis of the *Chicago Sun-Times*; Bernard Judge of the *Chicago Daily Law Bulletin*; Pauline Jelinek and Gina Holland of The Associated Press; Tony Mauro of the *National Law Journal*; Linda Greenhouse of *The New York Times*; Nina Totenberg of National Public Radio; Bernie Schoenburg of *The State Journal-Register* in Springfield, Illinois; and steadfast supporter John Wasik, who introduced us to Harry R. Booth.

Individuals who provided specialized help include John Maclean, son of Norman F. Maclean; David Kahn, author of *The Codebreakers*; Terry G. Seaks, an independent researcher at the National Archives and Records Administration; Penny Circle of President Gerald R. Ford's staff; Donald O'Harra, a local historian in Colchester, Illinois; Mrs. Luther M. Swygert, wife of Judge Luther Swygert of the Seventh Circuit; artist Judie Anderson; photographer Mary Jane Grandinetti; real estate title researcher Tom O'Connor of O'Connor Title Services, Inc.; the Rev. Nina D. Grey of First Unitarian Church of Chicago; public relations specialist Christina Tus of the Hilton Chicago Hotel; Andrew and Amy R. Gelman, owners of Justice Stevens's boyhood home; George G. Rinder and William J. Glick, boyhood friends of Justice Stevens; Elisabeth G. Hair, widow of Justice Stevens's boyhood friend Sam Hair; William J. and Peggy Stevens, nephew and niece-in-law of Justice Stevens; Sherry Goodman and Richard Watt, friends of Richard James Stevens; John G. Levi, son of Edward H. Levi; lawyer Wayne W. Whalen of Skadden, Arps, Slate, Meagher & Flom; and Philippa Strum of the Woodrow Wilson International Center for Scholars in Washington, D.C.

The production of this book could not have been accomplished without the careful volunteer copyediting of Mary L. Rosner and the professional efforts of the Northern Illinois University Press staff, who believed in this project from the moment they first heard about it: J. Alex Schwartz, Sara Hoerdeman, Tracy Schoenle, Julia Fauci, Susan Bean, and Linda Manning.

John Paul Stevens

The Flag

Returning from lunch, the nine justices stepped through a parted curtain behind their bench and settled into their chairs. The session of oral arguments was about to resume on this spring day in 1989. Like his colleagues on the Supreme Court of the United States, Associate Justice John Paul Stevens knew he was in for another wry performance by a celebrity lawyer named William M. Kunstler.

Outside, the March drizzle did not deter one hundred or so protesters demonstrating for free speech and making Kunstler's case on the sidewalk in front of the marble building in Washington, D.C. Damp American flags hung limply on their poles. Inside, the next case on the docket was *Texas v. Johnson,* in which the Court considered whether a Texas law making desecration of the nation's flag a criminal offense was constitutional. Making a crime of flag-burning seems easy to divide as a public issue—free speech versus mandated respect for country and flag. It was a well-worn debate that seemed unlikely to inspire any novel thinking, let alone unscripted drama. But Justice Stevens, then sixty-eight years old and in his fourteenth year on the Court, was having his own thoughts. No one flipped a coin in the ornate courtroom that afternoon, but there often was no better way of guessing Stevens's eventual vote on the case, even after comprehensive legal briefs had been filed by lawyers on both sides.

"To watch Stevens read a brief is to blow your mind," said one of his former law clerks, David J. Barron, who used to gather with his fellow clerks around the stuffed leather chair in the clerk's room where Stevens mulled new cases. "I've never seen anyone chuckle reading a brief. [He] sees argument and counter-argument at the same time."[1] Elizabeth J. Sesemann, one of his daughters who grew up at the Stevens dinner table as well as, occasionally, in the Stevens chambers, said, "I don't think what other people believe ever influences his decisions, *ever.*"[2]

In his more than three decades on the Court, Stevens consistently has been, by far, the Court's most prolific writer of special opinions, which are concurrences and dissents in which a justice expresses a viewpoint distinct from the majority. Concurrences and dissents may not directly affect the up-or-down outcome of the case at hand as the nine justices vote, but they often influence future Court actions. Special opinions are extracurricular work for justices that help reveal a justice's idiosyncrasies and make his or her mark on the law. According to data from the Court's 1986 term through its 1998 term, Stevens was the least likely of his colleagues to sign on to, or join, another's special opinion based on the percentage of special opinions he joined. But he was the most likely to have his special opinions joined by others, suggesting that his independence has had particular value to the Court.[3]

The political process of selecting the chief justice and eight associate justices of the Supreme Court, nine individuals whose decisions affect the lives of every American, is not well suited for recognizing such constructively independent thinking and installing it on the bench. Ideologues of the left and right want candidates for judgeships to recite current bumper-sticker slogans and expect fealty to superficial doctrines. Advocates of rival judicial disciplines want to see their adherents sitting on the bench and want them to follow rules for judging gleaned from arcane law journals. Confirmation hearings and debates in the U.S. Senate, in its duty to advise and consent to presidential appointments of federal judges, have been contentious and drawn out. A president, whose power to appoint federal judges is underappreciated by political analysts and historians, wants each White House nominee to be confirmed as quickly and painlessly as possible. The confirmation hearings for Sonia Sotomayor, President Barack Obama's Supreme Court nominee in 2009, demonstrated once again that would-be justices are advised to be bland and uninformative in the face of sound and fury from political partisans. A Supreme Court that results from such confirmation strategies on the part of the Senate and White House runs the risk of impeding fresh ideas in the law, diminishing productive political debate about the judicial system, and enlarging the public's misgivings about the third branch of government.

In this light, Justice Ruth Bader Ginsburg sees an ominous drift in the Court today—a balkanization of liberals against conservatives, with less cross-fertilization of ideas and fewer opportunities for independent, Stevens-style input in the opinion-writing process.[4] If the chill Ginsburg describes intensifies among the nine chambers, the Supreme Court will diminish as a contributor to democracy. The story of one justice in this generation, John Paul Stevens, points to a better way forward. Stevens literally skipped the partisan selection spectacle—not once but twice—in obtaining his black robes as a federal appeals court judge and, five years later, an associate justice of the Supreme Court. The unique circumstances of his appointments hardly lacked dramatic political backdrops. But the outcome, a jurist with no obligations to ideologies or sponsors, suggests that the judicial selection process, not political slogans or rules for judging, determines judicial performance. The process can be reformed to improve public confidence in the courts.

One way to restore independent thinking on the Supreme Court is to have more of it. If an independent judiciary is to be maintained, biographical markers that suggest freethinking deserve more attention in the nomination and confirmation exercises. What experiences in life indicate a prospective justice will make an evenhanded review of each case and pose creative solutions, the craft of judging that is Stevens's legacy? Which elements of his or her biography suggest that a justice can avoid being a captive of popular opinion or legal fads, not to mention hardened political or legal ideologies? Justice Stevens's long life and tenure on the federal bench invite an exploration of the origins, benefits, and risks of the judicial independence he so clearly prizes. That exploration is the goal of this book, as scholars await a final accounting of Stevens's tenure.

By personal inclination and professional strategy, Stevens avoids the spotlight. He often questions lawyers during the Court's oral argument sessions, but he seldom expresses his opinion on those public occasions. In *Texas v. Johnson*, it was different: Stevens stated his opinion. But none of those present—the other justices behind the winged mahogany bench or the litigants seated before them—shared his unique view of the controversy. An independent opinion, from outside the box of standard judicial reasoning, can surprise, frustrate, and confuse but often advance the process of interpreting law. Stevens, well known among constitutional law scholars for such twists and turns, took another detour in *Texas v. Johnson*.

The flag-burning case was one of the most closely followed and controversial cases of the decade. In 1984 Gregory Lee Johnson, known to his friends as Joey, was convicted of torching a U.S. flag—"desecration of a venerated object," according to the Texas statute—on the steps of the new city hall in Dallas, where Republican Party delegates and, in Johnson's view, their warmongering friends were holding the GOP presidential nominating convention. "I didn't actually ignite it," Johnson recalled. "I put the lighter fluid on it; other people lit it up."[5] (Someone else, with a different view from Johnson's, later gathered the remains of the flag and respectfully buried them in a backyard.)

The Supreme Court received the case in 1988 on an appeal by the Dallas County district attorney after a Texas appeals court sided with Johnson. By the time of the oral argument, the case was considered a dubious legal matter by parties on both sides. The new president, George H.W. Bush, had made devotion to the flag a hot-button issue against his Democratic opponent, Michael S. Dukakis. Film footage of flag desecrations was standard fare on the evening news. But despite such notoriety, the attorney general of Texas, a Democrat, and the Republican solicitor general of the United States under the previous president, Ronald Reagan, had declined to file briefs expressing their official views on the case. Having a Texas court side with a flag burner made the appeal look like a loser. Justice Harry A. Blackmun, in a memo to his Court colleagues, called it a "difficult and distasteful little (big?) case." Justice Sandra Day O'Connor said it was "an unpleasant case." Justice Antonin Scalia, in typical fashion, was more direct, saying the case "makes me sick."[6]

Still Kunstler, an icon of the protest movement of the 1960s whose clients had included Malcolm X and the Reverend Martin Luther King, Jr., planned to have a little fun before winning his case. He noted that the Texas law referred to "a national flag." "There are many national flags," he informed the justices. "I counted seventeen national flags. Each department here in Washington has a flag."[7]

A justice asked Kunstler, "Does the Supreme Court have a flag?" "I don't know, but the Republican Party has one," Kunstler replied. All but two of the nine jurists seated above him were Republican appointees, including Stevens, who was President Gerald R. Ford's one and only Supreme Court appointment.

Stevens listened to the uncharacteristically jocular courtroom banter and held his fire. He and Kunstler had much in common although one was a fierce advocate and the other, since joining the federal bench in 1970, embraced impartiality just as fiercely. Both were Phi Beta Kappa members who had studied literature at elite private universities (Yale University for Kunstler; the University of Chicago for Stevens); both received the military's Bronze Star for work in cryptography in the Pacific during World War II. Both were influenced by brothers to change their career goals and enter law school after the war with the subsidy of the G.I. Bill. Both men had married at the time of the war and divorced their wives more than three decades later, in their fifties. Both were seasoned skeptics concerning governmental power over individuals, although Kunstler played the part openly and Stevens, just as assiduously, did not.

With his tall frame, carefully unkempt hair, and reading glasses perched atop his forehead, Kunstler was far more recognizable to Americans than any of the black-robed justices. The opposing lawyer for Dallas County, Kathi Alyce Drew, was starstruck as she prepared to make her first appearance before the high court. She will never forget "the infamous William Kunstler." "He was seventy at the time; he looked like fifty-five," she recalled. "Instead of a briefcase, he carried a backpack and was accompanied by his two young daughters. I can honestly say he was friendly, courteous and, indeed, gallant. Certainly, I have never before or since had opposing counsel kiss my hand, but that is precisely what Mr. Kunstler did."[8]

Stevens and Kunstler, who died in 1995, were contemporaries in age and in their deep-seated instinct to question and, sometimes, tease authority. In July 2003, Stevens, dressed in shorts, tennis shoes, and a flowered shirt, led two librarians from Northwestern University on a behind-the-scenes tour of the Marble Palace, as the imposing U.S. Supreme Court building is known. He looked like the Florida resident he is for most of the year, "one of the most unassuming and grandfatherly persons I have ever met," recalled archivist Patrick Quinn.[9]

Stevens's thinner grey hair and heavier glasses made the Kunstler affectation of swept-back eyeglasses a risky move. Stevens prefers a more secure statement of nonconformity—the bow tie. He is a welcoming intellectual who never imposes his brilliance as a barrier to entry to anyone inquiring about the law. His humor frequently is directed at himself, and in one of his favorite laugh lines, he frequently points out that he volunteered for the navy on December 6, 1941: "I'm sure you know how the enemy responded the following day."

Another well-told example of Stevens lore, this one from the Court's law clerk grapevine, concerns an incident during a formal ritual at the start of each term when the new clerks are allowed into the justices' private dining room to mingle with the justices. At one such reception early in Stevens's tenure, when female clerks were still a novelty, a justice assumed a clerk was part of the waitstaff and asked her to serve coffee. The clerk complied. Seeing this awkwardness unfold, Stevens came to the rescue. "Thank you for taking your turn with the coffee," he told the clerk. "I think it's my turn now." He took the coffee pot and filled the clerks' cups.[10]

The late Albert E. Jenner, Jr., a former law firm colleague, said that Stevens writes "invitingly," a word seldom associated with legal texts. Justice William J. Brennan, Jr., gave a disarming answer when asked why Stevens writes so many dissents and concurrences. "One reason Justice Stevens often writes separately, I think, is that he can." Edward I. Rothschild, a former law partner, called him "plucky." Charles H. Percy, the U.S. senator from Illinois who in 1970 promoted his initial candidacy for the federal bench, said Stevens was "a man with a hard head." Justice Ginsburg, who was an advocate in several Supreme Court cases before joining the Court in 1993, recalled being on the opposite side of the bench from Stevens: "He didn't ask a lot of questions, but the ones he asked were very sharp."[11]

In books about the Court and rare mentions in the daily press, Stevens is characterized as a hermit in a monastery. (In an odd typographical error with ecclesiastical overtones, the index of lawyer David Boies's 2004 book, *Courting Justice*, lists "Stevens, John Paul III.") Public opinion surveys in 2003 and 2005 by the research service FindLaw ranked Stevens last in the percentage of Americans who named him as a member of the Supreme Court. (More than half the respondents in both surveys could not name a single justice; Justice O'Connor, who retired in 2005, was mentioned most often.). He's never been called a pope, but he frequently is described by an almost equally misleading term, "maverick." Even after three decades on the Court, Stevens was "as ever slightly removed from his colleagues," wrote Jeffrey Toobin, relating a scene from the memorial services for the late Chief Justice William H. Rehnquist. "Respected by his colleagues, if not really known to them, Stevens always stood apart."[12]

This image is vastly overstated, in part because Stevens, like most justices in the Court's history, does not hobnob with the press. The Court's inner workings are unavailable, except when leaked by off-the-record sources among clerks or justices anonymously pitching a point of view about a controversy. Certain justices give public speeches or testify before Congress. But the persona of justices at work centers on the mornings and afternoons of oral argument, beginning on the first Monday of October and extending until early June. After years of watching Stevens in action at these sessions, Nina Totenberg, National Public Radio's Supreme Court correspondent, compared him to another bow tie–wearing Midwestern lawyer, Joseph Nye Welch. Welch, an Iowa native, was the soft-spoken, self-described country lawyer who eviscerated Senator Joseph R. McCarthy in the Senate's historic Army-McCarthy hearings in 1954.

Stevens, the youngest son of a wealthy Chicago businessman who made it big in the 1920s, shelters his autonomy the way most lawyers shelter their clients. In his privacy, he feels safe, comfortable, and free but hardly disengaged. Not an outwardly religious individual, Stevens practices obscurity as an act of faith in the ideal of judicial independence.

The Founding Fathers decided that the new nation would be better served by institutionalizing independent power in a federal judiciary as a check on the two political branches, the executive and the legislative. In Article 3 of the Constitution, the Judicial Article, they gave federal judges lifetime tenure to isolate them from the ebb and flow of political sentiment. Their effort has had mixed results, especially on the Supreme Court.

As a court of review, the Supreme Court does not try cases, elicit facts, or declare guilt or innocence. Rather, the Court most often rules on how statutes and legal precedents were applied to cases by lower courts. Although they are supposed to be removed from politics, the inclinations of justices in interpreting law on review often are cast in partisan jargon. More than a century ago, satirical Chicago newspaper columnist Finley Peter Dunne declared, in the Irish brogue of his character Mr. Dooley, "th' supreme coort follows th' iliction returns."[13] Many Americans agree.

The flip side of Mr. Dooley's observation has been equally evident in recent years. Many candidates for political office follow court decisions and appeal for votes by reacting to the third branch of government. Some denounce "out of control" judges whom they would replace. Others list precious rights that would be imperiled if his or her opponent were to win and gain influence over judicial appointments.

In this contentious atmosphere, defining, let alone defending, an independent judiciary is a difficult and thankless task. Pressures on the Court to conform to contemporary public moods constantly emerge. Interest groups, such as the conservative Federalist Society and the liberal People for the American Way, identify and groom prospective judges of their liking, press for their appointment, and attempt to shape public discourse about the judicial branch. Analysis of the

Supreme Court by the news media and scholars typically is framed in the vernacular of political partisanship: "liberals" versus "conservatives," if not actual party labels, Democrat versus Republican.

Against this tide, the goal of judicial independence, in the simplest sense, seems to mean the absence of political calculation in resolving legal controversies. Yet, as former Stevens law clerk and Princeton University law professor Christopher L. Eisgruber notes in *The Next Justice: Repairing the Supreme Court Appointments Process,* justices make political decisions all the time: "The Court is indeed political, in the sense that we cannot expect the justices to interpret and apply the Constitution unless they make controversial, ideologically identifiable judgments about the meaning of its important, abstract provisions."

Contrary to the assertion by many judges, including Stevens, that justices act like baseball umpires, who call 'em as they see 'em under well-established and well-known rules, "the Constitution's abstract language makes it impossible for judges to behave like umpires, and every justice has an ideologically identifiable voting pattern," Eisgruber writes.[14] Indeed, a politically celibate judge could easily be an irresponsible judge. Demands for term limits for justices have increased in recent years, purportedly as a way of reconnecting the Nine, as the Supreme Court justices are sometimes called, with the world beyond their elite environs.

Still, few Americans would question the importance of an independent judiciary, not beholden to political parties or popularity polls. Chief Justice John Marshall, who in 1803 established the power of the Supreme Court to review acts of Congress, declared:

> The judicial department comes home in its effects to every man's fireside; it passes on his property, his reputation, his life, his all. Is it not to the last degree important that [a judge] must be perfectly and completely independent, with nothing to influence or control him but God and his conscience. . . . I have always thought from my earliest youth till now, that the greatest scourge an angry Heaven ever afflicted upon an ungrateful and sinning people was an ignorant, a corrupt, or a dependent judiciary.[15]

The writers of the Constitution were more precise and secular. They wanted federal judges to be independent of the congress and the executive branch because they understood the pitfalls of political behavior in a democracy. In part, they established lifetime appointments as a check on voters and absolute rule by the majority. In the *Federalist Papers (No. 78)* Alexander Hamilton stressed the risks of politicizing the federal judiciary by schemes other than lifetime service: "Periodical appointments, however regulated, or by whomsoever made, would, in some way or other, be fatal to [the court's] necessary independence. If the power of making them was committed either to the Executive or legislature, there would be danger of an improper complaisance to the branch which possessed it; if to both, there would be an unwillingness to hazard the displeasure of either; if to the people, or to persons chosen by them for the special purpose, there would be too great a disposition to consult popularity, to justify a reliance that nothing would be consulted but the Constitution and the laws." The Supreme Court itself, in a 1980 decision regarding judicial pay, affirmed Hamilton's view (*U.S. v. Hubert Will*): "A Judiciary free from control by the Executive and the Legislature is essential if there is a right to have claims decided by judges who are free from potential domination by other branches of government."

Moreover, the history of the judicial article, Article 3, indicates that the authors of the Constitution did not intend federal judges to be ruling elites in the mold of English judges. Rather, the early American system of justice evolved from popular reliance on juries drawn from local communities, not aloof jurists beholden to a king or an executive. Revolution–era Americans, in effect, preferred bottom-up, not top-down, justice. Indeed, Britain realized and accommodated this demand to some extent. Many of the judges appointed by the Crown for the colonies "were drawn from the same communities whose customary law they followed and defended," according to constitutional historian Jack N. Rakove. "But that sense of local accountability, coupled with the underdeveloped condition of the colonial bar, meant that few judges brought anything resembling legal expertise to their duties. This was little cause for alarm. That judges should be independent and honest was evident; whether they needed to be repositories of refined knowledge beyond the ken of ordinary citizens was less certain."[16] Yet neither the Founding Fathers nor subsequent supporters of judicial independence have provided a checklist for selecting judges most likely to fulfill that desire. Useful indicators of independence, drawn from evidence of a judicial candidate's past, are seldom discussed. Rather, confirmation hearings and media inquiries usually seek to uncover, however indirectly, the kinship of a candidate's views to political party platforms, especially left/right positions on abortion. Inquiring into biographical evidence that might foretell nonaligned thinking on the bench seldom occurs.

Sometimes a judge's independence makes headlines because he or she appears to break the tether to political sponsors. Certainly President Dwight D. Eisenhower did not expect the bold independent streak of his most famous court appointee, Chief Justice Earl Warren, a popular California governor and powerful Republican Party insider. During Warren's tenure in the 1950s, Eisenhower and the GOP rejected the liberal shift in favor of criminal defendants and chafed in the wake of the Court's ruling against segregated schools. Appointing Warren "was the biggest damn fool thing I ever did," Eisenhower said on several occasions.[17] More recently, many Republicans felt betrayed when Justice David H. Souter, a 1990 appointee of Republican President George H.W. Bush, began voting with the Court's liberal wing—Stevens and Democratic President Bill Clinton's two appointees, Justices Ginsburg and Steven G. Breyer.

President Ford never made an issue of Justice Stevens's liberal votes in civil liberties cases. Stevens's muted identity in the press as an unpredictable moderate shielded Stevens from detailed political scrutiny. The circumstances of Stevens's appointment to the Court, in hindsight, worked remarkably well in placing a freethinker on the bench.

Three weeks before Kunstler argued on behalf of Joey Johnson, he stood before the justices to present another case, that of a rock music promoter who claimed his free speech had been preempted by a New York City noise control ordinance applied by city officials to the Rock Against Racism concert in Central Park (*Ward v. Rock Against Racism*, 1989). In this case, Stevens sided with Kunstler, joining a dissent by Justice Thurgood Marshall. Marshall wrote that the majority opinion on behalf of New York City "eviscerates the First Amendment." Kunstler, however, did not win Stevens in the next free speech case he brought.

Rarely do Supreme Court spectators enjoy multiple outbursts of mirth during oral arguments. According to the transcript, Kunstler's presentation about flag desecration in *Texas v. Johnson* beat Drew's counterargument by a score of twelve to seven in the count of interruptions for laughter. Kunstler later won the case, as well, by a five-to-four vote of the justices.

But Kunstler's sprightly confidence in stating his case on that otherwise dreary day was punctured by a soft, steady voice from the bench that drew no laughs at all. John Paul Stevens, listening quietly to William Moses Kunstler's repartee, wasn't having it. The two men's middle names may have been drawn from the Bible, but Stevens was the one in the Old Testament mood. There was no friendly smile above the trademark bow tie.

Stevens never looks for fights or opportunities to dominate attorneys attempting to state their cases in the thirty minutes normally permitted for oral argument. At first, he wasn't convinced that the Texas appeals court decision required Supreme Court review. He had voted against hearing *Texas v. Johnson* when the case arrived on appeal.

At the justices' closed-door conference after the presentations by Kunstler and Drew, Stevens at first did not state his position. He passed when his turn came to vote on which side of the case he preferred. He favored upholding the lower court's ruling in favor of Johnson because of the law's vagueness. But he told his colleagues that Oliver Wendell Holmes, one of the Court's historical heroes, probably would have agreed with Chief Justice Rehnquist's vote against Joey Johnson.

Stevens resolved the conflict by reaching deeply inside himself, an unusual step for the dispassionate judge. Gregory P. Magarian, a former clerk, called Stevens's opinion "biographical. . . . It was very much based on his experience."[18] In a 2005 interview, Stevens acknowledged that his World War II experiences in the navy "had a profound effect on my feelings about that issue. I'm still convinced I was dead right."[19] In a personal note embedded in his dissent in a similar case decided the next year (*U.S. v. Eichman,* 1990), Stevens commented, ". . . Some now have difficulty understanding the message that the flag conveyed to their parents and grandparents. . . ." There was more. His adopted son, John Joseph Stevens, a troubled young man who had brushes with the law, lived on the periphery of society after returning from military service in Vietnam. In 1996, after unsuccessful Veterans Administration hospital treatments, John died of a brain tumor possibly associated with his military service.

There was a more complex biographical element to the case. To Stevens, the nation's flag deserves protection by the government—the "state interest," he called it—because the flag, more than any other national symbol or document, best expresses Americans' freedom to dissent from majority opinions.

Stevens had no difficulty allowing Joey Johnson to express his political opinions. He did have a problem with anyone who would damage, or, in the case of Kunstler, belittle, an icon of free thought and speech. So, after another justice implored Kunstler to quit kidding around at the oral argument, Stevens calmly, almost apologetically, teed it up. He was typically but, this time, ominously courteous.[20]

> [Stevens]—Mr. Kunstler, let me ask you—and maybe this gets a little bit away from the case—do you think there is any public interest at all in any of these regulatory measures about don't display the flag in the rain or fly it upside down or so [on]. Is there any state interest at all to support that kind of legislation?
>
> [Kunstler]—I don't know, but I don't think it matters, because they're not criminal statutes. They are recommendations. . . .
>
> [Stevens]—Do you think the federal government has any power at all to, to regulate how this flag is displayed in public places?
>
> [Kunstler]—I don't believe so. I don't—I'm thinking in my mind whether they have any injunctive power.
>
> [Stevens]—There is no state interest whatsoever?

[Kunstler]—I don't see any state interest whatsoever.

[Stevens]—I feel quite differently.

Several seconds of chilly silence drained away from the strictly enforced time that Kunstler had to state his case as the day's overcast sky entered the courtroom and Kunstler realized he was about to be, in the gentlest of ways, upbraided like a schoolboy.

He tried to change the subject in the vain hope of restoring his bonhomie: "I notice that Barbara Bush wore a flag scarf, for example. There are flag bikinis. There are flags everything. There are little flags that you put into a hot dog or a meatball and then throw in the garbage pail. There are flags under the Texas statute. . . "

Kunstler was missing Stevens's point and making things worse for himself. But he summoned allies to his rescue, citing comments on his side of the argument by Justices Byron R. White and Scalia. It didn't work. The soft voice was back, even more patient than before. Kunstler faced the inevitable:

[Stevens]—Let me go back to the "any state interest at all." Do you think the military would have legitimate interest in disciplining a member of the military who showed disrespect for the flag on public occasions?

[Kunstler]—You might have a case there.

[Stevens]—*You* might have a case there.

[Kunstler]—If a person joins the army, the flag has even a more peculiar significance to people in the army. I would have problems with it. I would represent such a person [laughter] because I would think there's something First Amendment in there. . . .

[Stevens]—I was only suggesting that maybe there is some, some identifiable state interest that's involved here.

[Kunstler]—Yeah. I'm not saying—I don't want you to get the wrong—

[Stevens]—I think you're acknowledging that there is.

[Kunstler]—impression that I'd say it's totally out of reach. I'm not saying that. I'm trying to confine it to this case.

[Stevens]—You did say that.

[Kunstler] (softly)—I know I did.

It was hardly a memorable episode in the history of Supreme Court theatrics. Accounts of the *Texas v. Johnson* oral argument overlooked the Stevens/Kunstler exchanges. Afterward, Kunstler and Johnson raised clenched fists of defiance as they walked down the expansive Supreme Court plaza steps. Kathi Drew was likewise enthused. "My husband had said, 'you're not going to get Stevens to vote for you.' I think Mr. Kunstler thought that he clearly was going to get Justice Stevens's vote. And I thought, 'No, he's mine. He's not yours.'"[21]

Stevens obtained something as well. The case he didn't want to hear and didn't win became a defining expression of his judicial career. To this day, he proudly cites his *Texas v. Johnson* dissent in speeches to fellow lawyers. In case after case, he has sought to clarify and resolve competing viewpoints through the "growth and power" of the "ideas of liberty and equality," as he wrote in his *Texas v. Johnson* dissent. For every American, Stevens's dissent holds up the U.S. flag as a license, a badge of authority, a "trademark," in Eisgruber's word, for freely expressing ideas and exercising the right to dissent. No one utilizes that power more than a Supreme Court justice. In that sense, Stevens's flag-burning dissents are biographical, as are his references to military service by himself and, though unspoken, his son.

Venerating the U.S. flag as a license, badge, or trademark of free thought seems a naive rhetorical contrivance, almost like the strained examples of flag displays offered by Kunstler. Stevens is no flag-waver. He opposes a constitutional amendment to protect the flag. His suit jacket lapel is not adorned with a flag pin. But three months after the *Texas v. Johnson* oral argument, he defended the stars and stripes in a rare courtroom display of emotion.

Justices never allow their clerks or staff, not to mention the public, into their conferences following oral arguments, nor do they announce in advance when they will issue their decision in a case. The advocates on either side of *Texas v. Johnson* were not present in the courtroom when the opinion was announced. The majority opinion, written by Justice Brennan, ruled against the State of Texas: "The State's interest in preventing breaches of the peace does not support [Johnson's] conviction because Johnson's conduct did not threaten to disturb the peace. Nor does the State's interest in preserving the flag as a symbol of nationhood and national unity justify his criminal conviction for engaging in political expression."

In the five-to-four vote, Stevens's dissent was not consequential to the outcome. But those who were there, including seasoned Court watchers, among them lawyers, academics, and journalists, said the somberly paneled room resonated with the sound of Stevens speaking in dissent. In the modern Court, justices rarely read their opinions aloud. Observers on this occasion recall a red-faced man releasing something well beyond the normal logic of judicial review. "I doubt anyone who was there has forgotten the moment," wrote Edward Lazarus, who was a clerk for Justice Blackmun at the time. "No person, even a supremely rational one such as Justice Stevens, reaches every decision by the cold light of reason. . . . As he read his dissent from the bench, Stevens's voice was raw with emotion. . . . As he reached his peroration, his face was flush, his eyes just shy of tears."[22]

"I never heard in his voice that amount of emotion," said Nellie A. Pitts, the tall, striking African-American woman who had traveled with Stevens from the federal court of appeals in Chicago and for more than thirty years was his secretary and the chief operating officer of the Stevens chambers. Pitts said the memory of the *Texas v. Johnson* dissent "will always be dear to me."[23] "It was very intense," recalled another witness, former Stevens law clerk Lawrence C. Marshall. "I had not ever seen him like that, visibly angry, red in the face. I understood that I could not understand it."[24]

It was short as judicial opinions go, just nine paragraphs. He circulated two drafts among his colleagues. The usual array of case citations was boiled down to just four. Stevens conceded that the

Supreme Court, under the Fourteenth Amendment, has the power to intercede in state laws to protect or limit the freedom of speech. "If judges had the souls of computers, this might therefore be a less difficult case. It has, however, an intangible dimension that is decisive for me," Stevens wrote in the initial draft.[25]

A separate dissenting opinion, written by Chief Justice Rehnquist and joined by Justices O'Connor and White, stressed what Rehnquist called the uniquely important role of the U.S. flag as a rallying symbol throughout the nation's history. Two hundred years of American history entitled the flag to "deep awe and respect," he said. Instead, he said the Court's majority opinion meant that "the government may conscript men into the Armed Forces where they must fight and perhaps die for the flag, but the government may not prohibit the public burning of the banner under which they fight."

In his final draft, which no other justice joined, Stevens looked deeper and asked what the flag symbolizes beyond national unity and purpose:

> Even if flag burning could be considered just another species of symbolic speech under the logical application of rules that the Court has developed in its interpretation of the First Amendment in other contexts, this case has an intangible dimension that makes those rules inapplicable. . . . A country's flag . . . signifies the ideas that characterize the society that has chosen that emblem as well as the special history that has animated the growth and power of those ideas. . . . It is a symbol of freedom, of equal opportunity, of religious tolerance, and of good will for other people who share our aspirations. . . . [Flag burning] involves disagreeable conduct that, in my opinion, diminishes the value of an important national asset. . . . The ideas of liberty and equality have been an irresistible force in motivating leaders like Patrick Henry, Susan B. Anthony, and Abraham Lincoln, schoolteachers like Nathan Hale and Booker T. Washington, the Philippine Scouts who fought at Bataan, and the soldiers who scaled the bluff at Omaha Beach. If those ideas are worth fighting for—and history demonstrates that they are—it cannot be true that the flag that uniquely symbolizes their power is not itself worthy of protection from unnecessary desecration. I respectfully dissent.

He still remembers it as one of his proudest moments on the bench, although it attracted no public reaction or support from his colleagues. Speaking of the Texas case and a subsequent flag-burning/free-speech case, *U.S. v. Eichman* (1990), he told an audience just a few years ago, "I remain firmly convinced that my dissents correctly interpreted the law—as well as the original intent of the Framers—and I must confess I am rather proud of what I had to say in those opinions."[26]

"I have a very wonderful job, and I happen to like it," Stevens told a judicial conference in 2007 in Hawaii. "I'm persuaded that I'm still performing in an acceptable manner. . . . There are times when a living person available who lived through some of those things that happened a good many years ago can make a contribution that others cannot make just on the basis of the written record and the like." Stevens disclosed that he had asked one of his colleagues, whom he did not identify other than by referring to that person as "he," to tell him when he should retire because of physical or mental impairment. Stevens quipped that this justice tells him yes at times, adding, ". . . he's apt to do it when he thinks I'm dissenting from one of his opinions." Stevens turned eighty-nine in April 2009.

"It is entirely appropriate to stay out of the limelight, because after all we do say a lot in our opinions, much more than most of you are willing to read," he said. "We are unique in our openness, in our duty to explain why we make the decisions we do, and I think it's perfectly appropriate for a justice to say, I've done the best I can to explain what my job is all about. Read what I've written."[27] Stevens's political leanings on the bench are subject to curiosity even after more than three decades of opinions from his chambers. In recent years, the Republican appointee has been labeled the senior liberal. Stevens asserts that he has not become more liberal. Rather, he says, the Court has become more conservative during his tenure, making him seem more liberal by comparison. Scholars tracking Supreme Court statistics reached the opposite conclusion. With its perennial tilt toward conservative rulings, the Court's annual conservative versus liberal scores, compiled in the Harold Spaeth Supreme Court Database, are little changed since 1975, when Stevens came on board.

In his first two decades as an associate justice, Stevens was not predictably liberal or conservative on civil liberties cases. But he underwent a pronounced change in the mid-1990s, becoming a consistent liberal, as his seniority and persuasive powers increased.[28]

In recent years, as he indicated in his remarks in Hawaii, Stevens has taken to injecting personal memories about his life and his work on the Court into his opinions. In the 2007 case *Morse v. Frederick*, his dissent recalled Prohibition, which he witnessed directly when it hurt his father's hotel business: "The current dominant opinion supporting the war on drugs in general, and our antimarijuana laws in particular, is reminiscent of the opinion that supported the nationwide ban on alcohol consumption when I was a student." More forcefully, in *Parents Involved in Community Schools v. Seattle School District No. 1* (2007), he drew on his early days on the Court in dissenting from a judgment that he said set back affirmative action programs for racial minorities: "It is my firm conviction that no Member of the Court that I joined in 1975 would have agreed with today's decision."

Nostalgia aside, many of his admirers in the legal profession and politics hoped that the election of President Obama, whose home in Chicago's Hyde Park/Kenwood neighborhood is just a few blocks from Stevens's boyhood home, would stoke the Stevens fire. "If you're going to talk about his legacy, you're going to have to talk about his legacy in the Obama administration, because I think he's really coming into his own," said longtime friend and admirer Abner J. Mikva, a former member of Congress, judge of the U.S. Circuit Court of Appeals for the District of Columbia, White House counsel, and a veteran of political reform efforts in Illinois.

Mikva, interviewed midway in the Court's 2008–2009 term, said that in more than three decades as an able practitioner of judicial craft on the Supreme Court, Stevens has made a transition from solitary puzzle master to intellectual leader. Stevens has begun to embrace the Constitution as "aspirational" in its service to American progress, Mikva said. "The Court has a role in helping push the ball when it stalls," Mikva said. "I think John came to that discovery later in life."[29]

CHAPTER ONE

The Family

A remark attributed to John Stevens in his senior-year high school yearbook was prescient, even though he probably never said it. Next to each senior's photograph, along with the customary list of school achievements, editors of the University of Chicago High School Class of 1937 yearbook published an amusing "expression" by the pictured senior. For John's entry, the phrase was "Well, no, because. . . "[1]

This polite overture to dissent correctly forecast one of Stevens's inclinations as a Supreme Court justice. Actually, the student editors invented most of the quoted lines, including John's, under deadline pressure. The words were "some smartass statement" that they imagined Stevens might say.[2] They were less successful in predicting Stevens's "destiny"—kindergarten teacher.

His parents intended that their youngest son remain in the bosom of the University of Chicago as long as possible. The university, founded in 1892 by John D. Rockefeller, is the anchor of Chicago's Hyde Park/Kenwood neighborhood on the city's sprawling South Side. Known as the Chicago base of President Obama, Hyde Park/Kenwood was Stevens's boyhood hometown, a formative locale much like Savannah, Georgia, was for Justice Clarence Thomas and the Lazy B Ranch in Arizona was for retired Justice Sandra O'Connor.

Stevens's childhood years were brilliant and tragic. He entered the world on April 20, 1920, the fourth and last of four children— all boys—of Ernest James and Elizabeth Street Stevens. The event prompted his father to seek a bigger house in Hyde Park. Elizabeth, the daughter of a wealthy Michigan City, Indiana, manufacturer, had met her future husband when they were students at the University of Chicago. In May 1920, they moved to 1314 East 58th Street, as Ernest put it, "on account of an increase in the size of my family."[3]

He and Elizabeth were able to make the upgrade effortlessly. Ernest's father, James, provided the money, a gift to his son in appreciation for his work in the family business. The house Ernest bought had been built a few years earlier for James Rowland Angell, a professor of psychology at the university and a disciple of pioneer educator and philosopher John Dewey. Angell sold the home to move to New Haven, Connecticut, where he became president of Yale University and a mentor to Robert M. Hutchins, who moved from Yale to become president of the University of Chicago during Stevens's college years. The spacious, three-story house, designed by noted Chicago architect Richard Ernest Schmidt, stands directly across 58th Street from Scammon Garden, a large parcel on the university campus that at the time was cultivated as a garden by students of the university's elementary school and, when they climbed the fence, served as an unauthorized football field for the neighborhood boys.

All four Stevens brothers attended the university's private elementary school and high school, known as the Laboratory Schools. The Lab Schools, opened in 1896, were the crucible of John Dewey's famous experiments in childhood education. A few years ago, in a tribute to Stevens, one of his former law clerks wrote that Stevens "in many ways is an intellectual heir of the Lab Schools' founder, John Dewey."[4]

Ernest's oldest son, Ernest Street Stevens, married the daughter of a high official of the university. Yet the family's fortunes were not tied to the school. The considerable family wealth reflected a business dynasty, which, at the time John was born, was expanding in insurance and hotel management. Stevens reported a modest net worth when he joined the Supreme Court. But he was born into one of Chicago's wealthiest families of the Roaring Twenties. In the insular Hyde Park community, populated by struggling academics as well as poor and middle-income workers of all races, the Stevens clan was on the highest rung. Politically, the family was conservative. "My grandfather was a very staunch Republican," recalled one of Justice Stevens's nephews, speaking of Ernest J. Stevens. "When household appliances would break down, he would say they'd gone Democratic."[5]

Since the mid-1800s, John's family on the Stevens side had produced mostly boys. John was the youngest of four brothers. His father was one of two children, both sons, of James W. and Jessie Stevens. James was the second oldest of six brothers. Before John's generation, the Stevens boys were men of business. The headwater of this entrepreneurial stream was the tiny town in west central Illinois of Colchester (the first syllable is pronounced as that in "collie").

Today the region around Colchester is best known as the home of Western Illinois University in Macomb. Some years ago, residents of the area dubbed it the Kingdom of Forgotonia, a place they complained was ignored by state political leaders and state largess. But in the post–Civil War era, abundant coal and a new railroad line lifted the economy of the region and turned Colchester into a bawdy boomtown. A few miles to the east is the Spoon River country, whose tragic small town characters were authentically immortalized by Edgar Lee Masters.

Socrates Stevens, the justice's great grandfather and one of Colchester's better-educated residents in the mid-1800s, contributed the Latin motto inscribed on the town seal in 1866: *multum in parvo* (much in little). The Stevens clan comprised prominent merchants and bankers in a town of just a single square mile. John's grandfather James helped expand the family empire by marrying Jessie Smith, daughter of a rival merchant, and later merging the two enterprises.

A centennial history of Colchester remarked, "It was said that to hear of Colchester without hearing of the Stevens Bros. would be like hearing of Washington, D.C., without hearing of the government."[6] Socrates and his wife, Amanda, are buried in a family plot north of the downtown. The plot is set off by four limestone corner markers, each carved with a family symbol, a letter *S* inside a circle. The Stevens grave site is unfilled. Colchester was too small for the Stevens boys.

James's younger brother Charles, barely out of his teenage years, was the first to depart. Later, he moved to Chicago and in the late 1880s, with James and three other brothers joining him, Charles established a retail store for silk fabric and made-to-order silk dresses on Chicago's bustling State Street. At the time of the 1893 Columbian Exposition in Chicago, Charles, at age thirty-three, was a heralded member of Chicago's business elite. He became one of the "Pioneers of State Street," a group of local commercial boosters that included Potter Palmer, Marshall Field, John Shedd, Elija Peacock, and John Pirie—names still revered in the city. The "Chas. A. Stevens" store name remained a prominent State Street destination for decades.

But brother James was restless. Amid a bout of family acrimony, he and brother Edward dissolved the Chas. A. Stevens & Bros. partnership and attempted to establish their own dry goods store featuring a broader line of products. James's split with Charles was aided by lawyer Frank O. Lowden, an up-and-coming star in the Illinois Republican Party. Lowden was the husband of Florence Pullman, daughter of railroad car manufacturer George W. Pullman. He served a term as Illinois governor from 1917 to 1921, as the Stevenses' business fortunes expanded.

James and Edward became convinced that more profit could be made in money. At the time, Chicago lacked a homegrown insurance industry. Premiums paid to New York–based insurers operating in the city typically were invested outside the area, a blow to the city's pride as well as its growth. James and Edward wanted to enter the business. Attracting an enviable list of initial investors and policyholders, including merchant genius Julius Rosenwald of Sears Roebuck & Co. and Illinois Republican boss William Lorimer, James and Edward took control of Illinois Life Insurance Company, which became the basis of an enormous family fortune. Energized by success, James divorced Jessie, his wife from Colchester, and married one of his young employees, Alice Marie Bradley.

The prosperity of the Roaring Twenties expanded Chicago's skyscraper profile and offered the Stevens brothers an opportunity to invest their insurance company profits locally. On a prime parcel in Chicago's central business district, they built the lavish

La Salle Hotel. "If you want to build that hotel, although I don't know anything about the hotel business, I promise you I will devote my life to making it a success" Ernest J. Stevens, James's son, told his father in 1907.[7] Operating a 1,100-room hotel was not enough. New York City hotel magnate Ellsworth Statler convinced Ernest that a hotel twice the size of the La Salle would be a more efficient moneymaker.

With plans on the city's drawing board for a new railroad station southeast of Chicago's main business district, in 1922 James and Ernest acquired a relatively inexpensive parcel on South Michigan Avenue, well off the city center. It was a gamble that became a family monument. Father and son erected a twenty-five-story hotel with 3,000 rooms—the world's biggest hotel at the time—designed by noted architects Holabird and Roche and named The Stevens.

Its hundreds of small sleeping rooms and comprehensive guest services were designed to be a first-class stopping-off place for thousands of traveling salesmen who came and went through Chicago's train stations. Drummers could enjoy a bowling alley and a movie theater and visit one of the hotel's three physicians, including a foot doctor. For wealthier travelers, a ramp for amphibian airplanes was installed across the street on the Lake Michigan shore. The Stevens opened in May 1927, shortly after John Stevens's seventh birthday. That year, his father reported an income of $212,788 ($2.52 million in 2008 dollars) and a net worth of $3.88 million ($46 million).

Illinois Life Insurance Company was a principal investor in bonds issued by the hotel, representing a risky concentration of the insurance company's reserves. One family controlled both entities. Ernest even solicited the $10 gold pieces that his grandfather James had given to John and his brothers. "Father asked us to turn over the gold to him in return for hotel bonds," recalled one of John's older brothers, William K. Stevens.[8]

The hotel lobby was adorned with statues cast by a distant relative of the future Supreme Court justice, noted sculptor Frederick C. Hibbard. The three youngest Stevens boys, Richard, William, and John, were models for the ornamentations, "displaying the pure spirit of mischief." John and Bill were depicted playing with a large fish. The images were used for bookends in the hotel library, and miniature sculptures were given as gifts to hotel patrons. A silhouette of John's mother appeared on rims of hotel dining plates. John worked as a bellboy.

John's great uncle Charles opened a branch of his lady's apparel store in the hotel. In keeping with a favorite Stevens family pastime, golf legend Chick Evans designed an eighteen-hole chip-and-putt golf course with natural grass, the High-Ho Golf Club, on the hotel's roof. Today visitors can see the family crest—an encircled letter *S*—above entrances to the hotel, now the Chicago Hilton and Towers.

The Stevens was a clubhouse for John, his brothers, and their friends. Where else to stage birthday parties? They posed for publicity photos in the hotel's 7,500-square-foot child care center called Fairyland. Among the early celebrity hotel guests he met were Charles Lindbergh, who made his historic flight in the year the hotel opened, and Amelia Earhart, a graduate of Hyde Park High School, not far from the Stevens home. Stevens, who became a pilot, often tells the story of meeting the world famous aviatrix at a hotel banquet in her honor: "I would like to repeat the gist of her inspiring message, but actually all I can remember is her suggestion that I had no business being out so late on a school night."[9]

Johnny, as he was known, excelled at the Lab Schools, where John Dewey's controversial child-centered teaching methods held sway long after Dewey left the campus in 1904. His freewheeling, optimistic approach to education dominated the instructional method. Dewey believed that children learn best through virtually unfettered experimentation and socialization, not regimentation and memorization.

Dewey owed much to Charles Darwin's theory of evolution. Education should be an unending process of discovering and adapting, of continuous trial and error, not rote learning, he wrote. "Children simply like to do things and watch to see what happens," he said. "But this can be taken advantage of, can be directed into ways where it gives results of value, as well as be allowed to go on at random."[10] He wanted children to understand, experiment, and make judgments, not simply remember.

Doing was central to learning in a Dewey school. In John Stevens's school days, Lab School students in the elementary grades built models of the historical settings they studied. They wrote and produced plays about concepts they encountered. Everyone participated in activity-based learning centered on the school itself as a community. "The girls had to take shop, and the boys had to take home economics," recalled one of his classmates, George Rinder. During his kindergarten year, students erected a miniature village, called "Our City," depicting in three dimensions their impressions of their environment. In Dewey's system, Scammon Garden was another classroom.

Teachers were researchers as well as instructors. As part of the Lab School's scientific mission, teachers compiled data as they taught. "We had an awful lot of tests," Rinder recalled of his grade school years. Accounts by several classmates indicate that Johnny was a model Dewey child, active in sports, a favorite among his classmates, and smart. Rinder recalled Stevens in the fourth or fifth grade earning extra credit by quickly solving problems in multiplication and division on a classroom chalkboard—while writing in Roman numerals.[11]

John's father left their Hyde Park home at 4 a.m. to manage the family hotels. But at night, he read classic literature to the boys in the family's well-stocked library. His mother was a teacher, an amateur watercolor artist, and poet, active in the Chicago chapter of the National League of American Pen Women. She was a practicing Christian Scientist in a family of casual Protestants, the only one to espouse much of a religious viewpoint. John's parents typified the philosophical divide evident in many prominent urban families of the 1920s—a hard-driven businessman, devoted to efficient materialism, and a faithful vessel of spiritualism, looking for something more.

Both John's parents were inherently optimistic and practical. Despite Christian Scientist teachings against the use of medical professionals, a doctor attended John's birth. Throughout the boys' childhood, Elizabeth kept an eye on her boys and their friends, watching through a large kitchen window in the home while they played in the family's high-walled backyard.

Ernest encouraged competitive sports but only up to a point. In a businesslike letter to one of the university's football lettermen, he wrote: "I am afraid the athletic activities in which your group of boys participate is much too strenuous for John. I have therefore told him not to go out with your group again."[12] John was just seven years old.

The family dog, a black-and-tan collie named Monday, after the day of the week on which he arrived, was John's close companion and the most undisciplined member of the Stevens household. The oldest boy, Ernie, was considerably older than brothers John, William (Bill), and Richard (who was called Jim from his middle name, James). The younger trio—and Monday—belonged to a rambunctious group that attempted to govern itself, at least as far as backyard baseball was concerned.

The Stevens boys and their neighborhood friends called themselves The Alley Bunch. Boys attending the Lab School and neighborhood public schools were members. "There was no social divide, except that we knew those attending private school had families of a bit more affluence than those of us in public school," recalled boyhood friend William J. Glick.[13]

"When we'd choose sides playing baseball John was always chosen last because he was the littlest," recalled boyhood friend Sam Hair in a 1975 interview with *The Charlotte Observer*.[14] The boys' rules for backyard baseball reflected a judiciously pragmatic interpretation of baseball law:

    1—Underhand easy pitching.

    2—Indian ball.

    3—Pitcher's hands are out.

    4—Over the fence is out.

    5—If a player is on base and a hit is made, the player must go home.

    6—If home plate is touched by an opposing player holding the ball, the player on base is out.

    7—If there is any dispute, a coin must be tossed to determine the decision.

8—If the ball hits Monday on a doubtful play, the play goes over.

9—A player on base can go as far as possible on any out, except a strike-out.

10—On June 10, provided that more than 15 five-inning games have been played, and provided that one team is more than one game ahead of the other team, the losing team must buy all the sodas, malted milks, and sundaes that the winning team can eat in one hour at Kuenster's Drugstore on 57th Street.[15]

June 10 was chosen as it was the start of the Stevens family's annual vacation a few hours' drive from Hyde Park. The Stevens family summer cottage in Lakeside, Michigan, was a Tudor mansion designed by Chicago architect Stanley Fairclough. The house contained "endless shelves of books filled with stories for everyone's imagination."[16] But the outdoors beckoned the big-city boys.

Lakeside was a summer retreat for many University of Chicago faculty and staff members and other residents of Chicago's South Side. Pioneer social activist Jane Addams, founder of Chicago's Hull House settlement house, was an early member of the local club, Chikaming Country Club, where Stevens learned "how to hit a tennis ball; how to miss a golf ball." The Chikaming clubhouse is a replica of William Shakespeare's father's house. The stone fireplace just outside the clubhouse is inscribed with poetic lines by Robert Burns: "But we have meat and we can eat. So let the Lord be thanked." "I have many wonderful memories," Stevens told a meeting of Michigan lawyers. "The unforgettable taste of fresh peaches and fresh corn, the splendor of thunder and lightning over Lake Michigan; the beauty of a clear, blue sky when the wind is from the northeast after a cold front has passed through."[17]

The Lakeside home became a refuge as well as a retreat, saved from creditors when the storms of the Great Depression hit the family. The playful statues of the boys had to be salvaged from The Stevens Hotel lobby and removed to the summerhouse after Illinois Life fell into receivership and the federal government took possession of The Stevens. The family's cascade from boom to bust was swift, tragic, and public.

In April 1929, a writer for a sophisticated and short-lived magazine, *The Chicagoan,* gushed about John's father: "Among all our hotel-men, Ernest Stevens is the dreamer extraordinaire. Shortish, solidly built, square-faced, he would never seem to the casual acquaintance the type of a visionary. . . . Of all Chicago hotelmen I know, how-ever, he seems to me to have the freest imagination, to be the most poet-like in his conceptions. I am inclined to believe Ernest Stevens is the most romantic."[18] What the Stevens family experienced, beginning a few months later, was anything but romantic. Despite his parents' best efforts to shield their children, including extended trips to resorts far from the city, in the 1930s John Paul Stevens wit-nessed the dismantling of his family's business accomplishments and its withdrawal from public view.

After the stock market crash in October 1929, the reaction of the Stevens men was to continue buying shares, maintain their opti-mism, and stick to their business. For decades, they had survived economic downturns with just such resolve and emerged richer every time. In June 1932, the La Salle and Stevens hotels, facing the sudden disappearance of traveling salesmen, went into "friendly" receivership on behalf of their creditors. Ernest was permitted to remain the manager of both establishments as Chicago prepared for its 1933 Century of Progress Exhibition. Much of Chicago antici-pated a fair as an economic antidote.

But with the Depression gripping the nation, public investors and policyholders of the Illinois Life Insurance Company filed suit. They charged that the Stevenses, in their effort to bail out their hotels, illegally had diverted insurance company assets, which should have been preserved to secure insurance policy cash values and provide policy loans for financially strapped policyholders.

When Illinois Life was forced into receivership, the federal Recon-struction Finance Corporation, an emergency agency established by President Herbert Hoover in 1932 and expanded by President Franklin D. Roosevelt, became a principal creditor. John's father and grandfather, both stalwart Republicans, left their company in hock to the government.

William Randolph Hearst's censorious newspaper, the *Chicago Herald and Examiner,* smelled a scandal in the downfall of the Stevens dynasty. A narrative about a rich Chicago family that had looked after itself at the expense of the little guy was perfect material for Depression-era journalism. The story dovetailed neatly with newspaper attacks on a more prominent Chicagoan, utilities entrepreneur Samuel Insull, who was accused of defrauding ordinary investors and was vilified by President Roosevelt. Stung by the publicity, the Stevens family was shattered by a bitter rift. Ernest's brother, Raymond, was said to have opposed the scheme to divert insurance assets to the hotels. But Raymond was accused in the newspapers of taking personal loans from Illinois Life.

On a Friday night in January 1933, Cook County State's Attorney Thomas Courtney took action on 58th Street. "The Stevens children were sent to bed so they could not see their father arrested," the *Herald and Examiner* reported the next day.[19] Courtney later claimed that he staged the dramatic arrest out of fear that Ernest would become a fugitive in Europe, as the infamous Sam Insull had done. "We are the unhappy victims of the depression and thanks to the power and influence of the *Herald & Examiner* we are now being held up to the public gaze as horrible examples—formally indicted as conspirators and embezzlers," Ernest wrote to a friend soon after his arrest. "For the last three years we have been doing our utmost to save the hotels and the Illinois Life from the ravages of the Depression but conditions kept getting steadily worse and although we have sacrificed our personal fortunes in the attempt, we have failed, with what result—Discredited & indicted & arrested in my home like a vicious criminal."[20]

The trauma had just begun. Two weeks after the arrest, four men brandishing a submachine gun, two shotguns, and a revolver ransacked the Stevens home in search of cash. Ernest and Elizabeth and two of their children, William, age fifteen, and John, age twelve, as well as the family cook and two maids were herded upstairs and held in a bedroom after one of the boys was forced to open a safe in the first-floor library, according to garish newspaper accounts. The men displayed badges when they entered the home but demanded "that million you have in tomato cans."[21]

Stevens's father suspected that the men were not robbers but agents of State's Attorney Courtney who were looking for evidence without a warrant. But he took the raiders' threats seriously. "I was afraid the children would be killed" if anyone revealed the incident, he told the Hyde Park police after refusing to report the incident for three days.[22] "We never thought they were robbers," said William K. Stevens, the third oldest brother. "But we were scared at the time, because the guys had guns."[23]

In March, Grandfather James suffered a disabling stroke from which he didn't recover. A few days later, Uncle Raymond shot himself in the head with a revolver in his family mansion, called The Meadows, in the wealthy northern suburb of Highland Park. He died an hour later, leaving John's father to stand trial alone for the family's alleged crimes. Ernest sent his wife and three youngest children to resorts out of the city to avoid the headlines. John, by that time a teenager, wrote to his father regularly to report his activities. In addition to early evidence of Stevens's poor handwriting, the chatty letters often contained his small cartoonlike drawings of his head.

The Stevens family pride, so evident in the Michigan Avenue hotel, worked against Ernest as he faced a jury. The intertwined nature of the family business, commonplace among entrepreneurs of the period, presented a confusing picture that suggested self-dealing and made the formal charge—embezzlement—seem plausible. The key testimony against Ernest came from Bert J. Stookey, a former Colchester neighbor who had married into the family and moved north to become the treasurer of Illinois Life. Stookey said he pleaded with James and Ernest to honor the demands of policyholders for the cash and loans entitled to them. Both sides in the case invoked the Great Depression. The prosecutor drew an image of the rich saving themselves at the expense of the poor. The defense saw the Stevens downfall as the sad fate of upstanding entrepreneurs trying to hold things together in hard times. The jury took just five hours to declare Ernest guilty and, by doing so, nullify the Stevens family grandiosity.

The *Herald and Examiner* coverage was typically colorful and judgmental: "As the verdict was read, Stevens sat rigidly for a moment at the counsel table. His hands clasped tightly and his face turned ashen. Then he fell forward onto the table but in a moment recovered and asked his counsel, Franklin S. Stransky, chairman of the Republican State Central Committee, 'What's the next move?'"[24]

John and his oldest brother, also named Ernest, were in the courtroom when the verdict was announced in October 1933. The *Chicago Times* reported, "The defendant's head fell when he heard the verdict, but his sons Ernest Jr., [sic] and John rushed to his side."[25] A boyhood friend remembered, "John was absolutely furious."[26] "The family was furious at the way the newspapers treated our father and the way the prosecutors treated the family," said William Stevens.[27]

Their father faced ten years in prison. But the Illinois Supreme Court took a different view of the facts and law in the case and, in December 1934, overturned the verdict. "The officers of the insurance company had a right and power to loan money to the hotel company," the court declared. "In this whole record there is not one scintilla of evidence of any concealment or fraud attempted. . . . It is a far cry from a mistake in investment made in good faith to a felonious fraudulent investment made for the purpose of converting the funds of the lender to the use of the accused."[28]

Even in victory, the Stevens family faced fresh humiliation. On October 23, 1934, the reversal of Ernest's conviction shared front-page headlines in Chicago newspapers with news of the death of Depression-era bank robber Pretty Boy Floyd. The family lost the hotels. In 1936, Stevens's grandfather James died heavily in debt, leaving a spiteful first wife who declared in a newspaper interview that she never wanted to leave Colchester. His second wife promptly went on a cruise aboard the ocean liner *Queen Elizabeth*.

John Stevens was eighteen when the Illinois Life's principal offices, a beautiful stone edifice on Chicago's North Lake Shore Drive, became the home of the Seventh Circuit U.S. Court of Appeals. The court remained in the former Stevens family headquarters until 1964, just six years before Stevens joined the court.

Most of the family blamed their hard times on the Depression, newspaper scandal mongers, an ambitious prosecutor, and the Roosevelt administration's eagerness to demonize legitimate businessmen as agents in the nation's ills. A retired leader of the Church of Christ, Scientist tried to console John's mother: "Turn away from person, place and thing, because they do not exist, and let the Principle and idea unfold as your mind and body at peace and immortal," wrote Helen B. Barrett.[29] Three months after the Illinois Supreme Court exonerated Ernest Stevens, his doctor advised him to "give up all business cares for the next 90 days at least and go to some place where you can have absolute rest."[30]

A few years before his death in 2001, John's second oldest brother, Jim, authored a critical account. In an unpublished play titled "J.W.'s Pride," Jim characterized his grandfather James W. Stevens as a wheeler-dealer blinded by his love of the family name; depicted his uncle, Raymond, as an honest businessman weakened by alcoholism; and hinted that a loyal but desperate Ernest, his father, had indeed sought to escape prosecution by fleeing to Greece with his wife and four sons. In the play's penultimate scene, Raymond ("R.W.") confronts his father: "You know damn well we are guilty as sin. Loaning money to that Stevens Hotel was not only stupid, but crooked. You didn't want your darling hotel that you were so proud of to go under. Your pride and joy. Pride. Pride. Your pride has destroyed us all."[31]

Justice Stevens takes a broader view of the work of his father and grandfather. "My father [who died in 1972] had a part in contributing to the skyline of Chicago, so I'm always very proud of this city," he told a Chicago-Kent College of Law audience in Chicago in 1992.[32] One of his prize possessions is an original 1924 drawing by the legendary *Chicago Tribune* editorial cartoonist John T. McCutcheon—the artist's depiction of Chicago's future skyline, including The Stevens. As Stevens described the cartoon in a 1984 speech to the Northwestern University School of Law, "a small figure is looking up at a Chicago skyline that contains a dozen magnificent structures that were then no more than a vision of the future but are now familiar landmarks of a great city. . . . The small figure, with his arms outstretched, summarizes what is happening in Chicago at that time in one word—'Gosh!'"[33]

CHAPTER TWO

The War

As John began his college years at the University of Chicago in 1937, he was one of many young people for whom the school's leafy quadrangles represented a port in a storm. His family, like many others, was undergoing a financial reversal as the Depression persisted. At the same time, his generation watched, and in many cases joined, a hot debate over whether America's young men should be sent to fight in Europe.

John's eldest brother, Ernie, scoured the nation looking for hotel properties and even newfangled motel properties that his father might purchase and manage. In 1938, his father submitted his resignation as manager of the Hyde Park Hotel, citing his inability to turn around the hotel's money-losing operations.

Later Ernie wrote to his father from Fort Myers, Florida, where he had relocated: "You wrote very longingly about the old days when you amounted to something. Let me remind you that the only people who amounted to anything in France about 1790 got their heads chopped off for the trouble. Please DO NOT amount to anything—be part of the people rather than above the people. . . . None of us want to be millionaires. This region is full of boom time millionaires—which after all is what your Father was—but they have learned that it was an illusion. The same applies to us—we had it but since it was NEVER in cash it, too, was an illusion so we might as well forget it."[1]

One of John's college classmates, Charles H. Percy, had witnessed his father's humiliation in losing his position as a bank officer in Chicago's North Side Rogers Park neighborhood. After the bank closed, the only job Edward Percy could find was as a night clerk in a run-down hotel. Young Percy, who later became a millionaire business executive and U.S. senator from Illinois, took nearly any job he could get, including a delivery route for the *Chicago Herald and Examiner.* He also sold magazine subscriptions and peddled his mother's cookies to his newspaper customers.

As a University of Chicago undergraduate on a scholarship, Percy operated a campus laundry business, ran a food-buying cooperative for fraternity houses, invented a student recruitment system for colleges, and still managed to be a big man on campus as a star swimmer and head of the inter-fraternity council. He was a self-described indifferent student. In later years, he liked to quote university president Robert Maynard Hutchins as telling young Mr. Percy, "You're the exact kind of student that I've been trying to keep out of the university."[2]

John Stevens, on the other hand, excelled as a scholar as well as a campus celebrity. He was named the head class marshal and elected to the Phi Beta Kappa honorary fraternity of scholars. He played for the school's undefeated tennis team in 1938. He was chairman, night editor, and occasional columnist for the student newspaper, *The Daily Maroon.* Among his job titles was sports editor, an assignment that became less rigorous after Hutchins, the physically and intellectually attractive young dynamo whom the University of Chicago had hired as its president in 1929, abolished intercollegiate football at the school in Stevens's junior year. The initials JPS, which litigants and Supreme Court scholars today recognize on opinion drafts and Court memoranda, first appeared as a moniker for his student society columns and editorials in the *Maroon.*

At home, his family's self-esteem and ambition were under repair. But on campus Stevens was surrounded by individuals for whom self-doubt and modesty were not issues. Chief among them was Hutchins, whose intellectual drive sowed the early seeds of Stevens's judicial craft. When Hutchins arrived from Yale, where he had been the law school dean, Chicago's undergraduate college had a reputation as a party school populated by callow offspring of the privileged and operated by the university primarily as a source of money for its graduate schools. The stock market crash and Hutchins's ascendancy prompted a no-holds-barred self-assessment of the role of the undergraduate college by students, faculty, administrators, and trustees. Hutchins reveled in debate. During his tenure, the urge to argue and counterargue, often impolitely, became the intellectual mortar of the Gothic limestone quadrangles.

To keep the pot boiling, Hutchins brought to the campus an irascible young Columbia University scholar named Mortimer J. Adler, who immediately repelled much of the Chicago faculty, which was Hutchins's purpose in hiring Adler. Hutchins and Adler jointly taught—"argued" might be a better term—a two-year honors course that came to be known as Great Books, which was offered to a few incoming freshmen, including Stevens. The course was a grilling for unsuspecting youth, especially those who were familiar with the college's former reputation for indolence. Hutchins's "remote but kind" teaching style contrasted with that of Adler, who "slapped the table and badgered students," according to one of Hutchins's biographers, Mary Ann Dzuback. Adler "pushed students to see the 'errors' in the books and contradictions between different authors' claims to truth. Just any response by students did not suffice. One had to take a position in light of the reading and present a logical argument for it that could withstand the assault of his aggressive questioning."[3]

Students were given an oral examination to determine their "capacity to talk sensibly about what they had read," according to a history of the Hutchins era at the university by William H. McNeill. In the course, McNeill wrote, Hutchins "was simply applying the case study method of Yale Law School to different and rather more complicated texts than those lawyers studied. And his aim was what it had been in law school: to understand the argument and to assess its validity by using simple logic and careful judgment."[4]

As head of the student newspaper staff, Stevens enjoyed another benefit of the Hutchins/Adler juggernaut. Circulation of *The Daily Maroon* spiked whenever it published their opposing views on controversial issues. Nonetheless, at the start of Stevens's senior year, the newspaper's four-member board of control, chaired by Stevens, declared that it would report such campus debates but take no editorial position on worldly issues. Instead, it pledged to focus its editorial attention strictly on student affairs. This decision reflected and endorsed Hutchins's sentiments about the university as an intellectual enclave.

When the Stevens board took over, the newspaper declared, *"The Daily Maroon* for 1940–1941 will not have a platform. As yet the Board of Control stands noncommittal on the issues of the day. . . . We shall depart from traditional *Maroon* procedure this year, and devote relatively little editorial attention to the problems of the world outside the university."* The statement of editorial policy appeared on the front page of the October 1, 1940, issue below the following headline: "Police Break Up Trotskyite Meeting: Protest Ensues." The meeting had occurred a few blocks from the Stevens home on 58th Street.[5]

Stevens did not participate in protest movements, although his membership on the executive committee of the Campus Peace Council indicated a preference for Hutchins's isolationist position on the proposition of war with Germany. He seemed to be a conformist in these years, reflecting the highest expectations of administrators and teachers, a view of him that is supported in a caption written by a fellow student editor on a Stevens senior photograph in the *Maroon*. Stevens, his fellow editor wrote, "walks on water."[6]

Classmate Perez Zagorin, who by contrast was a campus rebel, recalled in an interview, "Stevens was a person who was destined for success because he was in the center. Stevens was a person who was always correct, not in the sense of being intrinsically correct but in the sense of being accepted as correct. I don't know what Stevens ever dissented from. Stevens was one who ran with the hounds, rather than the hare."[7] Zagorin, whom the Stevens board fired in 1941 from his position as a regular guest columnist due to his alleged overstatement of his relationship to the newspaper at a left-wing conference, became a distinguished professor of early modern European history.

The *Maroon*'s professed neutrality on off-campus matters did not last long. In November 1940, the board of control endorsed Democrat

Franklin Roosevelt's reelection bid over Republican Wendell Willkie, saying Willkie was less prepared to start governing than Roosevelt was to continue, even for an unprecedented third term. The editorial, like most of the editorials during Stevens's senior year, was written by Ernest S. Leiser, who became a professional journalist and later the head of CBS television news. Stevens wrote few editorials and none on off-campus issues.

Regardless of their own views on public issues, Hutchins and Adler tried to shake whatever complacency Stevens and his fellow students may have enjoyed. So did Norman Fitzroy Maclean, one of the college's most popular teachers. Maclean began graduate studies in English literature at the university in 1928. "All my life in one way or another I've spent with the really elite young,"[8] Maclean recalled. "I do not feel any compunction about [not] being courteous to all people at all times, either in the classroom or anywhere else."[9] A *Maroon* reporter described his "satanic grin covering about two-thirds of his face."[10]

Stevens calls Maclean a mentor and "my inspiration."[11] Speaking to students at the university in 1979, he credited Maclean with teaching him the skill of reading and for influencing him to study English literature. "The study of English literature, especially lyric poetry, is the best preparation for the law. He taught me to read every word of a poem," he said. "That training helped me later, when trying to decipher law statutes."[12] Stevens's lifelong affection for English literature, especially the works of William Shakespeare, reflects Maclean's influence. "I thought it was important to teach Shakespeare once a year just to keep my literary values straight, so I wouldn't be running around, as I thought a lot of academic people do, exalting some second- or third- or fourth-rater," Maclean said.[13]

The author of the short novel *A River Runs Through It* (published in 1976), Maclean was as judgmental about his students as he was about fly fishermen in his beloved Montana. "When I am fishing and look upstream and see another fisherman coming down the opposite side I wait until I see him cast and then I say to myself, 'C minus,'" he said.[14] In Maclean, Stevens encountered a man of literature who, like his father in business, had no qualms about forming judgments, articulating an opinion, and steering clear of "second-raters."

But a simple intellectual life on the University of Chicago campus was not for Stevens. As Hutchins feared, the war in Europe intruded on the university. Events, as well as his own myopia and pride, caused trouble for Hutchins, just as they had for Stevens's father and grandfather. In early January, *The Daily Maroon* board announced a change in policy:

> . . . Over that period of three months, we changed our minds. We decided that too much space was being devoted to matters of little significance, even to University students. . . . We caution our readers of course that our answers are only partial, if only because of the limited extent of our own experience. But insofar as they are correct we would be intellectual cowards if we withheld them. . . . Perhaps it is an interest in the psychology of naughty children—but nevertheless numerous people have expressed indignation at what they have felt to be our lassitude in limiting ourselves to the relatively trivial. . . .[15]

Later that month, Hutchins followed suit, ending his public silence on the war buildup. In the campus field house, students trained in infantry drills, rifle target practice, map-reading, and first aid. Professor Maclean, dubbed "Dead-eye Norman" by the *Maroon*, taught marksmanship and helped recruit students to the military. But in a nationally broadcast radio address, Hutchins flatly opposed American participation in the war in Europe and even noncombatant aid to Britain. "We are drifting into suicide," he said. Adler disagreed with equal power: "Mr. Hutchins is basing his advice to the American people—that this country should stay out of the war—on certain practical judgments and not on principles." The *Maroon* published the statements of both men in full.[16]

At the end of January, Leiser wrote a four-part editorial, "America and the War," that dissected Hutchins's radio address and faulted what Leiser called "the weakness of his position." Aid to Britain, at a minimum, and military engagement "if Britain seems doomed" are required "if we are, in truth, to discover the new moral order for which we are searching as earnestly as [Hutchins] is," Leiser wrote.[17]

Stevens's father did not want his sons in the war. After graduating in the spring of 1941, Stevens returned to campus to begin graduate studies in English. By one account published in the *Maroon,* the young scholar was quite full of himself. The newspaper reported on a campus symposium on literary and art criticism staged in conjunction with the university's fiftieth anniversary celebration. Chicago professors, including Maclean, squared off rhetorically against academics from elsewhere. Stevens, in the standing-room-only audience, apparently did not know one of the Chicago contingent, a distinguished professor of French literature named Pierre Robert Vigneron. "Johnny, having spent too much time on the *Maroon* of late years to know much about the university, had never heard of Vigneron, and wanted to know where he came from," the *Maroon* reported. "When it was explained that he was a mainstay of our French department, John was vastly relieved. 'I was wondering if they had culture someplace else,' he explained."[18]

This suggestion of youthful intellectual conceit overlooks the fact that by this time Stevens was making his first sharp break with his family and his comfortable Hyde Park environment, thanks to a popular dean at the school. Leon Perdue Smith, Jr., a native of Georgia, received his Ph.D. at the university in 1930. His dissertation was titled "The Manuscript Tradition of the Old French 'Partonopeus de Blois,'" about a late twelfth- or early thirteenth-century romance poem of unknown authorship and fragmentary existence. Smith, born in 1899, was a dashing southern gentleman, a strikingly handsome man, an accomplished flute player, and a covert talent spotter for U.S. Navy intelligence. "He was the undercover guy," Stevens recalled.[19]

Like other veterans of America's radio signal code-breaking efforts in World War I, Commander Smith had been placed at one of the nation's elite campuses to indentify and recruit smart young men into the military's secret services. Mathematicians typically gravitate to the art of breaking codes and interpreting secret messages. But, as English major Stevens discovered, philology and cryptology have much in common. In an article about a badly damaged Partonopeus manuscript fragment, Smith wrote of "solving" abbreviated words "with normal practice" and expressed a scholar's thrill of the hunt.[20] As war loomed, Smith made a speech to Chicago businessmen in which he spoke of the legendary University of Chicago literary scholar John M. Manly, an expert on Chaucer and a worldwide authority on codes and ciphers. Smith predicted that the increased speed and complexity of military engagements since World War I represented a major challenge to the tedious, time-consuming work of code-breaking and reading enemy radio messages.[21]

With Smith's encouragement, Stevens enrolled in a program that was not in the University of Chicago's syllabus. In a speech to fellow cryptanalysts in 1983, Justice Stevens called it "the Navy's restricted correspondence course in cryptography." David A. Hatch, a historian for the National Security Agency, said: "In the 1930s and early 1940s, both the Army and Navy had correspondence courses in elementary cryptology that were sent to ROTC members and otherwise promising personnel."[22] The course was less instruction than it was a way to screen for the students who were the best and brightest, "a means of recruiting," Stevens said. "On December 6, 1941, having completed [the course], I went to the Great Lakes Naval Air Station, applied for a commission and passed the physical," he said.[23]

Stints in America's secret services in World War II often led to successful careers in the public and private sectors. Justice Lewis F. Powell, Jr., with whom Stevens served for most of Powell's fifteen-year tenure on the Supreme Court, had been a senior officer in the army's communications intelligence operation in Europe, directing relations between British and America cryptanalysts. Stevens, by contrast, was a junior officer destined for unglamorous duty in a place that, after Japan's initial attack, was considered by navy brass to be a career dead end—Pearl Harbor. "I learned what really lousy coffee tastes like, and eventually came to like it," Stevens said.[24]

Soon after Stevens set off for training in Washington, D.C., he completed another step away from his parents' desires. He married Elizabeth Sheeren, known as Betty, a vibrant, quick-witted girl he had met a few summers earlier in Lakeside. Her family was from Chicago's South Side but was not part of the Hyde Park/University of Chicago crowd. And she was a Catholic.

John's oldest brother, Ernie, took the long view in attempting to ease his parents' anxiety about their youngest child's independence in love and military ambition. Ernie did not even know Betty's full name when he wrote to his father in December 1941, but he was optimistic: "Please send us Bettys [sic] real name, address etc as we need it if she is to become a member of our family. It should be obvious that since John is free, white and 21 [he] is at liberty to choose anyone he wishes for his wife, and, since we all love John . . . we will love Betty just as much as anyone he might pick out." Ernie told his father that one of the happiest couples he and his wife knew in Florida was a Methodist married to a Catholic. "So I am absolutely sure that John and Betty will be very happy together," he wrote. As witness to the deflation of the family empire, Ernie seemed pleased with the budding adventurism in his youngest brother. He wrote: "We all love John (perhaps more than any of the others since he is the youngest and in some ways more like the rest of us.)"[25]

John and Betty were married in June 1942 in Washington, D.C. U.S. Naval Reserve Ensign John Stevens had moved there earlier in the year. His letters home in the weeks after the wedding confirmed his brother's prognosis and revealed no rift in the family over the marriage. They also indicated, however, that John, who worked odd and intense hours in secret, was concerned about Betty's adjustment to a new environment away from her friends. "Betty was a little lonesome at first," Stevens wrote to his father in August 1942. "She had a hard time getting used to Washington, which is undoubtedly the most confusing city in the world anyway. But now I am quite sure she is almost as happy about everything as I am."[26]

Stevens was assigned to naval communications work. His top-secret unit was code-named OP-G-20. He remained in touch with Dean Smith, who at age forty-three became a lieutenant commander and director of naval communications—the heart of the navy's code-breaking and deciphering efforts—in the Office of the Chief of Naval Operations. According to his letters, Ensign Stevens's life in the summer of 1942 was a combination of correspondence courses in navy regulations and courses in "my specialty, but that is, of course, not for publication."[27] John's "specialty" included daily watch shifts—often beginning at midnight—analyzing the sources and destinations of Japanese radio signals, a task called traffic analysis that, in effect, amounted to reading the address, postmark, heading, and signature of a letter rather than the letter itself. Traffic analysis also recorded the frequency of messages to and from ships, planes, and naval bases. Interpreting the body of an enciphered message might be useless if the identities of the sender and recipients were unknown. Moreover, information beyond the body of a message, when collated and studied as patterns, could be more informative than the message itself. The United States essentially had broken the Japanese radio code before the war. But making actionable interpretations of Japanese signals, which were frequently altered, continued until the war in the Pacific ended.

A War Department technical manual at the time described Stevens's job this way: "Traffic analysis is the process of extracting intelligence from radio traffic, without recourse to cryptanalysis of the text. It involves analysis of traffic volume, message length, direction of flow, call signs, operating instructions and procedures, precedence, time of origin, handling receipt, circuit construction and use of cryptographic systems."[28] For example, call signs were signals that identified the sender of a radio message. Using a chart to fool their enemies, each day the Japanese would, without altering the underlying code, assign a different call sign to various units in its vast communications network throughout the Pacific theater. Understanding the system of changing call signs enabled navy communications analysts to know who was sending a particular message to whom.

By the Fourth of July 1942, Stevens was proudly in charge of one of the watches. He told his father, "one of them was not running smoothly, and since mine was the best, they put me in charge of the poor one to straighten it out. It is now functioning properly."[29] Two weeks later, he again reported home: "I am now senior to all other watch officers but one. And I am much better than he, even if I do say so myself. I'm still on watch, with three other Ensigns and two yeomen under me. We have a darn good crew and have a lot of fun together as well as doing [our] work as well as it can be done." In the same letter, Stevens said, "Last Saturday I had lunch with Lt. Cmdrs. [Leon P.] Smith and [Ralph S.] Hayes," senior navy officers in naval intelligence. "I felt very important. Dean Smith is the same friendly person he was when he was in Chicago. He has his tennis racket here and is looking for somebody to play with. I don't know if it would be worth the trouble and expense to send my racket and shorts down. I probably wouldn't play very often anyway. As you may have gathered I am concentrating a little more on golf . . . using my new clubs while Betty uses the old ones."[30]

In early 1943, Stevens left Washington to join the OP-G-20 unit in Pearl Harbor. Betty moved back to Chicago, where she joined the ranks of thousands of women, known as Rosie-the-riveters, working in industrial plants that swiftly had converted to manufacturing armaments. She took a job at the Pullman-Standard Car Co. on Chicago's far South Side. The plant, established by George Pullman to make railroad passenger cars, began shipping armaments to the British before the United States joined the war. Its products included mortars, which the British called Lizas, shells, tanks, aircraft wings, and boats used to chase submarines.

When Stevens arrived in Pearl Harbor, an unseemly wartime political feud was underway in the U.S. Navy concerning the autonomy of the Pearl Harbor communications intelligence unit, code-named Station Hypo, versus the Washington headquarters, called Station Negat. Hypo was closer to the action and less by the book in its methods. Negat was closer to the top of the military hierarchy and more practiced in playing politics. Stevens was too junior in rank to be a combatant, but he contributed to the eventual recognition of Station Hypo as a vital though nonconformist part of the Allied victory in the Pacific.

Commander Joseph J. Rochefort, a pioneer Japanese code-breaker, led the small Hypo unit working around the clock in the cramped, dank basement of a navy administration building in Pearl Harbor. (In the 1976 movie *Midway,* he was portrayed by Hal Holbrook.) After the Pearl Harbor attack, military decorum was abandoned throughout much of Pearl Harbor, nowhere more so than in the basement. Formerly spit-and-polish navy band musicians from the battleship *California,* which was sunk in the attack, found themselves reassigned to employ their musical skills in inter-preting enemy radio signals in the top-secret basement. Stevens got to know the band members. "When I arrived at Pearl, the (Hypo) unit—then known as FRUPAC [Fleet Radio Unit, Pacific]—was still in the basement," Stevens recalled. He joined an "exceptionally fine bunch of men—both officers and enlisted—who worked in the unit. . . . Many of them were musicians, having been members of the band of a battle wagon."[31]

Stevens did not get a chance to serve under Rochefort. One of the navy's few experts on the Japanese language, Rochefort had been assigned to Pearl Harbor well before the December 7 attack. Afterward he did not escape suspicion and blame-shifting toward his unit's performance in the days before the attack. In the spring of 1942, he was the leader of a masterstroke of communications deceit that fooled the Japanese and tipped the navy to Japan's move on Midway Islands—a trick that led to one of the biggest Allied victo-ries of the war. But, once again, navy brass in Washington disagreed with and resented his analysis.

Several senior officers in Station Negat plotted against Rochefort. One of his rivals even used the navy's secret intelligence code system to convey this non-mission message: "Get rid of Rochefort at all costs," according to an account published in 1985 by Edwin T. Layton.[32] Layton was a Rochefort ally and a senior communications intelligence officer in Pearl Harbor at the time of Stevens's deployment there. In early 1943, when Stevens shipped out to Pearl Harbor, Rochefort had been ousted, ordered to a new assignment in Washington. "It was another blow to our morale," recalled one officer who served in the basement. "Communications Intelligence fell into a no-man's land between the Communications Division and the Intelligence Division of the Navy Department, subject to pressures, jealousies, and petty politics of both divisions. . . . The only probable explanation of what had happened to Rochefort is that he became the victim of a Navy Department internal political coup."[33]

Rochefort refused a Negat desk job and took command of a floating dry dock in San Francisco. Staffing at Station Hypo increased in the wake of Rochefort's departure, but the veterans in the basement wondered which side the reinforcements were on. "I was conscious of it," Stevens recalled. "When I arrived there, I was sort of a newcomer from the hostile territory. There was definitely friction at that time."[34]

Despite the intellectual appeal of the work, choosing communications intelligence duty was hardly a smart career path in the navy, especially in wartime. Since before World War I, old-timers in all military branches had regarded tapping an enemy's messages as ungentlemanly. Indeed, the Federal Communications Act of 1934 prohibited the interception of radio messages from foreign countries.

More important, junior officers were expected to serve time on ships at sea during combat in order to advance in the ranks. Few graduates of the U.S. Naval Academy at Annapolis aspired to land-based assignments in such fields as communications intelligence. For one thing, men steeped in enemy codes typically were kept off ships for fear that they would be captured and forced to reveal secrets. "Intelligence duty was suitable for reservists and dilettantes, but it was just marking time for career officers for whom gunnery and navigation were surer routes to flag rank," recalled Layton.[35]

Still, radio communications intelligence-gathering became sophisticated and effective under Rochefort and other practitioners. Competition with Station Negat in the wake of the Rochefort affair energized Station Hypo, as both stations struggled to interpret the same raw data from Japanese signals. The key to being first in solving a puzzle was teamwork, recalled Robert W. Turner, one of Stevens's fellow Station Hypo junior officers. Officers and enlisted men performed identical operations on hundreds of intercepted messages, twenty-four hours a day, seven days a week. Deviations from agreed procedures destroyed the uniformity vital to uncovering statistical probabilities in signal patterns. On the other hand, the work required solitary, creative thinking in detecting novel patterns.

Turner had these recollections of FRUPAC: Traffic analysts always worked a 24-hour shift, 8 a.m. to 8 a.m., so they could report

> . . . what the Japanese Navy was doing during that 24 hours. Those were man-killing watches, with usually a 2 or 3 hour nap in the evening but sometimes, during heavy action, working through without any sleep. . . . We were not being shot at, nor did we

shoot at anyone, so our off-time diversions would have been idyllic to much of the military. However, radio intelligence and traffic analysis was a key part of it, became obsessive, and people worked inordinate hours because they just couldn't drop an idea before running it to the end.[36] . . . You had all the resources available to you; you just needed the energy and the curiosity to follow up on it. . . . You can get real excited about this stuff. You have to figure these puzzles out. . . . John was very instrumental in breaking one of the call sign systems that was used toward the end of the war.[37]

"Our routines were more informal than many in the navy," Stevens said in his 1983 speech to fellow cryptanalysts. "For example, I remember Stanley Moe, a yeoman, who was our expert in reading enemy weather traffic."[38] Nothing in the nature of the work or the ages of the men separated Stevens from the men he commanded. Rank, like other military conventions, took a backseat. Moe recalled, "He was a very pleasant individual to work with and be around. I was then a junior enlisted man, and he was a very junior officer."[39] Stevens, Moe, and another enlisted sailor, Kenny Lee, "worked together around the clock for three or four days to break a new daily-changing call sign encipherment system, with the familiar weather intercepts providing the raw material for the reconstruction of what turned out to be a very simple strip cipher," Stevens said. "I remember the incident with particular pleasure because several days after we had the whole thing figured out, we were still getting messages from Washington advising us that they had received few values [plain text interpretations]."[40] Later he recalled of Washington, "They were so far behind it was almost embarrassing."[41]

Daily typewritten reports supervised by Stevens, Turner, and other watch officers were delivered to Layton, the liaison between the navy's communications intelligence operation in Hawaii and Admiral Chester W. Nimitz, commander of the U.S. Pacific fleet. Many of the typewritten reports during Stevens's tenure contain handwritten notations in pencil and the initials JPS.

Two days before his twenty-third birthday, Stevens reviewed a message that stayed with him the rest of his life. "I happened to be on duty when the message came in advising that our pilots had bagged a peacock and two sparrows," Stevens recalled.[42] The incident went down in naval history as the Yamamoto shoot-down. Revered in Japan and respected among U.S. naval veterans, even after the war began, Admiral Isoroku Yamamoto (the peacock) commanded the Japanese combined fleet. Although he had opposed his nation's plan to wage war on the United States, he was the architect and leader of the Pearl Harbor attack and Japan's war in the Pacific. Commander Layton, who spoke Japanese and had served in Japan before the war, knew him well. The two naval officers attended kabuki theater and played bridge together. In the summer of 1937, their staffs cooperated on the search for missing aviatrix Amelia Earhart.

On April 14, 1943, FRUPAC watch officers reported fragments of a message dated April 13 that they believed disclosed a plan by Yamamoto, "the Commander-in-Chief," to fly on April 18 from his headquarters at a former Australian naval base at Rabaul on New Britain Island to visit Japanese air bases a few hours away in and around Bougainville Island in the northern Solomon Sea. After quick review, Admiral Nimitz authorized a mission to shoot down Yamamoto's plane. "I was signing the death warrant of a man I knew personally," Layton recorded in his memoir.[43] A squad of Army Air Corps twin-engine P-38 Lightnings from Guadalcanal flew 410 miles at no more than 30 feet above the ocean to intercept the bomber carrying Yamamoto and a second bomber accompanying his plane (the two sparrows). The dead commander-in-chief was found in his grounded bomber, strapped in his seat, his sword at his side.

The Yamamoto shoot-down marked the beginning of the end of Japan's military offensive. But several issues presented themselves in the wake of the incident: Yamamoto was a voice of moderation in Japan who might have helped convince his superiors to end the war before the U.S. atomic bomb attack. It was unclear whom the Allies would face as his successor. U.S. intelligence officials also worried that a successful targeting of Yamamoto would reveal the extent of U.S. penetration of Japanese radio codes. A deeper question concerned the ethics of targeting an individual for assassination in wartime. "I had mixed feelings at the time, because, on the one hand, it was an important and successful operation but, on the other hand, it was a deliberate elimination of a specific individual rather than a nameless enemy," Stevens recalled.[44]

Official recognition for the men of FRUPAC never occurred until after the war, and even then the reasons for individuals' commendations were not publicized. The secrecy that surrounded their work was as rigorous as the work itself. On October 23, 1945, more than two months after the Allied victory over the Japanese, the Office of the Chief of Naval Operations issued recommendations for commendations for personnel who had performed communications intelligence work in the OP-20-G unit. Even then, details of the commendable individuals' performances were not disclosed.

His official resume notes that Stevens is a recipient of the Bronze Star, a medal authorized by President Roosevelt in February 1944 to recognize "heroic or meritorious achievement or service" in a noncombatant role; however, the October 23, 1944, navy memorandum recommending awards to communications intelligence personnel lists Lt. John P. Stevens, U.S. Navy Reserve, as the recipient of a more prestigious noncombatant award, the Legion of Merit.[45] The higher award, established by Congress in 1942, was intended to honor "exceptionally meritorious conduct in the performance of outstanding services" by U.S. and Allied personnel. Stevens was one of only two navy reserve lieutenants among twenty-seven communications intelligence officers recommended in the memorandum for the Legion of Merit medal. Another officer recommended was Captain Joe Rochefort. Apparently, Stevens's award was downgraded slightly.

Awards aside, Stevens acknowledged that he was shaped by his nearly four-year navy experience but never elaborated on his exploits. Like many other men and women who worked in intelligence, he was reluctant to talk about the work, although most records of the period have been declassified. Still, Stevens's characterizations of his wartime experience in Hawaii reflect a sense of his unit's independent, if unheralded, spirit. "Despite occasional problems with garbles, traffic analysis . . . made significant contributions to our understanding of what the enemy was up to," he recalled in his 1983 speech to fellow cryptanalysts. "Altogether, what I saw at Pearl convinced me that the value of the work done there—both before the war started and while it was being fought—was seriously underestimated by the folks in Washington."[46]

CHAPTER THREE

The School

For all but a few of the men at Station Hypo, the job was not only accomplished by the late summer of 1945, it was over. So, it seemed, was the past. Commander Leon Perdue Smith, Jr., the expert on ancient French poetry manuscripts who had introduced Stevens to the intrigue of deciphering enemy messages, returned to his native state to become a professor of romance languages and a dean at the University of Georgia. Lt. John Stevens did not return to literature studies at the University of Chicago. Following another mentor, his brother Jim, he applied to law school.

"My decision to go to law school was profoundly influenced by a letter that my brother Jim wrote to me shortly before the end of World War II in which he commented on the intangible benefits to members of our profession," Stevens told a bar association meeting. Richard James Stevens, called Jim, had died just a few days before the speech, at age eighty-six. Citing a biography published that year by David McCullough, Stevens said Jim's advice was "hauntingly similar to that expressed in a letter written in 1761 by a young lawyer named John Adams: "Now to what higher object, to what greater character, can any mortal aspire than to be possessed of all this knowledge, well digested and ready at command, to assist the feeble and friendless, to discountenance the haughty and lawless, to procure redress to wrongs, the advancement of right, to assert and maintain liberty and virtue, to discourage and abolish tyranny and vice?"[1]

Jim graduated from the University of Chicago Law School in 1938 and began practicing law in the city later that year. His partner in his early career was Alice Greenacre, a 1911 graduate of the University of Chicago Law School and one of Chicago's few prominent female attorneys in the mid-1900s. The same year he took up his law practice, Jim married Jane Coolidge, daughter of a wealthy Chicago industrialist and Jim's Lab School sweetheart.

Jim and Jane remained in Hyde Park for their entire lives, as liberal, active, and therefore typical residents of the university's community. Jim, who as a boy was known as "the master magician" for his skills at hat tricks and more, belonged to the Civil Rights Committee of the Chicago Bar Association and the American Civil Liberties Union. He was a founder of the Chicago Memorial Association, a cooperative that provided low-cost funeral services. Jim, like John, was a skillful duplicate bridge player. Unlike John, he was an enthusiastic singer, amateur playwright, and popular stalwart of his church, the First Unitarian Church of Chicago in Hyde Park.

John chose Northwestern University School of Law, just north of Chicago's downtown, rather than the University of Chicago Law School. His father had received his law degree from Northwestern, although he never practiced law. By the end of World War II the University of Chicago Law School had been more diminished by wartime faculty absences, and its student body and library were smaller than Northwestern's. Moreover, a four-year law school curriculum, implemented shortly before the war by University of Chicago President Robert M. Hutchins, was still in place.

Hutchins wanted to broaden the education of the would-be lawyer, supplementing training based in case studies with interdisciplinary courses in psychology, constitutional history, ethics, business organization, and economic theory to provide a realistic setting for mastery of details of law as actually applied in the courts.

By contrast, Leon Green, dean of the Northwestern law school, was in the process of compressing the standard curriculum to twenty-nine months from three years, in part by adding course work to the traditionally light summer schedule. "The time factor is important," Green reasoned. "A faculty cannot have all the time it desires. Costs to university and students would be prohibitive and students would be delayed too long in entering the profession."[2] An accelerated program aimed at returning veterans enabled Stevens to complete the work in two years. Green's practical approach to his school's calendar, as well as to legal education itself, appealed to young men who had just sacrificed as much as four years in military service. So did the G.I. Bill, a government program that subsidized tuition and living expenses for veterans entering any institution of higher education, including law school, regardless of the veteran's ability to pay.

By contrast, Hutchins's attitude toward the G.I. Bill was emblematic of the University of Chicago's ivory-tower mentality. By accepting G.I. Bill subsidies, Hutchins wrote in Collier's magazine, "colleges and universities will find themselves converted into educational hobo jungles. And veterans, unable to work and equally unable to resist putting pressure on the colleges and universities, will find themselves educational hoboes."[3]

Stevens's Station Hypo mate Robert Turner, who followed him to Northwestern's law school, recalled a different postwar environment: "The veterans were serious people. There wasn't much rambunctiousness. This was very intensified work. It was a rough row, and that's what we wanted. A bunch of guys dropped out after the first semester."[4] Navy men had an advantage over army veterans, because blue navy uniforms could be retailored more readily to appropriate suits for law school than could army olive drab.

Stevens cited one hardship: Dean Green "enforced some general rules that we considered arbitrary deprivations of liberty—no card playing at all was permitted in any part of the law school, not even a few hands of bridge while we consumed the contents of our brown bags during the noon break."[5] There was no summer vacation in the two-year program. "What the 'Greatest Generation' did after the war, be it law schools, technical institutes, medical schools, etc., derived, I think, both from a sense of duty engendered by the war and an innate feeling of having to 'catch up' for the time missed from civilian pursuits," said Turner.[6]

Four years older than typical law school students, veterans were closer in age to the faculty. In many cases, faculty members were themselves just returning from wartime service to the government. "The faculty was delighted," recalled Arthur R. Seder, Jr., an air force veteran who used the G.I. Bill to attend Northwestern's law school with Stevens. Seder and Stevens were so evenly matched in their classroom performances that they were named co-editors of the school's law review, a distinction normally awarded to a single high achiever. "There was a maturing influence and one of having assumed responsibility earlier than most kids before or since," Seder said. "People were willing to stand up and talk back to the faculty, and the faculty loved it."[7]

Beyond theories of law, Professor Homer Franklin Gary, who taught real estate law and engaged actively in progressive politics in Chicago, had a practical suggestion for his students. "He said lawyers are advised to devise some distinguishing characteristic" for their professional identities, Stevens recalled. "I was conscious of the fact that John Stevens was like John Smith."[8] The name soon became John Paul Stevens.

Stevens's law schooling moved through three stages. World War II veterans in search of a boiled-down, trade school education in how to practice law were disappointed at Northwestern and other major law schools. Before he decided to follow his brother's advice, Stevens said, "I recognized that the law provides for a set of substantive rules defining standards of conduct and prescribing the punishment that may be imposed for violating those standards. In retrospect, I now realize that my first vision of the law was one that might well have been satisfied by using mathematicians and computer programmers to administer the entire system."[9]

Stevens moved beyond this first stage. But he seems to have mastered one of its basic formulas—the application of established legal precedents by way of example or analogy to novel circumstances. For the school's law journal Stevens authored an anonymous review of government price-fixing complaints against the major Hollywood motion picture studios under the Sherman Antitrust Act of 1890.

Just as an English literature student might be asked to compare and contrast one poet with another, law students are expected to place the facts of a new case in the context of relevant statutes and precedents and, if possible, to "distinguish" the current case in terms of its distinct legal features. Many years later, Stevens acknowledged his authorship of the article, saying, "I made my first attempt to understand the Sherman Act in an unsigned 'Comment' on a topic that Professor [Nathaniel L.] Nathanson had suggested to me."[10] In "Price-Fixing in the Motion Picture Industry," Stevens cited a variety of related cases and litigants from different sectors of the economy, including a drug maker; manufacturers of electric lightbulbs, tires and wallboard; railroads; and a news organization. Unbiased, thorough case analysis and statutory research are expected from law students. But even a researcher may attempt to extend the law by stretching the goalpost beyond the available precedents, just as an appellate court judge might do.

In his article, Stevens stepped into a second phase of legal studies, a thicket sometimes called judicial activism. In endorsing a recent federal court antitrust ruling against three major film studios, Stevens wrote, "In order to support the decision against these three it may be necessary to decide that the motion picture industry requires greater control than the average industry."[11] Requiring "greater control" suggests the essence of judicial activism. To this end, he cited a five-to-three decision (Justice Robert H. Jackson did not participate) by the Supreme Court in 1945, *Associated Press. v. United States.* The Court ruled that The Associated Press, an international news gathering and dissemination agency, had violated the Sherman Act by permitting member news organizations to bar competitors from membership. The ruling against AP could have rested narrowly on straightforward issues in antitrust law. But justices in the majority and minority, no doubt driven by emotions sparked by World War II, introduced an overarching theme: the role of a free press in a democracy. Stevens cited Justice Felix Frankfurter's concurring opinion, in which Frankfurter embellished the majority ruling against AP: "But in addition to being a commercial enterprise, it has a relation to the public interest unlike that of any other enterprise pursued for profit," Frankfurter wrote. He continued:

A free press is indispensable to the workings of our democratic society. The business of the press, and therefore the business of the Associated Press, is the promotion of truth regarding public matters by furnishing the basis for an understanding of them. Truth and understanding are not wares like peanuts or potatoes. And so, the incidence of restraints upon the promotion of truth through denial of access to the basis for understanding calls into play considerations very different from comparable restraints in a cooperative enterprise having merely a commercial aspect. . . . A public interest so essential to the vitality of our democratic government may be defeated by private restraints no less than by public censorship.

Justice Frank Murphy, in dissent and in sharp contrast to Frankfurter, also drew from contemporary world affairs: "The tragic history of recent years demonstrates far too well how despotic governments may interfere with the press and other means of communication in their efforts to corrupt public opinion and to destroy individual freedom. Experience teaches us to hesitate before creating a precedent in which might lurk even the slightest justification for such interference by the Government in these matters."

These remarks by both justices were far afield from the straightforward issue of the case. Ironically, Justice William O. Douglas, widely regarded as an icon of liberal judicial activism, urged restraint upon his fellow justices in his concurrence and objected to "the broader issues which have been introduced into the discussion." Despite Douglas's advice, Stevens chose Frankfurter's sweeping perspective over Murphy's equally expansive view and then applied Frankfurter's reasoning to the motion picture industry. Stevens wrote: "Motion pictures are a great potential medium for dissemination of propaganda; they play an important part in the education of the people. It is possible that a few producer-distributors could achieve extreme political as well as economic power though monopoly."[12]

For support, Stevens cited a report by the Temporary National Economic Committee, a short-lived (1938–1941) creation of liberals in Congress and the Roosevelt administration late in the Depression era. The TNEC, as it was known, was staffed to investigate the evils of monopoly and the concentration of economic power. (Roosevelt had reversed his earlier opinion favoring monopolies as potential engines of economic recovery.) Among the committee members was Thurman Arnold, FDR's head of the Antitrust Division of the Justice Department and a skillful antitrust advocate.

Stevens quoted approvingly a monograph produced for the committee as follows: "The motion picture commenced as a novel and pleasing type of entertainment, but it has evolved into an important social and cultural force. In some senses it provides a common denominator to the feelings and aspirations of an entire people. Its importance must then be measured in terms other than the conventional one of dollars and cents."[13]

A year later, Douglas authored a landmark opinion for the Court that forced the studios to divest their movie distribution operations. In *U.S. v. Paramount Pictures,* Douglas derided the studio moguls as "those who have shown such a marked proclivity for unlawful conduct." Although he probably never saw the article of his future successor, Douglas indirectly rebutted Stevens's diversion from economic themes into free speech concerns: "There is a suggestion that the hold the defendants have on the industry is so great that a problem under the First Amendment is raised. . . . The central problem presented by these cases is which [movie] exhibitors get the highly profitable first-run business. That problem has important aspects under the Sherman Act. But it bears only remotely, if at all, on any question of freedom of the press. . . . "

Stevens was still learning. At the time that he was writing the article, he was taking Professor Nathanson's course in constitutional law. Nathanson, as Stevens recalled many times later, quickly erased any hopes students might have had for easy answers or sweeping applications of legal nostrums. Stevens said the course "came to be known as 'Nate's Mystery Tour.'" Students were expected to study and comment on Supreme Court opinions concerning constitutional controversies. "When we began to feel that we had at long last perceived the underlying issue that our professor was raising with us, we assumed that he would begin to provide us with some of the answers that we could use when the time of real decision— our final examination—arrived. . . . Categorical answers, however, were not forthcoming," Stevens recalled.

Rather, Nathanson raised fresh questions arising from "outside the record that we had been required to study," Stevens said. "Instead of answers, we had been given not merely another question, but a whole new line of inquiry to be used in seeking an understanding of a Supreme Court opinion." In particular, Nathanson introduced Stevens to what would be a major element of his jurisprudence: restraint. He "taught us to beware of 'glittering generalities,'" in the process of legal reasoning, Stevens said.[14] It was the very sin that Stevens had committed in the movie industry article.

Stevens's answer to a Nathanson question in the second semester of his constitutional law class, written in a blue book examination pamphlet, reveals the halting, trial-and-error steps that the first-year law school student took in reaching, perhaps against his instincts, a third step—an appreciation for judicial restraint. The professor's final question of the three-hour exam in May 1946 was this: "Of the United States Supreme Court, it has been said: 'All its wounds have been self-inflicted.' Discuss the soundness and significance of this statement in light of the Supreme Court's history."[15]

Near the end of his allotted time, pressed to complete the test, Stevens started and rejected two approaches to the quotation, which was based on the writing of former Chief Justice Charles Evans Hughes. At first, Stevens wrote, "The gist of the quote is that by not keeping up with social change, the. . . ." He scratched out those words, which implied an activist role of the Court that would have been controversial then and now. Next, he wrote, "The Supreme Court has made decisions which formed the basis for doctrines which later had to be overruled or modified because they were originally unsound." The "self-inflicted wound" was that having to revisit issues "often provides extra work" for the Court. Stevens, probably realizing that this utilitarian argument missed the point of the question, deleted this paragraph with an *X*.

Starting on a fresh page, with minutes ticking down, Stevens, who had just turned twenty-six, crafted his final answer. He listed examples of "wounds" to the Court's reputation caused by the Court when it reached beyond the narrow particulars of a case to impose what his professor had called "glittering generalities." First, he cited the tragic legacy of Chief Justice Roger B. Taney, an appointee of President Andrew Jackson who led the Court from 1836 to 1864 in a largely pragmatic and effective manner. Like the work of Taney's predecessor, the legendary Chief Justice John Marshall, "most of [the decisions] during Taney's [career as chief] also supported the fine standing of the court," Stevens wrote. He continued: "Probably because he wanted to shy away from controversies which threatened great harm to the court, Taney started the 'political questions' doctrine in *Luther v. Borden*"—an 1849 case in which the Court declared that certain issues are best decided by the political process through legislatures and the elected executive branch of government, not the unelected judicial branch. As Stevens was writing, Taney's political questions doctrine was not a purely academic issue at Northwestern University. The Supreme Court was considering a case brought by one of the university's political science professors, Kenneth W. Colegrove, who asserted that Illinois's method of apportioning legislative districts, including congressional districts, was an unconstitutional violation of the right to vote. In June 1946, with only seven justices on the bench, the Court voted four-to-three to reject the professor's claim. In his opinion for the Court, Justice Frankfurter invoked the Taney political questions doctrine.

Unfortunately for the nation and for Taney's place in history, Taney violated his own doctrine in the infamous case *Scott v. Sandford* of 1857. Stevens wrote: "Towards the end of his career, however, Taney's court was responsible for the greatest 'wound' the court ever suffered." Dred Scott was a slave owned by Dr. John Emerson, a U.S. Army surgeon. Emerson took Scott with him to free-soil areas of Illinois and the Wisconsin territory. But Scott lived in slaveholding Missouri when Emerson died. As was common at the time, the slave sued for his freedom in state court, saying he had gained his freedom when he lived in free-soil regions. Scott won. But Emerson's relatives appealed, and the Missouri Supreme Court rejected his claim. Scott then sued for his freedom in federal court. The Taney Court upheld the jurisdiction of the Missouri Supreme Court in the matter. But Taney's opinion went much further, endorsing extraneous claims by Emerson's relatives: Scott was not a person entitled to sue in federal court, and his residence in free-soil territories did not represent freedom because the Missouri Compromise, an 1820 act of Congress that established free territories, was an unconstitutional denial of property rights. The ruling enflamed the North and helped precipitate the Civil War.

"In the Dred Scott decision, because of the unfortunate decision to discuss the merits of the Mo. Compromise when the case had been decided on the jurisdictional issue, this court provoked a tremendous volume of hostile criticism," Stevens wrote. With time running out, he then listed other cases in which the Court issued "glittering generalities" that extended its reach into matters better left to legislatures, the executive branch, or state courts. For example, in *Lochner v. New York,* 1905, and *Hammer v. Dagenhart,* 1918 (better known as the Child Labor Case), the Court asserted laissez-faire capitalist theories, which were popular at the time among wealthy Americans, as its justification for barring states and even Congress from regulating on behalf of health and safety. In both cases, Justice Oliver Wendell Holmes delivered stinging dissents against judicial activism on behalf of a controversial theory of economics. Such "general propositions do not decide concrete cases," Holmes insisted.

In a similar vein, Stevens cited the *Hepburn v. Griswold* decision of 1870 in which the court, based on the "spirit" of the Constitution, outlawed an act of Congress during the Civil War that had authorized the use of government notes, known as greenbacks, as legal tender to satisfy debts in addition to gold and silver coins. The potentially disastrous decision quickly was overturned, but the entire "Legal Tender Cases" episode needlessly wounded the Court's reputation.

As time ran out, Stevens scribbled three common dangers in these examples of self-inflicted wounds: first, the Court annunciated bad public policy; second, it ventured into territory of policy making where the Supreme Court did not belong under the constitutional powers of the three branches and of the states; and, third, the particular facts and claims in the cases did not require the Court to issue sweeping decisions.

Nathanson gave Stevens an 88 on the exam, the second highest score in the class of seventy-six students. Arthur Seder received a 90. "Our standing was fractionally different," recalled Seder, who pursued a career as a private lawyer. "We were, I guess you would say, the class leaders. We were very good friends. I never thought of him as a rival. We respected each other's abilities, but I never thought we were trying to outdo one another."[16] Stevens finished first in the class.

The competition best remembered by the two men was a coin flip. The incident determined the path Stevens followed to the Supreme Court and, to a great extent, the kind of justice that Stevens became. In the spring of 1947, legislation enabling justices of the Court to hire two clerks, instead of one, passed Congress. Justice Wiley Blount Rutledge was looking for a second clerk for the upcoming 1947–1948 term. He contacted his friend and Northwestern law professor W. Willard Wirtz. The Rutledge/Wirtz relationship dated back ten years. Northwestern faculty members debated among themselves about whether to recommend Seder or Stevens. Seder recalled what happened: "Some members of the faculty got together to discuss this. In the end, they came to John and me and said they had this opportunity and did not want to decide between us."[17]

A coin was flipped in the office of the school's law review. The loser was to wait a year and, in a deal cooked up by Northwestern law professor Willard Pedrick, clerk for Chief Justice Fred M. Vinson in the 1948 term. Stevens won. "My hopes were really sunk at that point," Seder said.[18] Law professor Laura Krugman Ray concluded that Stevens was lucky in two ways: he was able to move directly to a Supreme Court clerkship, and he didn't get Vinson as a boss. Vinson was a far less able and conscientious judicial craftsman than Rutledge.[19]

Wirtz swung into action. Rutledge had hired Wirtz in 1937 when Wirtz, a native of DeKalb, Illinois, was completing his law degree at Harvard Law School; at that time Rutledge was dean of the University of Iowa College of Law. They were close allies in the thin ranks of liberal Midwest Democrats.

Wirtz's recommendation of Stevens to Rutledge was glowing, even for a man who is not shy about his enthusiasms. "Let me simply say that I consider Stevens to be one of the two most outstanding students whom I have ever worked with," he wrote in May 1947. "Stevens has the quickest, and at the same time best balanced, mind I have ever seen at work in a classroom. I have worked with him, too, in connection with two or three law review projects. The man is just as solid as he is brilliant. Beyond all this he has a personality which makes it a pure delight to work with him. I suppose that he is undoubtedly the most admired, and at the same time, the best liked man in the school."[20]

In a telephone conversation with Rutledge, Wirtz alerted his friend that Stevens came from a family of Republican businessmen in Chicago. "In other words, he's politically quite conservative," Wirtz said he told Rutledge. "Wiley Rutledge said, 'I think that's something I can take care of, don't you?' And I said, 'yes.'"[21]

CHAPTER FOUR

The Great Writ

The story of Stevens's career might have been quite conventional. But at important moments, unlikely characters stole scenes and prompted a more engaging plot. A scattershot public-interest advocate provided a venue for Stevens's nonconformist instincts. An irascible major league baseball team owner elevated him to the big leagues of law practice. An annoying gadfly of the Illinois court system helped launch him onto the federal bench. This parade of oddballs began much earlier, in 1947, when the chambers of Justice Wiley Rutledge encountered the Green Hornet.

An obituary writer for *The Washington Post* described James J. Laughlin as "one of Washington's most colorful criminal lawyers, . . . a member of the finger-pointing, Bible-quoting school of court-room oratory." His nickname, Green Hornet, drawn from a popular comic book character, referred to his stinging cross-examinations and courtroom harangues.[1] His clients included Mildred Gillars of Maine, known to Americans as Axis Sally, who was returned to America after World War II and tried for treason for allegedly airing Nazi propaganda on German radio broadcasts aimed at American troops. With Laughlin at her side, a jury found her not guilty on seven of eight charges. Another client was Charles Starkweather, whose murder spree in Nebraska and Wyoming at age nineteen with a fourteen-year-old female accomplice became material for movies and songs. Laughlin injected himself uninvited into Stark-weather's capital case in 1959 and won a brief stay of execution from a Supreme Court justice.

In 1947, the Green Hornet brought to the Supreme Court an appeal titled *Ahrens v. Clark* representing Paul Ahrens and more than 120 other German nationals, male and female, detained at Ellis Island as enemies of the United States even though fighting against Germany had ended. U.S. Attorney General Tom C. Clark had ordered them deported under the Alien Enemies Act of 1798 as "dangerous to the public peace and safety of the United States because they adhered to a government [that] is at war or to the principles thereof." Stevens does not recall seeing Laughlin in action or dealing with him, but the lawyer's last-ditch effort, which irritated several justices, pricked the curiosity of a freshly minted law school graduate. In the aftermath of World War II, few would have noticed or cared if young Stevens had left the Germans to their fate, which was a forced return to their Fatherland. But in his draft dissent for Rutledge, Stevens remarked, "This case presents a jurisdictional problem that has implications far beyond its immediate facts."[2] Stevens's interpretation of the case as a young law clerk came to life six decades later when Justice Stevens led the Supreme Court to rule, in the first of several cases arising in the 2003–2004 term from the government's treatment of detainees at Guantanamo Bay, Cuba, that federal courts have jurisdiction over the detainees and may decide "the legality of the executive's [President George W. Bush's] potentially indefinite detention of individuals who claim to be wholly innocent of wrongdoing" (*Rasul v. Bush,* 2004).

Most accounts describe the October 1947 term of the Supreme Court, when Stevens clerked for Rutledge, as undistinguished. (Supreme Court terms, which begin in October and end the following June, are designated by "October" followed by the year the term begins.) Law scholars generally dismiss the entire tenure of Chief Justice Fred Vinson, 1946 to 1953, as a "tiresome interlude"[3] between the progressive recasting of the Court by President Franklin Roosevelt and the arrival of Chief Justice Earl Warren. But as Stevens finished law school and prepared for his clerkship, some commentators were more optimistic.

Writing in the January 1947 edition of *Fortune* magazine, a monthly publication aimed at the nation's business elite, twenty-nine-year-old historian Arthur M. Schlesinger, Jr., noted the relative youth of the justices. The average age of what the article termed the "nine young men" was fifty-seven when the year began. Schlesinger found that the Court comprised a clear and appropriate balance between those who wanted to "play an affirmative role in promoting social welfare" (Hugo L. Black, William Douglas, Frank Murphy, and Wiley Rutledge) and those who wanted a "policy of self-restraint" on the part of unelected judges (Felix Frankfurter, Robert Jackson, and Harold H. Burton), with Stanley F. Reed and Chief Justice Vinson in the middle as swing votes. In this climate, Schlesinger expressed hope that the Vinson Court could rise above its internal personality conflicts, which were notorious, and become "one of the great creative Courts of history."[4]

That dream was dimmed by the early deaths of Rutledge and Murphy two years later. But as to the October 1947 term, a review published in *The University of Chicago Law Review* concluded, "Like America, the Supreme Court did not go anywhere very definitely in 1947–48." Nonetheless, "the application of the laws protecting competition did not retrogress, and there were some real advances for civil liberties."[5]

It was so hot in Chicago in the summer of 1947, as Stevens concluded his law studies, that mosquitoes in the city were dying from the heat. The heat seemed to follow him to Washington, D.C., as high temperatures for days at a time held in the upper nineties while John and Betty settled into an apartment on 16th Street just south of Meridian Hill Park in the DuPont North neighborhood, a few blocks north of the White House. It was their second move to the nation's capital.

The magnificent Supreme Court building on Capitol Hill was still new to the historical neighborhood, having opened just twelve years earlier. Though smaller, it was designed to be the co-equal of the U.S. Capitol, across First Street. Both featured Corinthian columns as reminders of the roots of democracy. And both had air conditioning, unlike most homes and public buildings in Washington at the time. "The justices' chambers were really quite comfortable," recalled Robert von Mehren, who clerked for Justice Reed in the 1947 term. "It was good to stay indoors."[6] Nonetheless, even hardworking Rutledge escaped Washington's heat—on the coast of Maine—after the unusually lengthy 1946 term finally concluded in the third week of June. He left fresh cases piling up in his chambers for review by his law clerks.

There is no more prestigious entry on a young lawyer's resume than having clerked for a Supreme Court justice. A clerkship, which typically lasts one year, represents a ticket to an exclusive club. A law clerk at the Supreme Court has three principal tasks: helping justices decide which cases to hear; conducting research into cases the Court agrees to hear; and assisting in writing opinions. The role of clerks in writing opinions—a perennially controversial topic— varied widely in the Vinson Court. Frankfurter used his clerks mostly to research footnotes. Vinson's clerks routinely wrote first drafts that became final drafts.

At that time, about 1,300 petitions arrived each year asking the Court to review lower court decisions. A dissatisfied party in a case petitions the Court to issue a writ of certiorari, a Latin phrase meaning that the Court seeks to remove a case from a lower court so that the Supreme Court may hear it and be made certain. The Court's discretion in accepting or rejecting petitions for certiorari, or cert petitions, is one of its greatest powers.

"The first two or three certs I picked up, I thought, Christ, they are impossible. They are very, very close cases," recalled Stanley L. Temko, a top student at Columbia Law School and the recipient of a Bronze Star in Europe. Rutledge had picked Temko as a clerk for the 1947 term. "If it was going to be like this all summer, this was going to be a hell of a job," Temko recalled.[7] But Temko soon got the hang of it and was pleased to pass on the techniques of cert review to his co-clerk. Stevens arrived in the third week of September, at the end of a week of vacation after law school.

Stevens and Temko squeezed into the room in Rutledge's chambers that previously had been assigned to a single clerk. Each of the one- or two-page cert memoranda they typed for

Rutledge contained a summary of the case, relevant law, and their recommendation on whether their boss should vote to grant or deny the petition. Stevens's typing skills, honed by writing daily summaries of radio messages sent by the Japanese navy, received another workout.

Rutledge was a stickler in the cert review process, as he was in every aspect of his job. He was just fifty-three when the October 1947 term began, but the self-inflicted strain of being thorough was showing. Many of these cases were filed by indigents and prisoners submitting far-fetched claims on their own behalf. It was easy to reject them. Vinson circulated a "dead list" of petitions he judged to be unworthy of the cert review by the full conference of justices. But the dead list "would bug Rutledge, who wanted us to look at it again," Temko said.[8]

In many respects, Rutledge, a former law professor and law school dean at Washington University in St. Louis and the University of Iowa in Iowa City, was the odd man out on the Supreme Court. He was not a multifaceted federal official or a seasoned Washington political coutier. His career highlights before joining the Supreme Court consisted of teaching and holding administrative posts at Midwestern law schools and nearly four years serving on the federal court of appeals in Washington. Rutledge had been an ardent Roosevelt supporter. But unlike several of his brethren on the Court, he was not a crony of Roosevelt or President Harry S. Truman. He was "a plain old shoe and one of the nicest guys you'd ever see," Temko said.[9]

His smile was too big for his face. It enveloped students, law clerks, friends, and associates of all sorts, most of whom came to express love for the man. He spent too much time responding to solicitations and salutations from practically anyone. Willard Wirtz, the Northwestern law professor who had urged Rutledge to hire Stevens and later was U.S. Secretary of Labor in the Kennedy and Johnson administrations, said: "He was one of the most human beings I have ever known. I have looked up to only four or five men in my life, and he would be one of them. He was an extraordinary combination of intellectual competence and human warmth. He had a terrible time arbitrating between his heart and his head."[10]

Rutledge generally got along with his Court colleagues, a noteworthy accomplishment at a time when the Court deserved the

description attributed to former Justice Oliver Wendell Holmes—
"nine scorpions in a bottle." At the end of the October 1945 term,
Justice Jackson, still in Germany directing war crime trials, grew
bitter over not being elevated to replace Chief Justice Harlan Stone.
In extraordinary cables from Europe to Congress, Jackson struck
out against Justice Black. He apparently believed that Black had
sabotaged his ambition to move to the Court's center chair. At the
same time, Justices Douglas and Frankfurter were engaged in a long-
running feud. In the summer of 1945, the justices could not agree
on a routine congratulatory letter to Justice Owen J. Roberts when
Roberts retired from the Court.

Thanks to well-oiled press contacts maintained by seasoned Washington insiders on the Court, internal disputes among the justices
were great fodder for newspapers. To an extent never seen before
or since, "the Justices, in effect, were put—or put themselves—in
the position of arguing their judicial philosophies both in their
opinions and in the popular press," wrote University of Chicago
law professor Dennis J. Hutchinson.[11] Headlines in *The Washington
Post* in June 1946 are almost unimaginable even in the intrigues of
contemporary Washington: "Supreme Court 'Feud' Flares Openly";
"President Reveals Futile Effort to Head Off Jackson's Blast."

Rutledge managed to avoid the infighting and damaging publicity.
He simply stuck to his knitting, focusing on the cases he was assigned.
In Douglas's words, Rutledge's "mill ground very, very slowly. He was
very, very, very conscientious, down to the last finest detail, and he
would write heavily footnoted opinions that sometimes seemed to
me to be useless expenditures of time and energy on a problem that
didn't need that detailed treatment. But that's the personality of the
man and he had to find his place in the mosaic."[12] Leaving behind
the Washington caldron, Rutledge traveled to the Midwest, to Lawrence, Kansas, for a series of lectures in December 1946. The talks,
which were published as a book by the University of Kansas Press,
were titled "A Declaration of Legal Faith."

Invoking "faith" is risky business for an appellate judge, who is
supposed to apply law to facts. But Rutledge said the war against
Nazism had arisen from competing ideas of justice, both of which
had inspired deep faith: "national and racial" justice for an aggrieved
state, namely Hitler's Germany, versus justice that was "inclusive of

humanity" on behalf of free individuals in lawful societies every-where. His faith resided with the latter. "I believe in law," he said simply. "At the same time I believe in freedom."[13]

Rutledge's focus on "faith" struck some of his brethren as naive. In a diary entry, Frankfurter quoted Reed as saying that Rutledge voted "wrong" on cases because "he is another one of those fellows who wants to do what he calls justice in the particular case without heeding the consequences in other situations not immediately before the Court, or in the general administration of justice."[14] In response, Frankfurter told Reed, "Rutledge evidently is one of those evangelical lads who confuse his personal desire to do good in the world with the limits within which a wise and humble judge must move. He will be very conscientious and very earnest and formula-ridden and perhaps too easily taken in by big, noble-sounding words."[15]

But in elevating the principles of justice over the "general admin-istration" of justice, in the October 1947 term Rutledge had allies among the Court's law clerks. In these years, many clerks were military veterans who were older and more worldly than their predecessors and more liberal than their bosses. "They weren't just kids right out of law school," Temko said.[16] He and Stevens turned twenty-eight during the term. Moreover, several clerks, including Stevens and Temko, had been military officers in the war. Yale University Law School graduate John B. Spitzer, a clerk to Justice Reed, had been a major in the U.S. Army's Special Branch. In a 2007 inter-view, Spitzer said he never knew that fellow clerk Stevens was also a cryptanalyst working on Japanese war communications. "Nobody talked about their war experiences," he said.[17]

The veterans knew how to acknowledge rank, even when it was not required. Rutledge "was annoyed that law clerks recently dis-charged from military service found it difficult to remain seated when a Supreme Court justice intruded on their labors," Stevens recalled.[18] Nonetheless, they were less likely to be cowed by profes-sors in law schools or bosses in black robes. "We used to joke that we were the supreme Supreme Court," Spitzer said. "We were not a modest group. We were impressed with our own importance, in a good-natured way." As a group, the clerks were more liberal than the justices, Spitzer recalled.[19]

The Court's 1947–1948 term is best remembered as one of several in which justices inched slowly toward a unanimous ruling in *Oliver Brown v. Board of Education of Topeka* in 1954, to overturn the Court's 1896 decision (*Plessy v. Ferguson*) legalizing racial segregation in public places, including schools. The Court heard three dozen cases concerning civil rights and civil liberties in the term. In January 1948 Stevens sat in one of the cane chairs on the south side of the courtroom to hear Thurgood Marshall, chief counsel to the National Association for the Advancement of Colored People's Legal Defense and Education Fund, present the case of one of Oliver Brown's constitutional law forerunners, Ada Lois Sipuel.

Marshall represented Sipuel, an African American who had been denied admittance to the University of Oklahoma's law school solely because of her race. The Court had ruled ten years earlier in another law school admissions case (*Missouri ex rel. Gaines v. Canada*, 1938) that states must not exclude racial minorities but must implement the "equal" side of the Court's "equal-but-separate" doctrine. The Vinson Court was willing to uphold that decision, but this time, in *Sipuel v. Board of Regents of the University of Oklahoma*, 1948, Marshall asked the Court to go further. "Classifications and distinctions based on race or color have no moral or legal validity in our society," he wrote in his brief. "There can be no separate equality."[20]

Marshall "was respectful, forceful and persuasive," Stevens recalled. But the Court upheld the status quo. Marshall filed a subsequent motion against Chief Justice Thurman S. Hurst and the Oklahoma Supreme Court to block enforcement of separate-but-equal treatment for Sipuel, who had married and bore the name Fisher (*Fisher v. Hurst*, 1948). In a three-page memorandum to his boss, Stevens advised Rutledge to use this motion to make a historic statement or, at least, to slow down the rush to dismiss Marshall's effort:

> If the petition is flatly denied, I would hold it long enough to write a dissenting opinion; if there is a chance of granting any relief, I would do so. . . . The mandate of this Court [in *Sipuel v. Board of Regents*] directs the state to provide [Ada Lois Fisher] with a legal education 'in conformity with the equal protection clause.' I would think it

possible to take judicial notice of the fact that (a) a law school for one student cannot be equal, even if you accept the equal but separate doctrine, and (b) the doctrine of segregation is itself a violation of the Constitutional requirement.

Stevens insisted that Marshall's motion was not premature or unwarranted: ". . . An opinion could be written explaining that at least for law schools, the constitutional requirement of providing equal protection was not satisfied by providing separate schools."[21]

Rutledge was not willing to go as far as his law clerk's proposal, which would effectively overturn *Plessy v. Ferguson* by means of an emergency motion. But his dissent stated that the Oklahoma state courts, regardless of the facility established for Fisher, had failed to obey the Supreme Court's order. "Oklahoma should end the discrimination practiced against [Fisher] at once, not at some later time, near or remote. . . . In my comprehension the equality required is equality in fact, not legal fiction," Rutledge wrote.[22]

If advocate Thurgood Marshall made a positive impression, advocate James Laughlin, representing the Nazi sympathizers detained on Ellis Island, did not. In his dealing with the Court, he was rude, ineffective, and unconvincing. Unlike Ada Lois Fisher and other African Americans who followed her in seeking constitutional rights, the individuals held under the Alien Enemies Act had few supporters. Nonetheless, Stevens saw a bigger question. "The petitioners in the *Ahrens* case were men whose application for habeas corpus raised an issue affecting every member of the community equally," he wrote later.[23]

Rutledge was the key to the Court taking up Laughlin's case, although he was not impressed by the lawyer's protestations. At first, Rutledge abandoned his normal alliance with liberals Black, Douglas, and Murphy and sided with Frankfurter and Jackson to reject Laughlin's plea. In his cert memo to Rutledge before the meeting, Stevens noted one of the Court's previous denials of certiorari in similar cases and recommended that "the petition for cert should be denied." But a final decision on whether to hear the case under a writ of habeas corpus was postponed. Justice Burton recorded on his score sheet for the conference, "Hold for WR," indicating that Rutledge was not finished reviewing a matter. A second look did not improve the merits of Laughlin's petition, as far as Stevens was concerned. Before the conference, when the case next appeared for a cert vote, Stevens again advised that it be rejected. But this time, Rutledge rejoined the liberal cohort of Black, Douglas, and Murphy to achieve the four votes needed to have the case heard. Stevens took a third look.

A 159-page retrospective on Justice Rutledge's jurisprudence published jointly in the year after his death by the *Iowa Law Review* and the *Indiana Law Journal* neither mentions *Ahrens v. Clark* in its seven articles nor even cites the case in an appendix listing Rutledge's opinions. But when Stevens, as a private attorney practicing in Chicago, wrote his memorial to Rutledge in 1964, he made the *Ahrens* dissent, in which he played a critical role, the centerpiece of his tribute. "It was his inclination to oppose a rigid rule limiting the power of a court to perform its function, particularly when that function directly involved the protection of individual liberty," Stevens wrote.[24]

The writ of habeas corpus, known as the Great Writ, is a building block of a free society and the foundation of a fair judicial system. The right of any person to seek a judge's review of the circumstances by which his or her liberty has been denied—by government agents or private persons—dates back at least to the Magna Carta in thirteenth-century England. "The privilege of the Writ of Habeas Corpus" was embodied in the first article of the U.S. Constitution, well before the Founding Fathers hammered out the Bill of Rights. The first law enacted by the first U.S. Congress authorized federal courts "to grant writs of habeas corpus for the purpose of an inquiry into the cause of commitment." The "privilege" of habeas corpus does not, by itself, grant or expand any rights. It exists prior to those rights. The writ of habeas corpus is the key to the jail, nothing more or less. A court may issue the writ at any time, from first arrest to years into a prisoner's term of confinement following a conviction and multiple appeals. It may be sought by a person detained or by anyone on behalf of the detainee. In U.S. law, the privilege is not limited to U.S. citizens.

The threat to habeas corpus embedded in *Ahrens* was hardly foremost in the minds of the litigants on either side. Rather, Laughlin claimed that his clients were not enemy aliens. He argued that the war was over and that the government's authority to deport alleged enemy aliens had expired. But his petition to the Court did not address what the Court eventually declared was the overarching question: Was the U.S. District Court for the District of Columbia the appropriate court for Laughlin to file his habeas corpus petition on behalf of individuals held in the jurisdiction of the U.S. District Court in New York City? In his pleadings Laughlin also ignored a second jurisdictional question: Why did he sue Attorney General Tom C. Clark, whose office was in Washington, D.C., instead of jailers or prosecutors in New York?

Despite Laughlin's apparent indifference, Chief Justice Vinson called jurisdiction in the case an "important issue." "There is a difficulty," he said in conference with his fellow justices. In the seven-to-two opinion against the detainees, Justice Douglas said the question was "whether the presence within the territorial jurisdiction of the District Court of the person detained is prerequisite to filing a petition for habeas corpus." He answered yes. Laughlin had brought his suit to Washington, D.C., the wrong court.[25] Having answered the first question, Douglas skipped the second question: "We do not reach the question whether the Attorney General is the proper respondent."[26] But by at least acknowledging the second question, Douglas allowed the core constitutional issue in *Ahrens v. Clark* finally to emerge.

Stevens, in a memo to Rutledge, planted the seed for what became the legacy of the case. The two questions were really one, and Douglas's reasoning might be backward, he said. If the attorney general, headquartered in Washington, D.C., was the proper target for Laughlin's habeas corpus action, then the federal district court in Washington was the proper court to receive his petition. "It seems to me that they are really the same issue," Stevens wrote.[27] A jurisdictional gap could arise in many circumstances whenever an official responsible for jailing someone escaped the reach of habeas corpus merely by residing far from the jail where he or she had placed suspects, Stevens reasoned. Justice could be imperiled, Stevens wrote, "even possibly from the willful misconduct by arbitrary executive officials attempting to overreach their constitutional authority. These dangers may seem unreal in the United States, but the experience of less fortunate countries should serve as a warning against curtailment of the jurisdiction of our courts to protect the liberty of the individual by means of the writ of habeas corpus."[28]

Rutledge realized immediately the importance to the writ of habeas corpus of joining the two questions and making the identity of the official being sued more important than the place where detainees were held. He shaped his dissent around Stevens's memo. "The question is whether the Attorney General is the proper party respondent," Rutledge wrote. Using phrases from Stevens's draft, Rutledge answered yes. Attorney General Clark "is in complete charge of the proceedings leading up to the order directing their removal from the country; indeed he claims to have complete discretion to decide whether or not removal shall be directed. In view of his all-pervasive control over their fortunes, it cannot be doubted that he is the proper party" to receive a writ of habeas corpus issued by the district court in Washington.[29]

Murphy, who initially voted to affirm dismissal of the case, wrote to Rutledge, "I now believe that you are right and that your opinion is a fine job. So I join you."[30] Black signed on as well. Still, attorney Laughlin lost by a vote of six to three. Deportations began that summer.

An unsigned review of *Ahrens v. Clark* in *The University of Chicago Law Review* in 1948—a rare contemporary analysis of the unheralded case—endorsed the Rutledge/Stevens dissent. Citing the plight of individuals detained outside the geographical reach of any federal district court, it urged that Douglas's "dubious statutory construction" be corrected by an act of Congress.[31] Separately, in its general review of opinions from the October 1947 term, the *Review* said, "The least satisfactory Douglas opinion from a purely technical standpoint was *Ahrens v. Clark,* holding that federal courts cannot hear habeas corpus actions when the prisoner is outside the territorial jurisdiction of the court." The review said that Douglas, in previous writings for the Court, had endorsed the opposite position and had agreed that the location of the jailer (in this case, Attorney

General Clark) established sufficient habeas corpus jurisdiction.[32]

Less than a year after writing his *Ahrens* opinion, Douglas backed down. "Habeas corpus is an historic writ and one of the basic safeguards of personal liberty," he declared in his separate concurrence in *Hirota v. MacArthur,* 1949. "There is no room for niggardly restrictions when questions relating to its availability are raised. The statutes governing its use must be generously construed if the great office of the writ is not to be impaired. . . . It has never been deemed essential that the prisoner in every case be within the territorial limits of the district where he seeks relief by way of habeas corpus." In 1973, two years before he resigned from the Court and was succeeded by Stevens, Douglas joined in an opinion by Justice William Brennan (*Braden v. 30th Judicial Circuit Court of Kentucky*) that appeared to overrule *Ahrens v. Clark* by a six-to-three vote.

When he accepted Rutledge's offer of a clerkship in the summer of 1947, Stevens agreed to stay for a second year, "if you decide that you would like to have me stay on." But he added, "frankly, my personal preference would be to stay only for one year."[33] Twelve months later, he was ready to move on, into the private practice of law.

The clerkship "gave one at the start of his legal career a view of the whole central structure from the top of the pyramid, and that was a useful experience," said former Reed clerk Robert von Mehren.[34] Like most other Supreme Court law clerks, Stevens had no reason to expect that the exact work of the clerkship would extend directly into his career. But in 2004 in *Rasul v. Bush,* Justice Stevens brought a string of judicial precedent full circle, back to the 1948 *Ahrens* dissent. Citing the Rutledge *Ahrens* dissent and the Brennan *Braden* ruling, Stevens rejected President Bush's effort to create a habeas corpus no-man's-land at the Guantanamo Bay Naval Station.

British citizen Shifiq Rasul and eleven other citizens of Britain, Australia, and Kuwait sued President Bush. The men had been captured in Afghanistan and Pakistan and turned over to U.S. officials during America's initial military response to the September 11, 2001, attacks on the United States. They claimed—and no information presented publicly in the case contradicted their claims—that they were noncombatants, having no affiliation with anyone associated with the September 11 attacks. At the time of the Supreme Court oral argument in their case, they had been held incommunicado at Guantanamo Bay for two years—without military or criminal charges filed against them and without legal counsel. In their case, titled *Rasul v. Bush,* the Court considered whether Guantanamo Bay prisoners could exercise the privilege of habeas corpus review in the federal district court in Washington, where Bush resided.

To refute the claim, the government relied almost entirely on a 1950 Supreme Court opinion by Justice Jackson (*Johnson v. Eisentrager*) that in turn was based on the majority opinion in *Ahrens v. Clark.* Yet the detainees' lawyer, John J. Gibbons of Newark, New Jersey, a former federal appeals court judge, did not seem to realize that Stevens was trying, as Stevens said to him from the bench, to "help you." The *Ahrens* ruling had been reversed, Stevens reminded Gibbons, implying that the dissent he had helped write in 1948 was the correct way to use *Ahrens* on behalf of his clients. Stevens had his work cut out for him since Gibbons hadn't made the trek in habeas corpus jurisprudence over many years from *Ahrens* to *Eisentrager*, which relied on *Ahrens,* to *Braden*, which Stevens maintained had overruled *Ahrens*:

> [Stevens]—. . . Once they [the justices] have overruled *Ahrens* against Clark, which they did, there is now a statutory basis for jurisdiction. . . .

> [Gibbons]—Your honor, respectfully, I do not think you can fairly read Justice Jackson's opinion as adopting the *Ahrens v. Clark* position.

> [Stevens]—No, but *Ahrens v. Clark* was the law at the time of that decision, and it was subsequently overruled, so that that case was decided when the legal climate was different than it has been since *Ahrens* against Clark was overruled.[35]

Despite this oral argument confusion, Stevens prevailed. In his opinion for the Court, joined by Justices Sandra Day O'Connor, David Souter, Ruth Bader Ginsburg, and Stephen Breyer, Stevens wrote that the habeas corpus privilege applied to the Guantanamo detainees, as Rutledge said it had applied to the Germans at Ellis Island.

Joseph T. Thai, a professor at the University of Oklahoma College of Law and a former Stevens law clerk, published a thorough analysis of the Stevens biographical overlay in *Rasul v. Bush*. He noted that when Justice Jackson wrote the opinion that the Bush administration relied on, Jackson seems to have intentionally ignored the implications that he was quite familiar with from the *Ahrens* case, including the jurisdictional gap in the habeas corpus statute.

Like the dog that didn't bark in a Sherlock Holmes mystery, Justice Jackson was all too familiar with the history of *Ahrens v. Clark,* including the Rutledge dissent, Thai wrote. Jackson failed to issue a warning. The Bush administration tried the same gambit, but the clue was exposed not by a singular detective but by a Supreme Court justice with a good memory. "The [*Rasul v. Bush*] case turned on dissenting views developed by a law clerk who just happened to serve as a Justice when, over fifty years later, the opportunity arose to vindicate those views, and he alone perhaps had the peculiar insight to seize it," Thai wrote.[36]

Dissenting in *Rasul v. Bush,* Justice Antonin Scalia charged that the Court was wrongly transferring military battlefield decisions into a federal court. But Stevens, as he had in 1948, turned the question around: "What is presently at stake is only whether the federal courts have jurisdiction to determine the legality of the Executive's potentially indefinite detention of individuals who claim to be wholly innocent of wrongdoing." This time, Stevens, as leader of a Court majority, was able to answer the question with a "yes." The case, in this respect, had nothing to do with the presence or absence of a war.

Many liberal heroes of American law, including Justices Douglas and Brennan, have contributed to the enshrinement of the habeas corpus principle. In *Rasul v. Bush*, Stevens joined that group, but with a unique "I told you so" reference to his work as a law clerk. His ability as a young lawyer to pluck a basic constitutional right from the inauspicious *Ahrens v. Clark* case demonstrated a budding judicial craft as well as a judicial philosophy.

CHAPTER FIVE

The Client

Not long after the clerkship with Justice Rutledge ended and John and Betty returned to Hyde Park, Stevens wrote to his former boss with some news: "Betty and I are making arrangements to adopt a baby as soon as we can." Leaving no doubt that he had learned a thing or two about the judicial traits of balance and deference, Stevens wrote,

> We did not specify the sex we desired, partly because we really couldn't make up our minds and partly because it didn't seem fair. Our friends, however, have criticized us severely on this count, saying that this is the one situation in which expectant parents have a choice, and that we have neglected a valuable opportunity. I think, however, that we avoided as much criticism as we incurred because, when first being told of our plans, women usually say how wonderful it is that we can pick a girl, whereas the men of course make the opposite comment. And the fun of wondering whether we will have a girl or a boy is the same whether the issue is resolved by an administrative agency or by some higher tribunal.[1]

Another reason for his neutral stance may have been decision fatigue. Stevens had been mulling his career choices with typical intensity. Law school deans at the University of Chicago and Yale University were interested. "After mulling over the problem of practice vs. teaching for the past month, I have finally decided, at least for the present, to go into practice," he wrote to Rutledge in September 1948.

Even after all the thought I have given the problem, I find it somewhat difficult to articulate the reasons for my decision. Perhaps the
main reason is that I really think I will enjoy practice more than
teaching. As part of the same reason, I think I need practical experience to round out my character. Almost my entire life has been spent
in scholarly circles, and even my navy work was largely of a scholarly
type. I think also that while I will learn something from seeing the
reactionaries' side of things, that my philosophy is sufficiently developed so that I will not be converted from my general point of view.[2]

Rutledge knew that President Harry S. Truman had influenced
Stevens's point of view. Stevens attended a 1948 White House
reception for federal judges that "generously included Supreme
Court clerks among the invited guests," Stevens recalled years later.
"I still remember vividly the impression he made on me when I was
introduced to him and Mrs. Truman in the receiving line. He was
a warm, friendly, decent person whom you could not help liking
immediately. A few months later I voted for Dewey, but as the election returns came in, I found myself quietly rooting for Truman."[3]
Justice Rutledge, an ardent Truman supporter who was thrilled by
the 1948 election results, had hoped that if Stevens did not choose to
teach, he would join the team of Illinois's newly elected Democratic
governor, Adlai E. Stevenson, an attractive, wellborn, and articulate
politician who was drawing eager liberals to Springfield in the same
way another Democrat, President John F. Kennedy, attracted them
to Washington, D.C., more than a decade later in 1961.

Walter V. Schaefer, one of Stevens's law school professors, had
taken leave from Northwestern to become Special Assistant to Stevenson. Schaefer had been one of Stevenson's closest advisers in
the 1948 campaign. After Stevenson's victory against incumbent
Republican Dwight H. Green, Schaefer became the architect of the
new governor's legislative agenda. Schaefer wanted to hire Stevens.

"I told him I would like to do it, and left the interview with the
impression that I should start packing in order to move to Springfield
immediately," Stevens told Rutledge in January 1949.[4] But by then
Stevens already had made a choice. After interviewing with about
fifteen Chicago law firms, he had joined Poppenhusen, Johnston,
Thompson & Raymond, an ambitious and fast-growing firm whose

partners included Floyd E. Thompson, a former chief justice of the Illinois Supreme Court and the Democratic candidate for Illinois governor in 1928. Among his better-known clients, Thompson had won acquittals in three separate trials in the mid-1930s of utilities mogul Samuel Insull. "By reputation it is one of the best firms in town," Stevens wrote to Rutledge. "And I am particularly favorably impressed by the young fellows I met there. Also by the fact that, contrary to the practice of most successful outfits in Chicago, there are several jews [sic] in the organization."[5]

But just three months into the new job, Stevens was looking forward. "I am fairly well convinced that I don't want to stay with such a firm for very long," he told Rutledge. One aggravation at the outset was the firm's policy of docking the pay of young lawyers for the day they spent at the Illinois Supreme Court in Springfield being admitted to the Illinois bar. "What I hope to do, assuming we could scare up some clients, is to hang out a shingle with one or two other fellows of about my age. But in any event, I plan to stay with Poppenhusen for at least a year (unless the state job should pan out) before making any changes."[6] The state job did not pan out, although Stevens's enthusiasm for Stevenson lingered. The post Schaefer initially offered went to a more senior lawyer. Instead, Stevens was in line for a position in the Illinois Department of Finance, which did not appeal to him. Working with Poppenhusen's best-known litigator did. He came under the tutelage and spell of Edward R. Johnston, one of the country's leading antitrust defense lawyers at the time. He was "a bear of a man," tall, barrel-chested—"a very tough guy," recalled two lawyers who worked with him.[7] His penetrating eyes and confident smile broke through the fog of corporate law to place his client's position foremost in the mind and gut of adversaries.

Johnston had practiced business law in Chicago since 1907, including a successful courtroom encounter with the legendary Clarence Darrow. He undoubtedly knew Stevens's father through fighting the Reconstruction Finance Corporation in Depression-era cases similar to Ernest Stevens's battles with the federal agency over the fate of the Stevens family enterprises. He won his antitrust spurs in 1925 when the Supreme Court upheld the right of his client, the Maple Flooring Manufacturers Association, to share price information among its member companies. Other trade associations, which were a principal target of antitrust enforcers, flocked to Johnston. "It is positively interesting to work with him during a trial because he is definitely an A #1 trial lawyer," Stevens wrote to Rutledge. "He also seems to me to be quite an exception among the trial anti-trust bar in his ability to understand and respect views with which he disagrees."[8]

Johnston may not have been one of the "reactionaries" Stevens expected to encounter in private practice, but he delighted in getting the better of New Deal antitrust lawyers, especially Thurman Arnold, who was President Roosevelt's antitrust chief and a close friend of Justice William Douglas. Recalling three separate cases involving Arnold, Johnston's memoir crows about the outcomes: "The decision was a great blow to Mr. Thurman Arnold, but it was decided and there was nothing he could do about it. . . . Mr. Thurman Arnold was outraged by the court's decision but there was nothing he could do about it, and we chalked up one more victory. . . . Mr. Arnold was so incensed by the decision of the Supreme Court that he prepared, or had prepared, a bill to be introduced in Congress."[9]

Working as an antitrust specialist under Johnston, Stevens enjoyed the competition but lost his first major trial. Johnston represented Phillips Petroleum Company, which supplied fuel to an intercity bus conglomerate, National City Lines, Inc. The government leveled criminal charges against National City Lines and its key officers as well as principal suppliers, including Phillips, General Motors Corporation, Firestone Tire & Rubber Company, and Standard Oil Company of California. The suppliers were accused of advancing cash to National City, enabling the company to acquire smaller bus lines in return for long-term, exclusive supply contracts.

Stevens was no stranger to such multifaceted litigation. A year earlier he had helped Justice Rutledge write an opinion for the Court on a technical issue in a case that rejected a pleading by the National City Lines defendants (*United States v. National City Lines,* 1948). Now, as a lawyer representing Phillips Petroleum, he was part of the National City Lines defense team, taking sides against the government.

In a similar vein, Johnston also represented Paramount Pictures, Inc., whose executives probably would not have appreciated law school student Stevens's argument in favor of special antitrust scrutiny of the movie industry. Concerning his work on the defense side of antitrust litigation, Stevens wrote to Rutledge, "This may surprise you."[10]

Johnston and Stevens collaborated on a 1949 law review article that argued that enforcement of "monopoly" should interpret the concept as a verb, not a noun. Whether or not industries such as the major Hollywood studios were "virtual monopolies," antitrust laws should break them up only if they were found to be engaging in harmful behavior, such as price-fixing or other forms of anticompetitive collusion. "It is not true that every monopolist monopolizes," Johnston and Stevens wrote, expressing a view contrary to federal antitrust philosophy from late in the Franklin Roosevelt era forward. "The fact that the [Sherman Act] uses the verb [monopolize], not the noun [monopoly], to define the crime is important."[11] That article for Northwestern's law review was an early statement of what became a discipline at a school on the other side of town. The self-styled Chicago School of Law and Economics was emerging at the University of Chicago under law school professors Aaron Director, brother-in-law of economist Milton Friedman, and Edward H. Levi, dean of the law school. The Chicago School, which applied mathematic models from economics as evidence to be used in legal analysis, taught that bigness in corporate structure could promote efficiency that benefited, or at least did not harm, consumers.

Debates over the theory and enforcement of antitrust law were by no means confined to the ivory tower in the postwar years. The Republican Party was torn between its legions of small-business owners who were vulnerable to the superior marketing and buying powers of chain stores and other giant competitors on the one hand, and Republican-registered captains of industry who were building and operating the big competitors on the other. One viewpoint both sides shared was suspicion of government intervention in private enterprise, a theme that a middling movie actor named Ronald Reagan seized to undertake a political career.

In his early years on the political stump, Reagan frequently began speeches to business executives by discussing Hollywood's antitrust problems as his way of establishing credentials in weighty economic issues. "It may seem presumptuous to some of you that a person in my profession would address you on the serious affairs of business and the world today," he said in remarks to an elite New York audience in 1959.[12] He went on to denounce Justice Douglas's 1948 ruling against major studios dominating movie distribution and to applaud the desirable "vertical structure" of the motion picture industry.

The fraternity of lawyers—nearly all were men—who worked on both sides of antitrust cases in the postwar era stood atop the legal profession at this time. Antitrust cases were rewarding, intellectually and monetarily, for plaintiff and defense lawyers alike. The best of the close-knit community were able to negotiate settlements among themselves. If negotiations failed, the protracted, Dickensian *Bleak House* nature of much litigation in this arena was of course no deterrent to comfortable careers in the law. The work required little empathy but a great deal of analytical power and persistence.

Companies threatened by antitrust actions paid dearly to avoid fines, corporate dismemberment, or public embarrassment, even when cases required teams of lawyers and dragged on for years. After World War II, the quickly expanding power of computers, which had established their practical use in the war, found a new venue for sorting and analyzing obscure data in antitrust litigation. In short, no other specialty offered as much opportunity to a young attorney seeking an elite professional network in which to build a career.

Working with Johnston, Stevens was at the epicenter of the antitrust bar. "I could no more have quit my job in the midst of the trial than I could have quit a championship (assuming I was a championship player) tennis match with the score tied," he told Rutledge amid the National City Lines trial. "Of course it was my first trial, and perhaps I will become more sophisticated later on, but I was certainly surprised at how adversarial I became in this adversary proceeding. Our job was to try to win this case and I had a swell time trying to win."[13]

But young Stevens drew his nourishment in law and economics from many wells. He attended the Chicago School, in a manner of speaking. In the 1954–1955 school year and again in the summer session of 1958, Stevens, as a part-time lecturer, taught Director and Levi's signature course, "Competition and Monopoly." His students remembered his informal, practical, "cheerful" teaching style as a welcome diversion from the survival-of-the-fittest rigor of the full-time law faculty. Stevens also taught at Northwestern's law school.

Despite his familiarity with Levi and Director and the respect they apparently had for him, he was not their disciple and was not regarded as a member of the Chicago School of Law and Economics. "No, he wasn't," Richard A. Posner, a judge on the Seventh Circuit U.S. Court of Appeals in Chicago and a leading figure among judicial conservatives who hailed from the law-and-economics fraternity, said in 2006. "The [Supreme] Court has become much more conservative in antitrust. Stevens has generally fought that trend, unsuccessfully."[14]

A much different source of Stevens's development as an antitrust lawyer was his Supreme Court mentor, Justice Rutledge. Rutledge's economic beliefs, based on his years as a teacher of industrial organization, reflected an old-school counterpoint to the rapid drift toward Chicago School thinking. He was a disciple of turn-of-the-century trustbusters, for whom corporate bigness was a prima facie menace.

While on the faculty of the Washington University School of Law in St. Louis, Rutledge told a congressional hearing the "growth of corporate enterprises has been drying up individual initiative and independence, drying up the life of the big town and the small town, and the hamlet. We are becoming a nation of hired men, hired by great aggregations of capital."[15] Rutledge taught that maximizing business competition, through aggressive enforcement of antitrust laws, was not just a theoretical economic goal. It also honored the essence of the Constitution and the American experiment. In his book *A Declaration of Legal Faith,* Rutledge tied antitrust enforcement to the original purpose of the national government:

> It was . . . to secure freedom of trade, to break down the barriers to its free flow, that the Annapolis Convention was called, only to adjourn with a view to Philadelphia. Thus the generating source of the Constitution lay in the rising volume of restraints upon commerce which the [Articles of] Confederation could not check. These were the proximate cause of our national existence down to today. . . . On [the Commerce Clause] as much as any other we may safely say rests the vast economic development and present industrial power of the nation.[16]

Stevens's debt to Rutledge is best reflected in his own reverence for the Commerce Clause of the Constitution, which grants Congress the power "to regulate Commerce with foreign Nations, and among the several States, and with the Indian Tribes," and for the Sherman Antitrust Act, which invokes the Commerce Clause. Shortly after joining the Supreme Court, Stevens cited Rutledge in his dissent in a case about anticompetitive behavior in the manufacture of candy vending machines (*Vendo Co. v. Lektro-Vend Corp.,* 1977). Stevens called the Sherman Act "the Magna Carta of free enterprise."

Later, in a rare critique of his own work, Stevens labeled as "unwise" his opinion for the Court outlawing California's medical marijuana use law (*Gonzales v. Raich,* 2004). In a speech to law students, Stevens said, "I have no hesitation in telling you that I agree with the policy choice made by millions of California voters, as well as the voters in at least nine other states, that such use of the drug should be permitted, and that I disagree with executive decisions to invoke criminal sanctions to punish such use."[17] Nonetheless, he said his ruling was compelled by the Commerce Clause. Sounding like Rutledge, Stevens wrote in his opinion:

> The Commerce Clause emerged as the Framers' response to the central problem giving rise to the Constitution itself; the absence of any federal commerce power under the Articles of Confederation. . . . In response to rapid industrial development and an increasingly interdependent national economy, Congress 'ushered in a new era of federal regulation under the commerce power,' beginning with the enactment of the Interstate Commerce Act in 1887. . . and the Sherman Antitrust Act in 1890.

Stevens said he could not agree to a "narrow interpretation of Congress's power to regulate commerce among the states that has been consistently rejected since the Great Depression of the 1930s."[18]

It's hard to see the Commerce Clause and the Sherman Antitrust Act as the cornerstone of a judicial philosophy that spans civil liberties as well as business transactions. But such a leap is required in explaining Stevens's lifetime work, especially his ability to meld conservative and liberal points of view. His approach toward freedom of speech and religious freedom, for example, is weighted heavily toward guaranteeing unfettered competition of ideas.

In addition to Johnston, Rutledge, and the University of Chicago, a more incidental contributor to Stevens's antitrust credentials does not appear in his official biography. While he was an associate in Johnston's law firm defending major corporations and trade associations against antitrust charges, Stevens was briefly a board member of the Citizen's Public Utility Committee for the Metropolitan Area of Chicago. The committee was one of several public interest organizations established over four decades by Chicago's pioneer consumer activist Harry R. Booth. Stevens's affiliation with Booth's organization was a special interest group activity that he otherwise avoided in his law career, except for bar association work.

Booth, a Hyde Parker, was an energetic gadfly. He "views the public interest as his private war," the *Chicago Sun-Times* wrote. Physically, he was the opposite of Edward Johnston. Booth was short and mousy and wore heavy, dark-rimmed eyeglasses on a decidedly non-intimidating face. He was disorganized about money and in his many legal pursuits against public utilities, railroads, government bureaucracies, and other powerful interests. But this graduate of the University of Chicago Law School was unrelenting in his campaigns against big business. Booth called himself a "public interest" lawyer, a novel term at the time. "I have sought to protect their interests from violation by huge utility companies," he said. "Harry Booth has no understanding of big corporations," a telephone company public relations official told the *Sun-Times*. "He often sees the devil in actions which are merely part of the routine operations of a large utility."[19]

Stevens's link to Booth's organization was his Northwestern law professor Nathaniel Nathanson, who sat on the committee's board and had clerked for Supreme Court Justice Louis D. Brandeis, a legendary opponent of corporate concentration. He worked in the federal Office of Price Administration; he was an active member of the Chicago Chapter of the American Civil Liberties Union. In September 1950, Stevens, Booth, and Nathanson formed a "committee of three" within the group to prepare court testimony regarding proposed rates for Illinois's telephone monopoly. Nathanson "suggested it would be good to have an opportunity to participate in rate hearings," Stevens recalled.[20] In January 1951, he reported to the group's board on efforts to oppose telephone rate increases. "Nat thought Harry was good for consumers but not good for himself," recalled Nathanson's wife, Leah. "Lots of people disliked Harry because he was so strong-minded about what he thought was right."[21] Booth had the distinction of having a dossier in the secret "Red" files of liberals that the *Chicago Tribune*'s arch-conservative publisher, Robert R. McCormick, maintained at the newspaper. According to a memo in the file, Booth was born in Lithuania, "then part of Russia," and was of "Jewish nationality."[22]

Booth's associates comprised a who's who of Chicago's left wing. He and Senator Paul H. Douglas had fought against the Samuel Insull utility empire in the 1930s. During the Great Depression, populist agitation against privately owned electric utilities was the centerpiece of liberal politics. Booth was named by Governor Henry Horner, a distinctly independent Democrat, to serve on the Illinois Commerce Commission, which set utility rates. In the 1940s, Booth worked in the Roosevelt administration's Office of Price Stability. In postwar years, many of Booth's friends belonged to the loose political coalition that helped Adlai Stevenson in his campaign for Illinois governor in 1948 and his unsuccessful campaigns for president in 1952 and 1956.

Despite the liberal credentials evident on its letterhead, the Citizens' Public Utility Committee was hardly a radical organization. While Stevens was a member, the board met, frequently on Saturdays, in the headquarters of the Chicago Bar Association, the watering hole of Chicago's legal establishment. Edward Levi helped organize Booth's committee.

In an era of intense public discourse about industrial conglomeration, Stevens's development as an antitrust lawyer avoided doctrinaire certitude. His experiences and associations spanned the range of attitudes about concentration of economic power in America. His unaligned stature in the highly partisan field reflected the ideological neutrality and equanimity necessary to represent clients of varied interests. He needed as much independent temperament as he could muster to handle his most celebrated client, baseball entrepreneur Charles O. Finley.

In the early 1950s, much of the national debate about business concentration played out in the House Judiciary Committee, chaired by New York Democrat Emanuel Celler. "Manny" Celler's strong words in the newspapers about antitrust enforcement were a key element of his political identity. As a platform for those words, he created and chaired Subcommittee 5, known formally as the Subcommittee on the Study of Monopoly Power, to investigate and hold hearings on corporate combinations. The subcommittee's ranking Republican member, Representative Chauncey W. Reed of suburban Chicago, was a lawyer who had sponsored railroad reorganization legislation. Reed belonged to a powerful Republican congressional contingent from Illinois that included Everett M. Dirksen. When a job opened in early 1951 for a staff lawyer representing the subcommittee's Republicans, Reed hired Stevens, who was then thirty-one years old and a protégé of antitrust powerhouse Edward Johnston.

As much as he admired Johnston, Stevens was looking for a change of scene. He and several other young World War II veterans who had signed on with Johnston's firm were annoyed by its bureaucracy and barriers to advancement. One of those vets, Edward Rothschild, had commanded a platoon of half-track mobile howitzers in Europe. He didn't like big organizations. "We were too old; we had been in the war; we were in this chicken-shit organization, excuse me; there was too much dead weight ahead of us," he recalled.[23] For the second time since Stevens obtained his law degree, John and Betty moved back to Washington, D.C., this time with two adopted children—John and Kathryn.

Stevens and his fellow congressional committee staff lawyers trudged through arcane antitrust probes of the newsprint industry, pharmaceutical retailing, an alleged international petroleum cartel, and proposed amendments to the Robinson-Patman Act of 1936, which regulates price discrimination by sellers of goods and services. In such a thicket of legal weeds, the manicured grass of baseball fields looked especially inviting. Chairman Celler knew that an antitrust investigation of major league baseball would draw press attention to an otherwise dreary topic.

A historic intersection of law and sports, which still intrigues baseball enthusiasts in the legal profession, occurred in 1922. Justice Oliver Wendell Holmes wrote for the Court that federal antitrust statutes did not apply to professional baseball teams. In an opinion widely considered one of the worst by the revered justice, Holmes held simply that major league baseball players did not engage in interstate commerce or, for that matter, in commerce at all, and therefore their teams were exempt from the Sherman Antitrust Act and the companion Clayton Antitrust Act. As a result, team owners were free to collude, particularly in dividing up the market and in maintaining their so-called reserve clause in player contracts, which bound certain players indefinitely to their teams and kept player salaries low.

Three decades later, in the summer of 1951, baseball's antitrust exemption remained in force, despite the start of nationally televised games and the expansion of federal antitrust enforcement to other national entertainment industries. Several lawsuits by ballplayers challenged the reserve clause and Holmes's ruling. But baseball owners and reporters covering the sport were convinced that overturning the exemption would ruin baseball's financial underpinnings and threaten the "integrity of the game."

If Celler hoped to raise the profile of his subcommittee on monopoly power, he succeeded. "I want to say . . . that I have never known, in my thirty-five years of experience, of as great a lobby that descended upon the House than the organized baseball lobby," he said. "They came to Washington like locusts."[24] A survey of baseball writers that Stevens compiled for the subcommittee found that the journalists overwhelmingly endorsed the reserve clause and believed that professional baseball should be allowed to govern itself, without regard to the Commerce Clause of the Constitution or federal antitrust laws.

Celler's baseball probe had a backstory: Emerging cities outside the northeast quadrant of the United States, and their representatives in Congress, wanted to host new major league teams. "Celler was trying to put the heat on baseball through these hearings to expand," recalled former baseball commissioner Bowie Kuhn. There were only sixteen teams in the National League and American League, and the owners guarded their territories jealously. Expansion, they feared, would spawn weak teams in secondary cities and dilute revenues of the sport. "If you drew a line from Chicago to St. Louis to Washington to Boston and back across they were all there," Kuhn said. "[Celler] felt that this was perhaps an example of the misuse of monopoly power to contain it in that area when other parts of the country would like to have major league baseball."[25]

At the end of July 1951, Celler convened hearings that brought some of the biggest names in baseball, on and off the field, to Capitol Hill. Despite their conservative political tendencies, team owners retained Paul A. Porter, one of Washington's most influential lawyers, a liberal lion of the New Deal era, and later a law partner of Thurman Arnold, to represent them at a time when Democrats controlled the White House and Congress. The conflicting theories and realities of baseball law were essentially nonpartisan.

Stevens, a lifelong baseball fan, presented to the subcommittee a history of baseball's legal standing and offered his assessment of the business's exposure to antitrust enforcement: "In view of many recent decisions expanding the concept of interstate commerce, it seems likely that the U.S. Supreme Court would agree with the Court of Appeals that baseball is interstate commerce. In summary, therefore, it seems fair to state that organized baseball is very probably interstate commerce; the question of the legality of its various agreements, however, has not been judicially determined." Existing contracts between teams and players may not violate antitrust laws, he concluded, but "it might be possible that . . . the agreements among the clubs setting up private methods of enforcement [of the contracts] would be illegal."[26] Within the subcommittee staff, Stevens's skepticism about baseball's antitrust exemption was shared by Republican and Democratic appointees.

The leadoff witness at Celler's hearings was Ty Cobb, the biggest vote-getter in the inaugural year of the Baseball Hall of Fame in 1936. In 1913, Cobb had demanded a salary boost and challenged the contract that allowed Detroit Tigers owner Frank Navin to bar him from switching teams for more money. Cobb had retired from the game in 1928.

Celler greeted him as the sports hero he was, despite his self-acknowledged reputation for violence and unscrupulous play. Under Celler's questioning, Cobb tried gamely to explain details about the structure of professional baseball that, he remarked at one point, were beyond his expertise. But near the end of the testimony, Stevens zeroed in on Cobb's actual knowledge of the game. "Would you say that the quality of play today is better, or about the same, or perhaps worse than it was when you were a player?" he asked. Cobb replied that "old-timers" like him often think things were better "back then" but that the conditions the players encountered had improved.

"Mr. Cobb, perhaps we could shorten this," Stevens interrupted. "You would say the conditions are better. But as to the quality of play, does the ballplayer play a better brand of baseball today?" In other words, had thirty years of exemption from federal antitrust laws improved the product offered to the public by the major leagues? "Absolutely, I do not think so,"[27] Cobb answered. In the vernacular of economic theory known to Stevens but probably not to Cobb, baseball's monopoly power had not increased consumer welfare, at least as far as this retired baseball legend was concerned.

Public hearings continued into October. Perhaps because he was a Chicago native and a Cubs fan, Stevens led the questioning of chewing gum magnate Philip K. Wrigley, president of the Chicago Cubs. Stevens saluted Wrigley as a "free thinker" among baseball owners but prompted him to acknowledge that the self-governance of the American and National leagues, free from antitrust constraints, needed improvement.

One exhibit Stevens presented on that point was the standard contract offered to prospective players in the All-American Girls Professional Baseball League, organized in 1943, when a wartime shortage of men led team owners to try something new. Stevens noted that the contract for the "girls" did not contain the controversial reserve clause. "That is correct," Wrigley said. "It was an idealistic, nonprofit operation. We went over the things that were generally discussed as being questionable, if 'questionable' is the right word, in baseball, and this was set up on that basis entirely."[28]

In the end, Celler's committee complained about the monopoly power of baseball owners but recommended no reform. Political reality trumped economic theory. A report issued in May 1952 said that, despite the harm to players, "the overwhelming preponderance of the evidence established baseball's need for some sort of reserve clause."[29]

Funding for Stevens's job as associate counsel to the monopoly subcommittee expired. He and Betty returned to their home in

Chicago. "The kids in particular seem awfully happy to be back," he wrote to E. Ernest Goldstein, general counsel of the subcommittee.[30] He rejoined his law firm, then called Johnston, Thompson, Raymond & Mayer, but continued to advise the subcommittee. The subcommittee staff remembered Stevens's prediction that Adlai Stevenson would and should be the Democratic candidate for president in 1952.[31]

In July 1952, Stevens, Edward Rothschild, and Norman Barry quit the Johnston firm and hung a shingle at 120 South LaSalle Street, the building where Rothschild's father, Isaac, had an office. It was a unique trio among Chicago law firms: a Catholic, Barry; a Jew, Rothschild; and a Protestant, Stevens.

Barry, an outgoing street fighter of a lawyer known as Jack, was politically connected in the Cook County Democratic organization through his father, who had been a state senator and was at the time a Cook County judge. Both Barrys had played football at Notre Dame and were popular members among the legions of Chicago's Notre Dame boosters. Rothschild was quieter but smarter. His father, who joined the firm as "of counsel," was a former Republican Illinois legislator and close friend of Walter Schaefer. A year earlier, Schaefer had won election as a Democrat to the Illinois Supreme Court, with Edward's help as campaign manager. Stevens, a registered Republican, was the only one of the three partners with no political entries in his pedigree. The Stevens name still had value in Chicago business circles, despite the family's Depression-era problems.

Later that year, Congressman Reed asked Stevens to return to the judiciary committee staff. He declined, telling him it did not seem wise to leave town after launching a new partnership in Chicago. But in 1953, after the election of Dwight D. Eisenhower as president, Stevens returned briefly to Washington as an unpaid member of the attorney general's Committee to Study Antitrust Laws. Republicans had recaptured the White House, in part by promoting the interests of conservative small business entrepreneurs who had become as anxious as liberal economists about the conglomeration of American business in the postwar era. The committee was one response to that concern.

Such volunteer work cost Stevens's fledgling law firm his work with paying clients but burnished its reputation as an antitrust shop that was able and willing to represent defendants as well as plaintiffs in the complex arena. Indeed, the firm added lawyers L. Edward Hart and William G. Myers, who had been working with Stevens on a massive and long-running federal price discrimination suit against the dairy industry [*United States v. Borden Co.*]. In 1962 Stevens argued the case before the Supreme Court on behalf of Bowman Dairy Co. of Chicago, Hart's principal client. The Court, in an opinion written by Justice Tom Clark, Truman's former attorney general, ruled against the dairies. In the mid-1960s, Stevens encountered Thurgood Marshall for a second time professionally, when Marshall as U.S. solicitor general picked up the Borden litigation.

The baseball world finally was undergoing change. In 1954, industrialist Arnold Johnson acquired the Philadelphia Athletics and moved the team to Kansas City, Missouri, breaking out of the northeast quadrant. Johnson was one of the capitalist cronies who controlled major league baseball. But when he died at age fifty-three in 1960, the successful bidder for his team did not belong to the club.

Insurance entrepreneur Charles Oscar Finley from La Porte, Indiana, wanted to own a baseball team. Charlie O., as he came to be known, was single-minded, ruthless, and crude in pursuing what he wanted. In hindsight, Finley came to be regarded as a breath of fresh air for the game, but his impulsive antics made the other owners squirm. Finley had become a major hindrance as team owners wrestled with the problems of expanding the game to new cities and dealing with the first-ever union of major league players that showed muscle, the Major League Baseball Players Association, headed by Marvin Miller, former chief economist for the United Steelworkers Union.

As usual, baseball's elite, exempt from antitrust rules against collusion, conspired to devise a plan for dealing with Finley. Three lawyers—Bowie Kuhn, representing the National League; Sandy Hadden, representing the American League; and Paul Porter, representing the commissioner of baseball—met in New York City.

"Finley's behavior was always unpredictable," Kuhn recalled.[32] Although he was a good judge of baseball talent, Finley's mercurial personality would have gotten him blackballed in any of the other owners' country clubs. He treated players with equal abruptness, fining and otherwise disciplining players for minor infractions. He fired his manager, Alvin Dark, and rehired him a few years later. "He was predictably unpredictable," Kuhn said. "And it was a time when we were very anxious to create a good working climate with the union. Finley's treatment of ball players was never good. Charlie was doing things which the union could seize upon and say the owners were behaving unfairly. It gave the union leverage."

Worse, he had enraged Kansas City's civic establishment by announcing that he might move the team just three seasons after he acquired it. Missouri Senator Stuart Symington angrily threatened to revisit baseball's antitrust exemption in Congress. Someone had to get Finley under control. Porter, who had known Stevens since the days of the Celler antitrust hearings, "came up with the idea of Stevens," Kuhn said.

Earlier, Finley had retained one of the nation's celebrity lawyers, Louis Nizer, to be his muscle against fellow team owners and other perceived antagonists. But Nizer's flamboyance nearly equaled Finley's. The trio of baseball lawyers decided that Stevens could provide temperamental balance and asked Hadden, on behalf of the American League, in which the A's played, to approach Finley with the idea. "Remarkably enough—he wasn't a guy who took suggestions easily—he liked it," Kuhn said. "He thought it was a good idea. I could not have been more delighted."

Finley's antagonisms extended beyond his fellow team owners. In labor negotiations with players association head Marvin Miller, "Finley would never sit still in a chair," Miller remembered. "He would get red in the face to an alarming degree. He would cuss, not at you individually but at the situation. . . . Every once in a while Stevens asked for a recess and walked out with Finley and then came back."[33]

"John would let Charlie do his thing, and then John would give Charlie some advice, and that's what he would do," said former law partner Alan L. Unikel, who worked with Stevens on Finley-related matters. "He was soft-spoken. When Stevens raises his voice, he's on the wrong side of the case."[34]

The chemistry between Finley and Stevens prompted several lines of speculation. William Myers, who joined Stevens's law firm in 1955, agreed that the two men seemed like an odd couple. But he noted that Finley in 1964 was trying to relocate the Athletics to Oakland, California, a move that required approval of other owners. "Charlie was concerned about getting the proper vote of the owners and wanted to have an antitrust person, I'm guessing, as a threat if the deal wasn't approved," Myers said.[35] The fact that Stevens had shown no ideological bias in antitrust circles made him a less predictable and therefore more credible counsel for Finley, who viewed the antitrust law not as legal doctrine but as the ace up his sleeve.

Stevens's bona fides as an antitrust combatant were no secret. In 1961, Byron R. White, the deputy attorney general in the Kennedy administration and future Supreme Court justice, interviewed him for the job as head of the Justice Department's antitrust division. Stevens and White had met each other in Hawaii as fellow navy officers. "I never had to give him a definite answer because [Attorney General] Bobby Kennedy had other plans," Stevens recalled.[36] In the years before civil rights enforcement became the trademark of the Justice Department, antitrust was high on Robert Kennedy's agenda. Lee Loevinger, who regarded antitrust enforcement as a "secular religion," got the job.[37] He hailed from the Minnesota Democratic-Farm-Labor Party, whose founders included his father and Hubert H. Humphrey, the Democratic whip in the Senate. But Stevens clearly had made the big leagues in antitrust law. The Finley/Stevens personality mix made sense, as well, said former Athletics star Ken Harrelson. "Hawk" Harrelson was a colorful and assertive player whom Finley released from the A's in a pique of anger. "Charlie was an enigma," Harrelson said. "He liked to talk to people who were almost the antithesis of him."[38]

The personalities of Stevens and Finley had at least one thing in common: an ability to focus single-mindedly on the goal at hand, independent of distractions that might have sidetracked others. The best analysis of the Stevens/Finley relationship probably was expressed by Stevens himself. In 1972, after he had joined the federal appeals court in Chicago, Stevens testified by way of a deposition that was read to the jury in the trial of a lawsuit brought by a former Oakland A's official, William Cutler. Finley had hired Cutler as his vice president for baseball operations in late 1967 and fired him six months later. Cutler sued for back pay, claiming that Finley had misrepresented his job description. Stevens testified that he had forewarned Cutler before he signed with Finley: "You and I both know that Charlie is a difficult man to work for. Before you take the job, you have to commit yourself." Stevens added, "Bill knew he had to be prepared to get along with Charlie."[39] Cutler won his case, nonetheless. After the verdict, the jury foreman told a reporter: "I thought Finley was an ass. A hard-nosed, successful businessman, yeh. I was impressed with him because he is very successful at what he does. But the way he handles people rubbed me wrong. I saw him chew out his own lawyer in the hall and I didn't like that."[40]

Stevens and Finley remained an unlikely pair until Stevens went on the federal bench in 1970. Kuhn recalled that some in baseball's establishment who had cheered Stevens's role as a calming influence on Finley were not pleased at how well Stevens succeeded in relocating the A's. "I didn't think it was a good move but I did attribute the ability of Finley to pull it off to having John Paul Stevens as his lawyer," Kuhn said.[41]

Just days before the start of the 1968 baseball season, Finley refused to come to terms with Oakland officials over use of the newly constructed Oakland-Alameda County Coliseum. "He was the kind of negotiator who wanted to squeeze that last drop of blood," said Coliseum general manager William Cunningham.[42]

Once, Finley and his lawyer walked out of a late night meeting in the newly built Coliseum, intending not to return. "Charlie insisted if we couldn't get an agreement we should storm out of the meeting," Stevens recalled.[43] But the negotiating ploy went awry. The two men exited the building and found themselves in the middle of nowhere, with no automobile, taxicab, or public transportation available at the new facility. They had to return to the meeting to ask for a ride.

As the meetings dragged on and opening day approached, "John Paul Stevens pulled out his pen and stuck it in Charlie's hand and said, 'sign,'" Cunningham said.[44] Despite chronic dissatisfaction by A's fans with the Coliseum as a baseball venue, the team generated an exciting but brief dynasty, winning the World Series three years in a row—in 1972, 1973, and 1974.

"The interest of his client determines what the lawyer will seek to accomplish," Stevens noted in a speech after he joined the federal bench. As he worked to solidify the move of the Athletics to Oakland,

> I naturally became convinced that the result we sought was not only in my client's best interest, but also in the larger sense in the best interest of 'baseball'—a sort of mystical concept that owners, fans, and players may understand in somewhat different ways—and [that] the interest of fans everywhere would profit from the move. . . . It is amazing. . . how often the advocate becomes sincerely convinced that the cause of justice really requires vindication of his client's interest. . . . I by no means suggest that a lawyer exercises no independent or neutral judgment in advising and representing his clients. But it is a fact that a lawyer's initial analysis of a new problem is naturally affected by his knowledge of what his client wants to accomplish. It is quite different in the judging business. We have no client to tell us how a case should be decided.[45]

Practicing antitrust law in the era of the Chicago School of Law and Economics demanded rigorous analytical skills to answer the riddle, "When does a monopolist monopolize?" Lawyers with such abilities might not be the first people to look to for someone with the skills to smooth the rough edges of an impulsive impresario who was making his mark on one of the nation's greatest monopolies, Major League Baseball. In representing Charlie Finley, Stevens exercised both talents.

JUSTICE JOHN PAUL STEVENS

Photo by Steve Petteway. Collection of the Supreme Court of the United States.

John (*left*) and brother William at the Stevens family summer home in Lakeside, Michigan, August 1923. Stevens Family Photo Collection, Chicago History Museum (ICHI-61173).

Elizabeth S. Stevens and son John at Stevens family summer home in Lakeside, Michigan, August 1923. Stevens Family Photo Collection, Chicago History Museum (ICHI-61172).

James W. Stevens (John's grand-
father) and wife, Alice, at Stevens
family summer home in Lakeside,
Michigan, July 1923. Stevens
Family Photo Collection, Chicago
History Museum (ICHI-61170).

Stevens boys (*tallest to shortest*):
Ernest S., Richard ("Jim"),
William, and John with Elizabeth
S. and Ernest J. Stevens (*standing*)
and unidentified child caretaker at
Stevens family summer home in
Lakeside, Michigan, August 1923.
Stevens Family Photo Collec-
tion, Chicago History Museum
(ICHI-61171).

John in backyard of family home in Chicago's Hyde Park neighborhood, year unknown. Stevens Family Photo Collection, Chicago History Museum (ICHI-61177).

John and Stevens family dog, Monday, outside family home in Chicago's Hyde Park
neighborhood, year unknown. Stevens Family Photo Collection, Chicago History
Museum (ICHI-61179).

(left) The Stevens hotel on South Michigan Avenue, Chicago, circa 1927, Chicago History Museum (ICHI-61180).

(below) Stevens family at the Stevens hotel, 1927 *(left to right)*: Ernest J., Alice, James, Elizabeth, John, William, Richard, and Ernest S. Courtesy of the Hilton Chicago.

Three Stevens boys, William, John, and Richard ("Jim"), in the Stevens hotel (1928).
Collection of the Supreme Court of the United States.

Chicago Tribune, "Jury Convicts Ernest J. Stevens," October 15, 1933.

Courtesy of the *Chicago Tribune* Archives. All rights reserved. Used with permission.

Norman F. Maclean, 1970. Photo by Leslie Strauss Travis. Courtesy of John Maclean.

Leon Perdue Smith, Jr., circa 1947. Special Collections, University of Maryland Libraries.

Lieutenant John Stevens in Hawaii, circa 1943.
Collection of the Supreme Court of the United States.

Left to right: Communications traffic analysts Robert L.J. McKee, Robert W. Turner, and John P. Stevens at Station Hypo, Hawaii, circa 1943. Collection of the Supreme Court of the United States. Courtesy of Robert W. Turner.

Professor Nathaniel L. Nathanson, November 11, 1983. *Chicago Tribune* staff photo. Courtesy of *Chicago Tribune* Archives. All Rights Reserved. Used with permission.

Justice Wiley B. Rutledge, circa 1943. Photo by John F. Costelloe, Library of Congress, Rutledge Collection.

Charles O. Finley at Comiskey Park, Chicago, 1963.

Photo by Luther Joseph, *Chicago Daily News*. Courtesy of the *Chicago Sun-Times*.

Arthur La Frana, February, 1955,
Chicago Tribune staff photo.
Courtesy *Chicago Tribune*
Archives. All rights reserved.
Used with permission.

(opposite page) John Paul Stevens
and Sherman Skolnick, 1969.
Photo by Larry Graff. Courtesy of
the *Chicago Sun-Times,* © 2009.

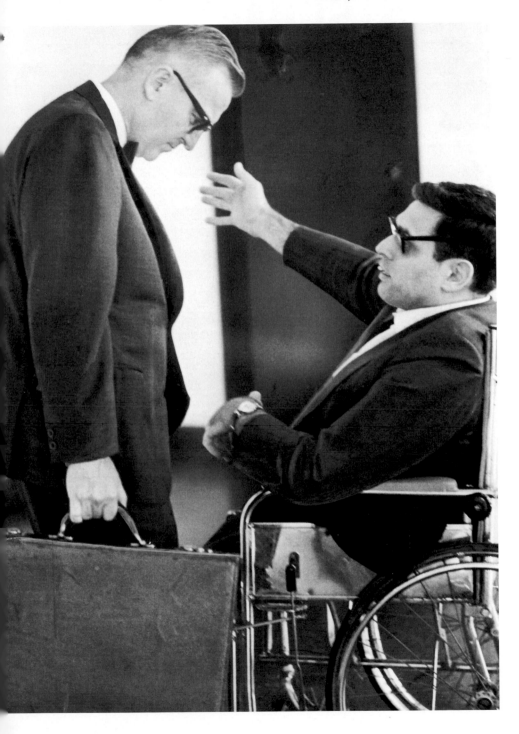

Walter V. Schaefer (*seated, at middle*) campaigning for Illinois Supreme Court, 1951. Chicago History Museum (ICHI-61166).

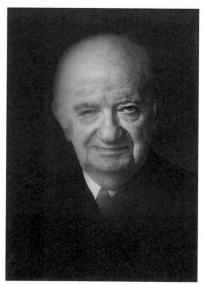

Judge Julius J. Hoffman, circa 1982. Chicago History Museum (ICHI-61169).

Senator Everett M. Dirksen (*left*) and Charles H. Percy, 1964.
Photo by Robert W. Kelley, Time & Life Pictures/Getty Images.

(*above*) Charles A. Bane. Chicago History Museum (ICHI-61168).

(*right*) Judge Robert E. English, September 30, 1953. *Chicago Tribune* staff photo. Courtesy of *Chicago Tribune* Archives. All rights reserved. Used with permission.

U.S. Seventh Circuit Court of Appeals, February 1972. *Standing, left to right*: Judges Robert A. Sprecher, Wilbur F. Pell, Jr., Walter J. Cummings, John Paul Stevens, Roger J. Kiley, Otto Kerner, Thomas E. Fairchild. *Seated, left to right*: Judges Win G. Knoch, R. Ryan Duffy, Chief Judge Luther M. Swygert, Court Clerk Kenneth J. Carrick, Judges Latham Castle and John S. Hastings. Wilbur F. Pell, Jr., Collection. Courtesy of the Law Library, Indiana University Maurer School of Law.

(above) Father James Groppi at a press conference, December 10, 1969. *Chicago Tribune* staff photo by Bill Bender. Courtesy of *Chicago Tribune* Archives. All rights reserved. Used with permission.

(right) Senate Judiciary Committee, 1975. *Left to right, at table*: Senator Charles H. Percy, Judge John Paul Stevens, Attorney General Edward H. Levy. Senator Charles H. Percy Papers, Chicago History Museum (ICHI-59958).

(right) Left to right: Betty Ford, President Gerald R. Ford, Elvera Burger, Chief Justice Warren E. Burger, Betty Stevens, Associate Justice John Paul Stevens at the Stevens swearing-in ceremony, 1975. Courtesy of Gerald R. Ford Library.

(below) U.S. Supreme Court, 1977. *Left to right*: Associate Justices John Paul Stevens, Lewis F. Powell, Jr., Harry A. Blackmun, William H. Rehnquist, Thurgood Marshall, William J. Brennan, Jr., Chief Justice Warren E. Burger, Associate Justices Potter Stewart and Byron R. White. Photo by Yoichi Okamoto © Okamoto Photo, 2009. Print courtesy of Mrs. Luther M. Swygert. Photo reproduction by Judie Anderson.

'OK Betty, I'll consider a woman for the Supreme Court . . . Now let me in

Editorial cartoonists reacted to Betty Ford's preference for a female Supreme Court nominee, 1975. Cartoon by M. Stimson, *Houston Post* (*Houston Chronicle*).

Maryan and Justice John Paul
Stevens. Collection of the Supreme
Court of the United States.

Political cartoon sent by Justice Stevens to Justice Harry A. Blackmun in May 1988 with the
note, "Harry, you may enjoy this one." Cartoon by Tom Toles. Toles © 1988, *The Washington
Post*. Reprinted with permission of Universal Press Syndicate. All Rights Reserved.

"I don't know about you, but my confidence in the judge as an impartial guardian of the rule of law wasn't that high even before the Supreme Court ruling."

(above) Cartoon based on Justice Stevens dissent in *Bush v. Gore*. Cartoon by Robert Mankoff © 2000, *The New Yorker* Collection from cartoonbank.com. All rights reserved.

(left) Maryan and Justice John Paul Stevens at Fordham (University) Law School symposium, 2005. Photo by Robert Daniel Ullmann © Robert Daniel Ullmann.

(above) Left to right: President George W. Bush, Chief Justice John G. Roberts., Jr., Jane Marie Roberts, and Justice John Paul Stevens leaving the White House East Room after the swearing-in ceremony for Roberts, 2005. Photo by Joe Raedle, Getty Images News.

(right) Chief Justice John G. Roberts, Jr., and Justice John Paul Stevens on the Supreme Court steps, 2005. Photo by Joe Raedle, Getty Images News.

Justice Stevens winding up to throw the ceremonial first pitch before the start of the game between the Chicago Cubs and the Cincinnati Reds at Wrigley Field, Chicago, on September 14, 2005. *Chicago Tribune* staff photo by Nuccio DiNuzzo. Courtesy *Chicago Tribune* Archives. All rights reserved. Used with permission.

(left) Justice John Paul Stevens at a bridge tournament, 1994. Photo by Brad Markel © 2009.

(below) Justice John Paul Stevens bobblehead doll, made by Alexander Global Productions, Bellevue, WA, for *The Green Bag: An Entertaining Journal of Law*. Photo by Bill Barnhart.

Justice Stevens's hole-in-one plaque, 1990. Photo by The Oyez Project, with the permission of Justice John Paul Stevens.

President Barack Obama with Justices Stevens and Kennedy (and retired Justice Souter in background) at the investiture of Justice Sonia Sotomayor, August 2009. Photo by Steve Petteway. Collection of the Supreme Court of the United States.

Supreme Court of the United States, September, 2009. *Standing, left to right*: Associate Justices Samuel A. Alito, Jr., Ruth Bader Ginsburg, Stephen G. Breyer, Sonia Sotomayor. *Seated, left-to-right*: Associate Justices Anthony M. Kennedy, John Paul Stevens, Chief Justice John G. Roberts, Jr., Associate Justices Antonin Scalia, Clarence Thomas. Photo by Steve Petteway. Collection of the Supreme Court of the United States.

CHAPTER SIX

The Senator

Three years before he became a judge, Stevens's preference for evenhanded first impressions appeared in the *Chicago Tribune* in a letter to the editor about a major controversy in Chicago. In August 1967, the city unveiled in its Civic Center plaza a gigantic rust-colored steel statue donated by Pablo Picasso. No one knew what the unnamed structure was supposed to depict, but nearly everyone had an opinion.

"Apparently, there are two principal schools of thought about Picasso's contribution to Chicago: that it is a great work of art; that it is a hoax," Stevens wrote on the day of the unveiling. In what may be the only public reference Stevens ever made to his political party affiliation, Stevens said, "both schools are correct, and therein lies the true genius of the masterpiece. It is unquestionably an imaginative and dramatic representation of an elephant. What could possibly amuse its creator more than to persuade our wonderful mayor that the Civic Center should be decorated with a world-famous statue of an elephant? Only a truly great artist could work such a miracle" of presenting a 162-ton Republican totem to decorate the front yard of the Democratic organization of Mayor Richard J. Daley.[1]

Like many Chicagoans, Stevens had no trouble viewing nearly every public phenomenon in his hometown through the lens of local politics. He was a well-informed spectator but not a player. He enjoyed his momentary stint as a *Chicago Tribune* critic of art and politics so much that, like most of his favorite anecdotes, the Picasso elephant story appeared in Stevens's speeches throughout the years. But riddles in law easily lose their parlor-game charm. "One of the contrasts between art and law is that mystery, ambiguity, and suspense are virtues in art, but not in law," Stevens said in 1992, marking the twenty-fifth anniversary of the installation of the Picasso statue.[2] When Picasso's mammoth but lighthearted statue was unveiled in downtown Chicago in the summer of 1967, the nation's system of laws was under attack. Less than three weeks earlier, President Lyndon Johnson had named Illinois governor Otto Kerner to chair a commission on deadly urban riots, which had just rocked Detroit, Newark, Cincinnati, Atlanta, and other cities. Chicago and its legal system were spared that year but not the next.

In those years, Republicans held several key positions in Illinois, including the two U.S. Senate seats and the presidency of the Cook County Board. They controlled both houses of the legislature. Democrats occupied the governor's mansion and the state's most important address, Chicago City Hall. Illinois voters were evenly divided between Republicans and Democrats.

For leaders of both parties, judgeships—elected state judges as well as federal judges appointed by the president upon the recommendation of the state's U.S. senators when they share the same party affiliation—were valuable patronage rewards to political supporters and cronies. In Chicago, the city's judicial system also represented an insurance policy for local politicians engaged in dubious election practices and everyday corruption. Indeed, the best analysis of Chicago political strategies in the close 1960 presidential victory of John F. Kennedy over Richard M. Nixon was aptly titled *Courthouse Over White House*. Author Edmund F. Kallina, Jr., demonstrated that the race that mattered most in Chicago that year was the election of the chief Cook County prosecutor, not the election of an American president.

Chicago lawyers in the 1960s played local politics in two venues, regardless of their party registration. First, city politics mattered, because hardly any lawyers wanted to offend Mayor Daley or his organization. Doing so would mean a loss of business and a cool reception in the courtrooms of state and federal judges. Second, many lawyers sought professional stature in the equally entrenched political system of the Chicago Bar Association. Membership on bar association committees and leadership was part of professional development and marketing at a time when lawyers were discouraged from advertising.

By the mid-1960s, the world outside Chicago was intruding on Chicago and CBA politics. The Great Society program of President Lyndon B. Johnson, especially under his Office of Economic Opportunity, recruited dozens of aggressive young anti-poverty lawyers in major cities. These lawyers claimed a broad social mission. In Chicago, they rebelled against the entrenched Daley political machine and challenged the state and city bar associations that were dominated by well-paid corporate lawyers employed by major law firms. The young turks, as they were sometimes known, believed that bar associations should become more engaged in sponsoring legal services for the poor. What became known nationally as the "counter-bar movement" began to jell in Chicago.

"Dissatisfaction was rife within the legal profession, particularly among younger lawyers," wrote American Bar Foundation researcher Michael Powell in his history of a breakaway group, the Chicago Council of Lawyers. "There was little evidence that the profession put the public interest before its own. Indeed, to many observers the profession and its associations seemed at best self-serving and at worst tied to special interests."[3]

Meanwhile, debate over a proposed new state constitution for Illinois presented an opportunity to replace the system of electing state judges with a system whereby judges would be appointed by the governor from a list compiled by a blue ribbon committee. Illinois voters rejected the so-called merit selection provision of the proposed constitution, but the idea helped spur public scrutiny of the bench.

In a little-noticed comment, the Republican candidate for Illinois governor in 1964, Charles H. Percy, a self-admitted law school dropout, told the liberal reform group Independent Voters of Illinois that he wanted to "remove the selection of judges from the election process"—a seemingly benign reform but an affront to the state's Democratic and Republican leaders.[4] Percy lost to the incumbent Democrat, Governor Otto Kerner, who was a product of the Cook County Democratic Organization, but two years later Percy won a seat in the U.S. Senate.

On a separate track, the CBA experimented with reform, hoping in particular to quell complaints by lawyers at small firms. When Stevens applied for membership in the CBA in 1949, his independent streak peeked through. Neither of the two sponsors he was required to list came from his employer, the fast-growing Poppenhusen firm. Instead, he chose his brother Richard James (Jim) Stevens and one of Jim's Hyde Park colleagues, a progressive Republican named Burton H. Young. Both lawyers worked at small firms. Young, an espionage specialist in World War II, ran for Congress in the 1954 GOP primary but was dismissed by Chicago's Republican newspaper, the *Chicago Tribune,* as one "who favors recognition of Red China."[5]

Stevens became active in the CBA's Younger Members Committee, which in the early 1950s investigated the shortcomings of Chicago's municipal court system. The municipal court heard cases of minor violations of city ordinances. "The nits and lice of the legal system would end up there as judges and lawyers," recalled Abner Mikva, a member of the committee with Stevens. But the CBA Board of Managers ignored the committee's work.[6]

After the formation of the Rothschild, Stevens & Barry firm in 1952, Stevens's participation in CBA activities expanded, reflecting the CBA's greater attentiveness to small firms. He focused on antitrust issues, becoming chair of the CBA's Antitrust Committee in 1959. He joined the CBA's Candidates Committee, which reviewed contenders for local judicial posts and published recommendations. By 1962, Stevens won a seat on the governing CBA Board of Managers, succeeding his partner Edward Rothschild as a small-firm representative.

As he labored in the vineyards of CBA politics, Stevens understood the limited civic role of the CBA during the Richard J. Daley era: "On more than one occasion in the 1960s, Mayor Daley informally expressed his gratitude to the officers of the Chicago Bar Association for providing him with a proper justification for refusing to endorse a political supporter who had earned the Mayor's patronage but was not qualified for judicial office," he recalled.[7]

Stevens's elevation to the Supreme Court of the United States from the Seventh Circuit U.S. Court of Appeals in 1975 put him at the pinnacle of the legal hierarchy. In a 2006 letter to a law school dean, former President Gerald Ford declared, "Normally, little or no consideration is given to the long term effects of a President's Supreme Court nominees. . . . Let that not be the case with my Presidency. For I am prepared to allow history's judgment of my term in office to rest (if necessary, exclusively) on my nomination thirty years ago of John Paul Stevens to the U.S. Supreme Court."[8] Yet in some ways Stevens's appointment to the federal appeals bench in Chicago five years earlier by President Richard M. Nixon marked a more distinct moment in the evolution of the nation's judicial selection system. Coming as it did from the playing fields of Illinois and Washington politics in the 1960s, Stevens's Seventh Circuit appointment turned out to be a milestone of judicial independence.

In 1966, Congress expanded the Seventh Circuit, representing Illinois, Wisconsin, and Indiana, from seven judges to eight, along with several retired judges who heard cases on occasion. All but one was a creature of partisan state or local politics to some degree. F. Ryan Duffy, who at age seventy-eight was an appointee of President Franklin Roosevelt, had been a Democratic U.S. senator from Wisconsin; Thomas E. Fairchild had been attorney general of Wisconsin and an unsuccessful Democratic candidate for the U.S. Senate against incumbent Joseph R. McCarthy; Elmer J. Schnackenberg, a Chicago Republican, had been speaker of the Illinois House; Roger J. Kiley had been a Chicago alderman and high-ranking member of the Richard J. Daley Democratic organization. Walter J. Cummings was a former U.S. solicitor general in the Eisenhower administration. Only Thomas S. Hastings, a Republican from Indiana, had no political office title on his resume.

At that time, few notable cases reached the Seventh Circuit. The most celebrated controversy in the mid-1960s was *United States v. Hoffa*, 1966. The court threw out the conviction of James R. Hoffa, head of the International Brotherhood of Teamsters, who had been convicted of mail fraud and conspiracy. In 1965, the court moved from the former headquarters of the Stevens family insurance business on North Lakeshore Drive to the thirty-story Everett McKinley Dirksen United States Courthouse at Dearborn and Adams streets in downtown Chicago, a starkly elegant steel-and-glass structure designed by Ludwig Mies van der Rohe. Mostly the court received little publicity. Judges enjoyed a relaxed lifestyle, which typically included lunches at nearby private, men-only clubs and a thin docket of cases each summer. But in the years 1968 though 1970, a confluence of events disturbed the placid Chicago court system and began a period of reform.

Chicago joined the list of so-called riot cities in April 1968, as entire blocks of the city's West Side were destroyed by fire after the assassination of the Rev. Dr. Martin Luther King in Memphis. The Circuit Court of Cook County struggled to process hundreds of persons arrested in the following days. Justin A. Stanley, CBA president for 1967–1968 and one of the city's most prominent corporate lawyers, formed a bar committee on civil disorders to develop a plan for handling the cases and to recruit CBA members as volunteers for the county public defender's office. "This well-devised mass-arrest volunteer program not only was a model for other cities similarly disturbed but also served notably in the turbulence that shook Chicago during the Democratic convention that August," wrote Herman Kogan in his centennial history of the CBA.[9] In August, concerted political radicals and blithesome youth descended on Chicago for the Democratic National Convention. They came to protest the Vietnam War, expose the embattled state of urban poor, and rebel generally against the older generation. Mayor Daley and many other Chicagoans regarded their arrival as an invasion by alien forces. The convention and its aftermath fractured Chicago's legal community into its own generational divide.

Another spark for reform went almost unnoticed. A month after the Democratic convention, Seventh Circuit Judge Schnackenberg, a Republican, died, ending fourteen years on the bench. The vacancy gave the first opportunity for a Republican president to place a judge on the Chicago appeals court since 1959. In the wake of urban unrest and the Democratic convention disorder, Richard Nixon campaigned successfully on a law-and-order theme. Having two Republican senators available in Illinois to make recommendations should have made the job simple. But the state's senior senator had peculiar problems with judgeships.

In December 1968, Harold E. Rainville, Senator Everett M. Dirksen's top Illinois adviser, wrote a confidential memorandum to his boss: "You know the problems which have arisen in the operation of the Federal District Court in Chicago. Basically, it is not poor work, but no work on the part of two judges: Parsons and Lynch."[10] James B. Parsons, a Kennedy appointee, was the first African American named to a lifetime post on a federal district court. William J. Lynch, a Johnson appointee, had been Mayor Daley's law partner. Both were heavy drinkers, Rainville reminded Dirksen. "Washington must be fully aware of the problem since at judicial conferences it has been necessary to force open the room of Lynch to find him and get him back on his feet. It is an open secret to judges throughout the country and can't long be kept out of the press."[11] With respect to both judges, Rainville, who was known among Illinois's political operatives as "Rainey," added a warning: "If drunkenness and poor work are a basis, then impeachment is possible."[12]

Dirksen, who became the senior senator from Illinois after Charles Percy defeated three-term Democrat Paul Douglas in 1966, was a master of the craft of federal patronage appointments. In 1962, he had persuaded Democratic president John Kennedy to appoint a Republican, Bernard Decker, to the Federal District Court in Chicago, over the strong objection of Douglas, a legendary figure in Kennedy's party. At the time, Dirksen was Senate minority leader, a powerful post that was crucial to the Kennedy legislative agenda. Douglas held no leadership title. Rainville held the fort in Illinois, while Dirksen worked his charm in Washington. "Rainey was Dirksen's alter ego," said George M. Burditt, a former Illinois state legislator who ran unsuccessfully as a Republican for the U.S. Senate in 1974. "He was a very well educated and knowledgeable guy in the legislative process. He wasn't a really likeable guy."[13]

Getting rid of a life-tenured judge was harder than having one appointed, especially considering the backgrounds of Lynch and Parsons, as Rainville noted in a memo to Dirsken: "This is a bad time for the Nixon administration to face a charge of racial discrimination. It would not be a good time, either, to face an irate Mayor Daley if his law partner were attacked."[14] Rainville advised that a pending bill in Congress providing incentives for federal judges to retire after five years of service might give Lynch, age sixty, a hint. His solution for Parsons was even more cynical. Parsons, at age fifty-seven, had no interest in retiring, Rainville said. "That leaves [the] only easy out to move him up to the appellate bench where it will have less impact on the court."[15]

In addition to Rainville's scheme, Dirksen saw the Schnackenberg seat as a chance for him to provide a plum job to one of his downstate supporters. Before Schnackenberg died, four of the five active judges from Illinois on the Seventh Circuit hailed from Chicago. Dirksen, whose home was Pekin, Illinois, just south of Peoria, wanted to spread the wealth. With a newly elected Republican president, Dirksen stood a good chance of handing the Schnackenberg seat to a downstate GOP kinsman. Meanwhile, Charles Percy, whom Dirksen derisively called "the Junior Senator,"[16] wanted a say in federal appointments from Illinois.

A name on no one's list for the Schnackenberg seat or any other federal appointment was John Paul Stevens. Stevens was building a successful and lucrative law practice. In addition to their adopted children, John Joseph and Kathryn, he and Betty had two daughters of their own, Elizabeth Jane, born in November 1961, and Susan Roberta, born in June 1963. They lived in the upper-middle-class North Beverly neighborhood on the Southwest Side of Chicago; or, as locals would emphasize, they lived in Christ the King Catholic parish and sent their children to the parish school. Betty attended church regularly; John did not.

John took flying lessons and bought an airplane, a bit of ostentation, daring, and convenience duly noted among his peers in Chicago's legal community. "He was quite a glamorous figure," recalled Frank J. McGarr, who had been a lawyer for Illinois Attorney General William Scott and was named to the U.S. District Court in Chicago in 1970. "He flew his own plane."[17] In the pivotal year of 1968, Stevens worried when his son, John Joseph, volunteered for army duty and was sent to Vietnam. According to his sisters, John was a troubled youth. "A little wild," said Susan. "I think today Johnny would be diagnosed with attention deficit disorder."[18] His father was proud but anxious about his son's decision.

But Stevens's most harrowing experience that year occurred nine days after his forty-eighth birthday. The Cessna 172 airplane he was piloting on takeoff from the Ottawa, Illinois, airport was buffeted by wind turbulence and ended up in a ditch. His passenger, law partner John J. Coffey III, recalled: "We lifted off and did not have adequate airspeed to climb. The stall warning came on. John did exactly the right thing. He headed down, but a cross wind headed us right into a plowed field. We hit a ditch. I'd never been up in a private plane before. My first experience was not a good one."

When the two returned to their office on LaSalle Street, Coffey said, partner Jack Barry, the most acerbic lawyer in the firm, remarked, "I wouldn't even drive with that guy."[19] Stevens's law practice, especially client Charlie Finley, kept him on the road, or in the air, quite a bit. On off days, he routinely flew back and forth across Lake Michigan to the Stevens family compound in Lakeside, Michigan.

According to his daughters, Betty ran the household. Betty, the more outgoing of the parents, was an excellent cook and loved dinner parties. She and John were avid bridge players, but Betty was the better player, according to fellow bridge club members. "My mother was a fabulous bridge player," Susan recalled. As Susan grew older, "she tried to teach me, but she was so advanced that she couldn't break it down to the most rudimentary skills."[20] The Stevens household was structured to a great extent around the parents' bridge schedule. When Elizabeth, called Liz, and Susan were growing up, a housekeeper had to stay in the home until Betty returned from her afternoon games. John and Betty frequently played in the evening games as well. The children did not learn the game. "Because we lived it so much, there is no way I wanted to learn this," said Liz. "They were very serious. This was not a little club kind of thing. They went to national tournaments."[21]

When John was working, Betty's partner often was a friend and neighbor, Maryan Mulholland Simon. "Betty was the better player. But Maryan was a quick learner," recalled Carol LaBarge, a member of a bridge club the Stevenses frequented.[22] Maryan attended a Catholic girls high school in Chicago and was a 1952 graduate of Saint Mary's College in South Bend, Indiana, the sister school to Notre Dame University. "She was smart," recalled Saint Mary's classmate Nancy Barker. Like Stevens, she knew something of Shakespeare, having played the Earl of Gloucester in a college production of *King Lear*. "She was a wonderful, cool girl. She knew what she wanted. If she started to knit a sweater, the sweater would be done in a week," Barker said.[23] Maryan's father, Clem B. Mulholland, was a prominent builder on the Southwest Side. Ronald Simon, a hospital executive, and Maryan Mulholland were married in 1953 and had five children.

"My mother and Maryan were in the same bridge club," said Liz. "They all played together. In Beverly, there was a whole pile of people in the same bridge club. . . . Her children used to baby sit for me."[24] Beverly was—and is—a popular enclave for Chicago Democrats. City rules require many public employees to live inside its borders. The Nineteenth Ward, which includes Beverly, is home to the city's South Side Irish political contingent, whose legendary names include John Duffy, Thomas Nash, and Dan Ryan, the latter of which is the namesake of Chicago's Dan Ryan Expressway.

Stevens's roots were English, not Irish, and he was a Republican. But he was not political. William J. Bauer, one of the Chicago area's most politically astute Republicans and a Seventh Circuit judge, quipped that Stevens's only political expression in the 1960s was on occasion "to applaud vigorously" when his former University of Chicago classmate Charles Percy ran for office as a Republican.[25] On the other hand, Democrat Abner Mikva recalled that Stevens sent him a small check when he first ran for the Illinois legislature in the 1950s. More problematic to many, Stevens rooted for the North Side Chicago Cubs in the core fan base of the South Side Chicago White Sox.

In a roundabout way, baseball, not Illinois's other favorite pastime, politics, explains Stevens's emergence as a public figure. In June 1969, allegations broke in the newspapers that two of the state's supreme court justices, Ray I. Klingbiel of Moline and Roy Solfisburg of Aurora, had accepted bribes.

An unkempt, physically disabled, and unrelenting civic scold named Sherman H. Skolnick, who called himself a legal researcher, accused the two Republicans of having received shares of stock in a newly formed Chicago bank after giving a favorable ruling in the appeal of a criminal case against the bank's general counsel, Theodore J. Isaacs. Isaacs had been a major promoter of the bank's stock when it was organized a few years earlier. He also had been a close associate and political adviser of former governor Otto Kerner.

Skolnick, who was confined to a wheelchair, was known around state and federal courts in Illinois as an annoying meddler in the justice system. Formally he was a "pro-se" litigant, a person who files suits without benefit of formal legal counsel. He never liked Stevens, but Stevens later honored "the unexpected merit we found in the [Skolnick] allegations" as a factor in his insistence to his fellow juistices that they not routinely dismiss pro-se complaints.[26] Skolnick's charges rocked the Illinois legal establishment, which was already witnessing a generational rebellion. Five days before Skolnick filed formal charges in Springfield, about three hundred lawyers, mostly young progressives still reeling from the treatment of individuals in the King riot and Democratic National Convention, met in a basement auditorium of the Peoples Gas Company, Chicago's natural gas utility, to organize a new bar association for the city, the Chicago Council of Lawyers.

When the legislature, already annoyed by state judges' perpetual demands for higher pay, moved to investigate Skolnick's charges, the state's legal establishment rallied. The Chicago and Illinois bar associations, at the request of the Illinois Supreme Court itself, agreed to air the dirty laundry left over from the *People v. Isaacs* matter. The court selected Frank Greenberg, incoming CBA president, and Henry L. Pitts, incoming president of the Illinois Bar Association, for the commission. In turn, Greenberg and Pitts, both senior corporate lawyers, chose three of their peers as commissioners, and the five picked Greenberg as chairman. Greenberg and Pitts proposed Chicago lawyer Milton I. Shadur, secretary of the CBA, as counsel to direct the investigation. But Shadur never got the job.

The forty-five-year-old Shadur worked for a small Jewish firm whose partners included Abner J. Mikva and Arthur J. Goldberg, the latter of whom was a former U.S. Supreme Court justice and U.S. representative to the United Nations. The job as counsel to the Greenberg Commission, as it was called, was hardly a plum for Shadur. No lawyer eagerly seeks to engage in a public investigation of judges he or she may later face across the bench. Moreover, the work would be pro bono—without pay. "I said I'd just as soon not," Shadur recalled telling Greenberg and Pitts. "They said we're going to have a press conference tomorrow, and we are going to announce that you are going to be representing the commission, so hold yourself available."

Early the next morning, Greenberg and Pitts phoned Shadur. "Did you ever sue Phil Wrigley?" they asked. "I said, yeah." William Shlensky, a young lawyer in his firm who owned ten shares of Chicago National League Ball Club., Inc. (the Cubs), was suing Philip K. Wrigley for his failure to exercise due care and proper business judgment. Wrigley's sin? His insistence on banning lights and night baseball from Wrigley Field, despite the fan appeal and potential income from television advertising.

"I said what does that have to do with it?" Shadur said. A lot. To add prestige to the commission's work, Greenberg had convinced Edwin C. Austin, a name partner in Wrigley's law firm, Sidley & Austin, to be a member of the commission.[27] "Austin and Phil Wrigley regarded [the Shlensky suit] as some kind of communist plot," recalled Howard J. Trienens, one of Austin's partners. Austin already was miffed that the Greenberg Commission's undertaking would disturb his summer plans, Trienens recalled. "When Shadur's name was mentioned, he wanted no part of it."[28]

Shadur said he warned Greenberg and Pitts, "If you got a lawyer who's going to be influenced in that way by an extraneous consideration, you're dealing with a very hot potato on this commission.

How is it going to be when it comes to exercising any courage? I was really horrified. How can you practice law with integrity and have the sense that clients' views can compel you to do something you would not otherwise do?" But Shadur was benched for another player. "I wasn't looking for this in the first place," he recalled. "I said, in the words of the immortal Sam Goldwyn, include me out."[29]

Next, Greenberg turned to the lawyer from another small firm who had just been named to chair the CBA's standing Committee on the Judiciary, John Paul Stevens. By this time Stevens was nationally known in the legal community as a major league baseball lawyer. He had objectively interrogated Philip Wrigley in congressional antitrust hearings in the 1950s. He passed the Austin/Wrigley test. The bigger test was administered by Chicago's newspapers—especially the *Chicago Daily News*—which were skeptical about whether lawyers could investigate judges. Skolnick, who brought the charges, refused to cooperate and continually denounced the investigation as a whitewash.

At first, Stevens and his staff of volunteer investigators felt doubts as well as pressure. Joseph E. Coughlin, one of the young lawyers volunteered by his law firm to work with Stevens, recalled, "The initial estimates of what we were up to was that [Skolnick's allegation] wasn't anything serious at all." Despite the rebellion underway among many young Chicago lawyers, the Stevens team was not composed of insurgents. "There was a generational divide, but we were much more respectful of authority," Coughlin said. "There was a presumption that everything was fine."[30] But depositions by key figures in the scandal, mostly obtained by Stevens and his chief assistant, Chicago lawyer Jerome H. Torshen, uncovered solid evidence of improper relations between Theodore Isaacs and the two justices, as well as intriguing tales of cover-up.

The public testimony surprised those expecting dry exchanges between chummy lawyers. Robert J. Seltzner, an editor for *The Daily Calumet* in northwest Indiana who initiated the press probes of Sherman Skolnick's charges, said: "I was astounded . . . to hear Stevens attacking, not only making presentations. I could hardly believe my ears when Stevens conducted himself like a veteran prosecutor dealing with hardened criminals."[31]

Still, the central question was, What to do? "What's the punch line?" recalled commission lawyer Nathanial Sack. "The original assignment to the commission [by the Illinois Supreme Court] was vague on that." The court had instructed the commission to "conduct an investigation of the specified charges but . . . not adjudicate the rights or liabilities of any person." The court's instruction seemed unsatisfying, especially in light of the hours of pro bono work required and the obviously prosecutorial nature of the probe. "I remember saying as my advice that if you shoot at the king, shoot to kill," Sack recalled. "John looked at me and he smiled. It kind of penetrated his consciousness."[32]

In its July 31 report, the Greenberg Commission, armed with the Stevens team's findings of fact, pressed the envelope of its own formal instructions to the team. It concluded that Justices Solfisburg and Klingbiel had engaged in "positive acts of impropriety" that tainted the court's decision regarding Isaacs and—the punch line—that public confidence in the Illinois Supreme Court "can best be restored by the prompt resignation of the two Justices."[33] One commissioner, Mason Bull of downstate Morrison, a former president of the Illinois Bar Association, dissented from the call for resignations, saying it was beyond the scope of the commission's duty. The two accused justices resigned in August.

Stevens's star rose in the Illinois legal community, especially among leaders of the Chicago Bar Association, because of his expeditious, soft-spoken handling of the Illinois Supreme Court scandal. On the other hand, his partners were pleased to see him return to fee-generating work. But, unknown to them, events were unfolding that took Stevens away permanently from the private practice of law.

Early in his first term, Senator Charles Percy did not see himself as a judicial reformer, despite his early endorsement of merit selection of state court judges. Judicial selection was not a high-profile political issue nationally or among voters in Illinois. But after Richard Nixon's victory in 1968, the junior senator from Illinois was determined to play a role in recommending any federal appointments from his state, especially judges.

Percy's relationship with Dirksen was a political marriage of convenience between two starkly different individuals—Percy, the all-American boy who became briefly the great hope of the national Republican Party, and Dirksen, the grizzled veteran legislator with an arresting voice whose dominance of legislative issues was nearly equal to that of the president he most admired, Democrat Lyndon Baines Johnson. In most venues, Dirksen and Percy seemed to get along, even as their supporters worked against each other behind the scenes. But on federal appointments, the two men sometimes disagreed. In particular, after Nixon won the White House, Percy publicly rejected Dirksen's choice for U.S. attorney in Chicago. His resolve was stiffened when Dirksen told him that he planned to recommend a federal judgeship for a lawyer Percy had fired years earlier for unethical behavior when Percy was president of the Chicago-based photographic equipment maker Bell & Howell Company.

The two GOP senators attempted to divide appointment endorsements for such posts as U.S. marshal and district court judge, often angering downstate Republicans who thought they already had deals with Dirksen. Tom Merritt, a state senator from Hoopeston, Illinois, complained to Dirksen: "I was shocked to hear that you and Senator Percy had made a division of appointments to Federal positions, . . . the final outcome being that Senator Percy had named an individual from St. Clair County to the post of U.S. Marshal for the Eastern District of Illinois." Merritt said Dirksen's aide, Harold Rainville, had promised that the job would go to the Vermillion County sheriff. "This has brought about unrest and tension, which is not good for the Republican Party in this area, and neither is it good for the image of you and Senator Percy." He asked Dirksen and Percy to "correct the wrong that has been done."[34]

In a barely civil reply to Merritt, an aroused Dirksen gave no ground:

> Let me ask you what you would do if you were one of two Republican Senators called upon to agree on seven Federal positions in the state, all of them identified with the Federal Court system or the prosecuting branch. . . . There is a good line of communication between

myself and Senator Percy, because we discussed this whole matter in
my office on several occasions. He had a list and I had a list and we
tried in the spirit of accommodation to agree. That is precisely the
whole story.[35]

One name they jointly endorsed, with no opposition, was Chicago lawyer Charles A. Bane for the Elmer Schnackenberg seat on
the Seventh Circuit. Rainville's scheme regarding Judge Parsons
and Dirksen's hope for a downstater on the court were set aside.
Bane was a high-profile utilities lawyer with an impressive resume
in civic, academic, and Republican Party affairs. He was a friend of
Dirksen's and a longtime supporter of Percy's political ambitions,
dating back to before his 1964 race for governor. Within weeks of
Schnackenberg's death, Justin Stanley, the immediate past president
of the Chicago Bar Association, urged Dirksen to recommend Bane,
who was one of the CBA's most active members.

In early March 1969, Percy presented to Dirksen five names for
the Schnackenberg seat; the lead name was Bane's. One of the
others was a state appellate judge named Robert E. English, who
"is supported by Congressman [Donald H.] Rumsfeld."[36] John Paul
Stevens was not on the list.

Dirksen informed Nixon's Deputy Attorney General Richard G.
Kleindienst, "The Junior Senator and I have agreed to submit the
name of Charles Bane for the vacancy on the Seventh Circuit."[37] The
case for Bane seemed settled. President Nixon formally nominated
him at the end of May. But Bane almost immediately was damned
by two of the most fearsome antagonists a public figure in Chicago
ever encountered: the Internal Revenue Service and *Chicago Daily
News* columnist Mike Royko.

On May 28, the day news of Bane's nomination was first reported,
Royko disclosed that a Cook County judge would oppose Bane's
nomination because Bane was anti-Semitic and was complicit in a
"Jewish quota" among owners in Bane's luxurious co-op apartment
building on Lake Shore Drive.[38] The judge, Jacob M. Braude, had
warned Percy and Nixon privately by letter in mid-April that he
would cause trouble for Bane, but the Royko column was a bomb-
shell.[39] "There seems to be trouble written in the stars for federal

judges this year," Royko wrote. Two weeks earlier, Supreme Court Justice Abe Fortas had resigned amid an ethics scandal stoked by the Nixon White House. "Even Charles Bane . . . is about to have problems," Royko said.[40] Bane vigorously denied Braude's charges and presented support by a prominent Jewish resident of the co-op building in question.

Dirksen and Percy attempted to keep the nomination alive in June, but the IRS matter could not be overlooked. Unbeknownst to Dirksen or Percy, the IRS had accused Bane of deducting personal expenses as business entertainment expenses in connection with his law work, especially his representation of Commonwealth Edison Company, Chicago's electric utility. Deputy Attorney General Richard Kleindienst "asked Bane to attempt a settlement with the IRS. Bane tried, but because of the IRS' intransigent position, Bane feels it would be wrong to settle and asked us to withdraw his nomination," White House aide Egil "Bud" Krogh wrote in an internal memo at the end of July.[41] "Dick Kleindienst told me the Bane nomination is dead," Krogh informed Nixon.[42] Bane asked that his nomination be withdrawn.

Nearly a year after Schnackenberg died, his Seventh Circuit seat remained empty. Then, on September 7, 1969, Everett Dirksen died at age seventy-three of complications from lung cancer. "That broke the logjam," said William Bauer.[43] Percy was now the senior senator from Illinois.

Judicial appointments suddenly were on the front burner, in Washington as well as Illinois. A few weeks before Dirksen's death, Nixon had nominated Clement F. Haynsworth, Jr., of South Carolina, for Abe Fortas's seat on the Supreme Court. Questions about Haynsworth's ethics arose immediately, along with liberal opposition to Nixon's so-called Southern Strategy of pandering to southern whites. Meanwhile, Michigan Congressman Gerald Ford, with the encouragement of the Nixon White House, was threatening to seek the impeachment of another justice, William Douglas.

Back in Illinois, the state supreme court had just been tarnished by the resignations of Justices Solfisburg and Klingbiel. If that weren't embarrassing enough for the state's legal community, on September 24 a trial of eight political radicals opened in Chicago in the federal district court of Judge Julius J. Hoffman. Chaos ensued in and outside the courtroom, leading Hoffman to order one defendant, Bobby Seale, bound and gagged; he later excluded Seale from the trial.

Amid the turmoil in the judiciary, Percy's staff was urging him to become more systematic in handling patronage, from high-profile judicial appointments to obscure commissions and boards, given his new status in the post-Dirksen era. Aide Joseph A. Farrell told Percy that now that he was the senior senator from Illinois, he needed to establish a network of sources, or "references," to suggest names for all sorts of federal jobs. Percy lacked sufficient staff for the task, but ignoring patronage would cripple him politically as he advanced toward his 1972 reelection bid, Farrell warned. "You need a filing system of references appropriate to the professional and political information needed. Bert Jenner is virtually our only oracle now."[44] Albert E. Jenner, Jr., a ubiquitous lawyer and Republican insider, was a partner in Stevens's former law firm, which in 1969 changed its name to Jenner & Block. Among Jenner's clients was Theodore Isaacs in his appearance before the Greenberg Commission.

At the same time that Percy needed a patronage management upgrade, prominent lawyers in Chicago were looking for a way to cleanse the roster of the Illinois judiciary. In early October, Robert S. Ingersoll, chief executive of Borg-Warner Corporation in Chicago and a director of Percy's former company, Honeywell, told Percy that lawyer Justin Stanley "would like to have twenty minutes to one half hour of your time to discuss our judicial system."[45] Percy had many lawyers on his list of supporters, many dating back to his run for governor, including "Charlie" Bane and "Bert" Jenner, both listed as "personal friend."[46] Neither Justin Stanley nor John Paul Stevens was among them.

A few weeks later, Stanley and Percy breakfasted in Washington's swank Cosmos Club, initiating a series of meetings and letters that lasted the rest of Percy's senatorial career. "To my mind, the subject of the functioning of the courts is, as I indicated, of paramount importance and I think the entire judicial system has to undergo the most careful scrutiny," Stanley wrote in a follow-up letter to Percy after the first meeting.

All sorts of people are beginning to speak out about this, from Chief Justice [Warren] Burger down to newspaper columnists. While in no sense do I condemn either the basic system or all judges, it seems perfectly clear to me that such things as delays, incompetence, lack of imagination and, in some few cases, venality threaten a breakdown of the entire process. Much of the trouble is traceable directly to the attitudes of the political parties which both in the elective and appointive process have not regarded the naming of the best judges possible as a matter of decisive importance.[47]

In particular, Stanley cited his friend Carl McGowan, a downstate Democrat, a close associate of former Governor Stevenson, and one of Chicago's most respected lawyers. McGowan and Stanley had been classmates at Dartmouth College and Columbia Law School. In 1963, President Kennedy had placed McGowan on the U.S. Circuit Court of Appeals for the District of Columbia, where he served ably on active and senior status until his death in 1987. "He should have been appointed to the Seventh Circuit but politics prevented it," Stanley wrote to Percy, echoing the complaint of many of Chicago's leading lawyers.[48]

Stanley and Percy, both enthusiastic strivers, hit it off. For one thing, Stanley was no stranger to politics. He had won the presidency of the CBA and was beginning the spade work for becoming president of the American Bar Association in 1976. "That is something people don't just call up and hand you," he recalled years later. "You have to try to get it after you decide you want to do it. And we put together a so-called campaign which necessitated the persuasion of the state delegates to nominate you. . . . It's a political process and you have to have some organizing ability, some sense of what to do and what to say to achieve this."[49] In 1974, Stanley joined a Percy exploratory committee regarding a possible campaign for president in 1976. The effort faded after Richard Nixon resigned and President Gerald Ford became the Republican standard-bearer. But Stanley won his ABA campaign.

After the Stanley/Percy get-togethers and letter exchanges began, Percy's interest in the federal judiciary blossomed, just as judges and would-be judges were making national headlines. At the end of

November, Percy joined sixteen fellow Republican senators in voting against confirming Clement Haynsworth for the Supreme Court. A few months later, he opposed Nixon's substitute choice, G. Harold Carswell, another southerner. Carswell had a debatable record on civil rights and lacked maximum support from the American Bar Association. Percy had been on the fence regarding Haynsworth, but he opposed Carswell almost from the start, with solid approval in his office's polls of Illinois voters. The Senate rejected both men, infuriating Nixon. Political reporters speculated about how Nixon would take his revenge on the GOP defectors in the Senate.

Percy adviser Farrell cautioned his boss that he faced "a serious loss in the White House. Most of the major spear carriers and the President himself will at least tend to write you off. . . ."[50] Sara Evans Barker, a lawyer on Percy's staff at the time and later a federal district judge in Indiana, recalled, "The Justice Department wasn't interested in going out for Senator Percy's agenda."[51]

Back home, Percy enjoyed the financial and advisory support of a cadre of wealthy young Republican lawyers, investment bankers, and business executives, most of whom had attended Ivy League schools, notably Princeton University, and, along with Percy, lived in the wealthy northern suburbs of Chicago. These men were pragmatic, worldly, and ambitious in their politics as well as their professions. Chief among them was congressman and Princeton graduate Donald Rumsfeld.

When the Charles Bane nomination went down in flames, Rumsfeld quickly revived a name he had favored since Schnackenberg died, Robert English of Winnetka, the heart of Rumsfeld's North Shore district. English, a judge on the Illinois court of appeals, was a Princeton trustee and mentor to Rumsfeld. He had long been active in Republican politics. Investment banker Edgar D. ("Ned") Jannotta of William Blair & Co., one of Rumsfeld's closest friends, informed Percy: "I have known Bob English since my high school days, when he steered me to Princeton. . . . He was particularly helpful . . . in the initial Rumsfeld campaign and he has a strong record in Republican participation and leadership."[52]

Justice Stevens often cites his work for the Greenberg Commission as the springboard to his career in the federal judiciary. Yet on September 22, 1969, shortly after the Greenberg report and the resignations of Solfisburg and Klingbiel, Percy wrote to Nixon's Attorney General John N. Mitchell, recommending English for the Seventh Circuit. "Judge English has been recommended to me by the most respected lawyers and civic leaders in Chicago," Percy declared. "Thus, Judge English is my sole nominee."[53] Among the lawyers endorsing English were Frank Greenberg and Henry Pitts, chair and vice chair of the Greenberg Commission; the Chicago and Illinois bar associations; Illinois's Republican Governor Richard B. Ogilvie; and the *Chicago Tribune*. Richard W. McLaren, head of the Justice Department's antitrust division and the most high-ranking Illinoisan on Attorney General John Mitchell's staff, added his support for English. Nixon had a mercurial relationship with the American Bar Association regarding the ABA's process of vetting prospective Supreme Court nominees. But his justice department routinely sought ABA comments on other federal judicial nominations.

It was well known that English, at sixty-one years old, was a year beyond the threshold the ABA preferred for incoming lifetime federal judges. What few knew was that English had been rejected twice by ABA screeners, once by the standing committee, which included prominent Chicago lawyer Miles G. Seeley, and again by a panel of lawyers from outside Illinois who were not involved in the initial review. Kleindienst delivered the news to Percy aide Joseph Farrell at the end of January 1970: "[Kleindienst] noted that these second reviews more often than not result in qualifying the candidate. That was not the case with English—they turned him down again," Farrell wrote to Percy. "While they see him as a superb lawyer and fine person he is seen, almost unanimously according to [Kleindienst], as not possessing judicial temperament: he is dilatory and very indecisive according to ABA. Justice will not send the nomination forward. He said the matter had been discussed with Mitchell who concurs."[54]

Another complication was the fact that Percy's sway over judicial appointments by Nixon was weaker now than it was when Dirksen was comparing lists of names with the "Junior Senator." The new junior senator, former Illinois House Speaker Ralph T. Smith, a Republican appointed by Governor Ogilvie after Dirksen died, endorsed Percy's selections, but it wasn't working.

In late January 1970, Jack E. Walker, the new speaker of the Illinois House, urged Smith to support English but added what many political observers in Illinois believed: "I have heard a rumor to the effect that because Chuck voted against Haynsworth that John N. Mitchell . . . may be putting the 'hammer' down on him."[55]

Meanwhile, Percy's stable of lawyers advising him on judicial appointments was growing and aging. Three senior members of the Chicago bar, Glen A. Lloyd, William H. Avery, and Hammond Chaffetz, whom Percy aide Joe Farrell called a "troika," began supplying names to Percy.[56] Lloyd, born in 1895, Avery, born in 1905, and Chaffetz, born in 1907, represented the graybeard side of the generational spectrum in the Chicago bar, just as Percy was beginning to listen to the relative youngsters in the Chicago Council of Lawyers. Bert Jenner, the Percy "oracle," remained in place as a source of names, but he was proving to be a liability. Jenner apparently misled Nixon about Percy's position on Haynsworth. One man then under consideration, Philip W. Tone, was a colleague of Jenner at Jenner & Block, but in a memo to Percy, Joe Farrell cautioned, "Being Jenner's friend could hurt him."[57]

Hammond Chaffetz was regarded nationally as a leading antitrust lawyer. He joined the Justice Department's antitrust division in 1930 under President Herbert Hoover, on the recommendation of Harvard Law School professor Felix Frankfurter. Chaffetz got the job after his law school classmate Alger Hiss turned it down to become a clerk for Justice Oliver Wendell Holmes. In the Eisenhower administration, Chaffetz was a senior member of Attorney General Herbert Brownell's National Committee to Study the Antitrust Laws, which included a young Chicago lawyer named John Paul Stevens. The two men had worked together on a gigantic antitrust case that came before the Supreme Court in 1966 involving milk producers [*Federal Trade Commission v. Dean Foods Co.*]. Solicitor General Thurgood Marshall represented the government against Chaffetz's and Stevens's clients.

In Washington, meanwhile, Nixon's antitrust chief, Richard McLaren, a longtime professional associate of Stevens in Chicago, had John Mitchell's ear in resolving judgeship problems in Illinois. McLaren was a Yale graduate and a member of the North Shore Republican contingent led by Rumsfeld. Later in his first term, Nixon became bitterly disenchanted with McLaren and his aggressive stance on antitrust enforcement. But at this time, McLaren was a White House darling who was orchestrating a Nixon/Mitchell plan to apply strict antitrust scrutiny to the nation's bulging conglomerates, especially in the media and entertainment industries, which Nixon never liked.

The files of Senators Percy and Smith contain no evidence that Stevens ever put his name forward for a judicial post or that anyone else recommended him. "I don't think I ever heard him mention being a judge," said former law partner Edward Rothschild.[58] But at the beginning of February 1970, "the troika" presented a list of names to Percy that for the first time included Stevens. The accompanying handicapping note, written by Farrell based on the troika's input, mentioned Stevens's antitrust work, his scholarship, and "good judicial temperament." There was no mention of the Greenberg Commission. Farrell added cryptically, "Some question about intellectual integrity since has talked on both sides of issue."[59] Though brief and unattributed, Farrell's comment about talking on both sides might have appealed to Percy, who disliked groupthink and political ideologues. A 1982 law review article, after inspecting Stevens's private practice and published writings on his antitrust specialty, endorsed Farrell's analysis in a more positive tone: "Stevens' litigation tactics as a private practitioner provide little insight into his philosophy of antitrust. He appeared to take his clients as they came, plaintiffs and defendants alike, and fashioned his arguments to fit their circumstances."[60]

Percy later recalled his re-acquaintance with an old college friend: "Early on the committee came up with the name J.P. Stevens. I asked if that was John Paul Stevens. They said yes. I said, 'He was a classmate with me at the University of Chicago. In our senior year, he was chairman of the men's honorary society and I was chairman of the inter-fraternity council. He was the smartest senior in our class."[61] Stevens's story, told by Kenneth A. Manaster, one of Stevens's investigators on the Illinois Supreme Court case, was different: "Probably Stevens's practice of using his middle name professionally had caused Percy not to recognize that this was the same John Stevens he had known some thirty years earlier."[62]

Either way, it was in Percy's interest to minimize their former association. The best story, which happened to be true, would be that Stevens simply was a highly qualified lawyer who had not sought a patronage job. If he could place Stevens on the federal appeals court, one step below the Supreme Court, Percy knew he could inaugurate a new regime for making judicial appointments in Illinois.

Eventually, "Percy's perspective on the judiciary was that anybody who applied would not be considered," recalled Milton Shadur, whom President Jimmy Carter named to the federal district court in Chicago in 1980 with Percy's support.[63] But Percy's merit selection initiative would fail if Stevens refused or if Nixon continued to stonewall Percy's selections.

Initially, Stevens balked, according to subsequent interviews with both men. In 2005, Stevens gave his recollection in a magazine interview. He acknowledged being reluctant because of financial considerations: "Well, I was. I was just beginning to have a feeling of some security, and I thought my practice was successful and if I had a little more time, I would have been more financially secure. But nonetheless I was certainly interested, and when I got the telephone call from a member of his staff asking me to meet the senator, I of course agreed. . . . I met with him on a Saturday morning to discuss—supposedly—my views about some candidates that he had in mind for two or three vacancies. And we talked a little bit, then he said, 'Well, would you be interested?' I said, 'Well, Chuck, I hadn't really thought about it.'"[64]

In a 1998 oral history interview, Percy gave his version: "He said, 'Let me think it over and talk to my family. I just can't give you an answer.' He went home and called me back the next morning and said, 'No, I can't do it. I've really got to educate my kids. I've got to make enough money for that and other expenses. Why don't you name me six years from now and that would be fine.' I said, 'Look, John, in six years I may not be senator. In six years we may not have a Republican president, either. In six years, you ought to be on the Supreme Court.'"[65] (. . . At this point in their conversation, Percy told author Robert Judd Sickels, "I crossed my fingers behind my back."[66]) "'Take another night, talk to your family, and think it over,'" Percy told Stevens. "He then accepted the next day."[67] Stevens told Manaster that Percy just "happened to hit it right."[68]

Percy recommended Stevens to John Mitchell at the end of February, but Nixon did not make the nomination until September. The Schnackenberg vacancy existed for two years, despite the Seventh Circuit's growing backlog of cases. Meanwhile, Stevens hedged his bets. In March, he was named second vice president of the Chicago Bar Association, a step toward becoming CBA president two years hence. His law firm was expanding and seeking new quarters on the prestigious top tenant floor of Chicago's First National Bank Building, based in large part on Stevens's revenue-producing capacity.

There is no evidence that Richard Nixon became personally involved in any Seventh Circuit appointments. But Chicago lawyers eager to break the logjam, as William Bauer put it, approached the White House directly. In mid-March, Justin Stanley wrote to Franklin B. Lincoln, a former Nixon law partner, urging action on Stevens and other judicial prospects favored by Percy. Lincoln forwarded the letter to Mitchell, who gave a form-letter response: "We appreciate Mr. Stanley's interest and the recommendations he has submitted will certainly have our consideration."[69]

In May, Stevens's law partner Jack Barry complained to Thomas P. Ford, an official of the exclusive Wall Street private bank Brown Brothers Harriman, at an advisory board meeting they attended at Notre Dame University. On Barry's behalf, Ford contacted a friend in the White House, Peter M. Flanigan. Since Stevens's name first surfaced, "nothing has been heard," Ford said, adding that he had no stake in the matter. "Apparently, the problem is that the firm is a small one and having Mr. Stevens sitting on his hands waiting to hear makes it a little difficult to run the operation."[70] Flanigan, who had been Nixon's deputy campaign manager in 1968 and held the title assistant to the president, replied that he had talked to "the appropriate people in the Justice Department" but "no decision has been reached as yet and unfortunately they were imprecise as to exactly when a decision would be made."[71]

Near the end of June, Percy, with Senator Smith's approval, tried a new tactic with Mitchell. "In accordance to what I understand was a suggestion from your department," he submitted to Mitchell a package of five names, including Stevens's, for judgeships on the appellate and district courts in Chicago. "We are hoping that these recommendations can be processed rapidly, in order to fill vacancies on both courts," Percy wrote.[72] But this gambit, which included resubmitting Robert English's name but for the district court, failed. For one thing, it looked like a traditional political fix. For another, Mitchell rejected three of the names, including English, citing ABA concerns.

In Chicago, Percy's frustration on judicial appointments generated little sympathy beyond Justin Stanley and the troika of elder lawyers. Judson H. Miner, one of the founders of the Chicago Council of Lawyers, recalled that when he asked one senior member of the Chicago bar about the Percy Five, he was told that no one cared. "The notion that people were going on the federal bench and no one said 'boo' struck me as goofy," Miner said.[73]

Miner and other young council founders started meeting regularly with Percy, bouncing names around the room in what appeared to be a companion bookend to Justin Stanley and the troika. "He enjoyed the candor," Miner recalled.[74] Everyone in the meetings agreed that Stevens was the name to begin a new process of judicial selection. Percy agreed not to push any candidate the council opposed, including Rumsfeld's man, English.

By September, Percy aide Joe Farrell was dealing directly with Nixon antitrust chief Richard McLaren to end the standoff. McLaren agreed to become Stevens's champion. In mid-September, Nixon nominated Stevens for the Seventh Circuit post, carrying an annual salary of $42,500 (about $225,000 in 2009, adjusted for inflation). Frank McGarr, the fifth name in the Percy Five, was nominated for the district court. At an otherwise perfunctory confirmation hearing before the Senate Judiciary Committee on October 1, 1970,

McLaren appeared as a witness to offer Nixon's, and his own, blessing to Stevens.[75] Stevens's law firm canceled its relocation plan.

Percy continued to have trouble with the Nixon White House and later with the Reagan White House regarding judicial appointments. But as early as April 1970 Farrell was citing the "PR possibilities" of "judicial excellence" as a Percy mission and urging his boss to prepare an article on the subject for a national publication.[76] By the time Percy was defeated for a fourth term in 1984, nonpolitical judicial selections and more credible federal courts in Illinois had become central elements of his political legacy.

For his part, Stevens moved onto the federal bench in Chicago, and later the U.S. Supreme Court, in much the same way the Picasso statue landed in Chicago's Civic Center Plaza. His lack of political resume made him a mystery to litigants and law scholars. Like Picasso, he did little to clear up the matter.

CHAPTER SEVEN

The Bench

When John Paul Stevens took his seat on the Seventh Circuit at the end of the 1960s, his fellow judges welcomed another shoulder at the wheel. The Civil Rights Act of 1964 and civil liberties decisions by the Warren Court, notably the *Miranda v. Arizona* (1966) ruling on criminal suspect rights, were percolating up to federal courts of appeal, expanding court dockets. Appellate courts were being asked to weigh the letter and intent of these statutes and rulings, often for the first time. The delay in getting new judges confirmed had hobbled the court for two years. Another Seventh Circuit newcomer, former FBI agent Wilbur F. Pell, Jr., of Indiana, had been appointed by Nixon a few months before Stevens.

Unlike the Supreme Court, federal appeals courts may not select the cases they will hear. Cases simply arrive over the transom. Typically, panels of three judges review briefs, hear oral arguments, and select one member of the trio to write an opinion. With Stevens on board, panels typically heard six cases a day, four in the morning and two in the afternoon. On occasion, the entire circuit bench, which numbered eight active judges when Stevens joined, reviews a decision. The court was receiving more than a thousand appeals per year, up from slightly more than three hundred cases ten years earlier.

Stevens found relief in the routine. The frequent travel necessary in his private practice, "that sometimes made me go back and forth across the country like a yo-yo," ended, he said.[1] He became a daily train commuter, traveling between Dirksen Courthouse and his home. Chief Judge Luther M. Swygert, an avuncular jurist who enjoyed playing Santa Claus at Christmastime, pushed to keep the court's growing docket under control. Doing so required expeditious and collegial work, a form of male bonding that eased Stevens's transition from private lawyer to appellate judge. Camaraderie was a vital component of efficiency.

At one point, Swygert proposed to open a sundeck on the roof of the thirty-story Dirksen Courthouse, with the stipulation that it be restricted to Seventh Circuit personnel. He envisioned lounge chairs and umbrellas against the sun. "The idea we had worked out is that we would not have all of the roof, but part of the roof in the center, enclosed so people couldn't walk out and fall," recalled Swygert. The idea was approved reluctantly by the U.S. General Services Administration, the federal agency that manages the building, but it never got off the ground. Among other objections, the GSA feared snipers might take potshots at judges from nearby skyscrapers. "One of the points that I think was well taken was that there would be nothing secret about it, and of course, the [*Chicago*] *Sun-Times* and the *Tribune* would be delighted to talk about the judges sitting on the roof of the federal building sunning themselves," Swygert said. "I think it was rather a 'far out idea' to start with, maybe a little eccentric, and also, it was classified as my colossal failure. It got no support."[2]

As it was, aside from occasional newspaper stories published after court clerks handed out opinions in the building's press room, Seventh Circuit judges and the inner workings of the court received almost no media attention. Reporters covering the building "had virtually nothing to do with appeals court judges and, in fact, were shooed away by law clerks and court functionaries whenever we visited their rarefied environs," recalled former *Chicago Tribune* federal building beat reporter Richard Phillips.[3]

Stevens's judicial skills incubated in this lofty isolation. He called it "on-the-job training," a phrase he applied repeatedly throughout his judicial career. "I frequently thought of myself as a new law student," he said of his early days on the Seventh Circuit.[4]

On the other hand, Stevens knew the drill of appellate review. He was the first judge on the Seventh Circuit bench who had clerked for a Supreme Court justice. His boss, Justice Wiley Rutledge, had been intense in his analysis and expansive in his writing, but Stevens remembered that Rutledge moved the assembly line of the Court's docket along in a timely fashion. Stevens was trained in judicial job efficiency. He also had a head start on a philosophy of judicial independence, thanks in part to two experiences in the tumultuous 1960s.

Not long after the end of the riotous Chicago Seven trial of Democratic National Convention protesters, the Judiciary Committee of the Chicago Bar Association, with Stevens as chair, undertook a probe of "questions concerning the conduct of the trial" and the trial judge, Julius J. Hoffman.[5] Hoffman's imperious rulings and remarks had been a national embarrassment to the federal judiciary.

A month after the trial ended with convictions and an appeal process was underway, Hoffman made matters worse by attending a reception in the Nixon White House and the annual Gridiron dinner of Washington reporters. The seventy-two-year-old judge was cheered on both occasions.

Condemning Hoffman was a clear shot for progressive lawyers everywhere. But Stevens knew that the case against him wasn't that simple. For one thing, Hoffman's background conflicted with his antics during the Chicago Seven trial. A year after President Eisenhower appointed Hoffman to the federal district court in Chicago in 1953, he had published in the *American Bar Association Journal* a balanced, convincing rebuke of McCarthyism and a strong defense of civil liberties. Had they read it, the Chicago Seven (originally, the Chicago Eight, before Hoffman ejected defendant Bobby Seale) and their lawyers likely would have approved.

Amid the communist scare of the fifties, fomented by Wisconsin senator Joseph R. McCarthy, Hoffman had written: "Even if we were in imminent danger we could find some better defense than the abandonment of our rights. To give them up in order to make it easier to catch those who threaten them would be like robbing a man of his valuables today in order to prevent a possible thief from stealing them at a later time. Such an absurdity should remind us that we must not take our Constitution for granted but that in our schools, our courts, our forums and our homes we must continue to sell the bill of rights."[6]

Also, respected lawyers defended Hoffman's harsh courtroom discipline as a permissible judicial reaction to the orchestrated chaos staged by the defendants and their lawyers, including William Kunstler. "We have always had self-proclaimed revolutionaries in this country, but the carrying of tactics of revolution into the courtroom itself in criminal trials is a fairly recent development," Frank Greenberg, president of the Chicago Bar Association, told a rare CBA press conference.[7] No judge may allow the transformation of a courtroom into a stage for anarchy, even if a defendant must be shackled and removed, he said.

Stevens remains somewhat sympathetic toward Hoffman. "He had been a fine judge; he had been a better scholar than most members of the bench," he said years later. But judicial demeanor was important as well as judicial scholarship, he said. "I think he just felt he was going to be on center stage on a matter of national interest for quite a while and it just kind of overcame him. He tended to be a martinet and was particularly concerned about anything that was disrespectful of him."[8]

Stevens's committee and the CBA board of managers, which included Stevens as the CBA's newly installed second vice president, shelved its probe of Hoffman pending the outcome of the defendants' appeal. The decision spared Stevens unneeded publicity in the Nixon White House on the threshold of his nomination to the Seventh Circuit. The CBA did not resume the investigation.

After Stevens was named to court, one of the Chicago Seven defendants, David T. Dellinger, told a group of law students that Nixon wanted Stevens on the court to support the government and uphold convictions. The daughter of one of Stevens's friends had heard Dellinger's remarks. "It was totally untrue," Stevens said. "They said Attorney General Mitchell had met with me and I had made this promise; but I never met Mitchell."[9] In fact, Stevens asked his fellow judges to keep him off the panel that would be considering the case, citing his participation in the short-circuited CBA probe.[10]

In 1972, the Seventh Circuit overturned the Chicago Seven convictions and rebuked Hoffman. "The district judge's deprecatory and often antagonistic attitude toward the defense is evident in the record from the very beginning. It appears in remarks and actions both in the presence and absence of the jury," the three-judge panel found in *U.S. v. Dellinger.* "We conclude that the demeanor of the judge and prosecutors would require reversal if other errors did not." The lengthy opinion, which occupied three judges almost exclusively for most of 1972, was written by Judge Thomas E. Fairchild of Wisconsin, who had run unsuccessfully as a Democrat against Senator McCarthy twenty years earlier.

The Hoffman story demonstrated the advantage of obscurity on the bench. With the chambers of the other Seventh Circuit judges filling the twenty-seventh floor of the Dirksen Building, Stevens had been assigned alone to the twenty-sixth floor. When he first saw his solitary L-shaped suite of four rooms, he recalled, "they were being used as a storeroom, with stacks of books and papers piled virtually everywhere."[11] The identity of the main tenant on the floor was not well known: The Chicago office of the Central Intelligence Agency liked being cloaked in the virtual invisibility of the appellate court one floor up. "They decided to put the CIA in with the Seventh Circuit because it was a kind of sleepy place. Nobody came around," recalled the court's executive administrator Collins T. Fitzpatrick.[12] Stevens never complained about his downstairs status and managed to stay out of the news throughout his tenure.

Another lesson in how not to be a judge accompanied Stevens to the Seventh Circuit. The Greenberg Commission had focused on two Republican members of the seven-member Illinois Supreme Court, Roy Solfisburg and Ray Klingbiel. But Stevens could not ignore the behavior of one of the Democrats, Justice Walter Schaefer, his former law school professor and contact for a potential job in the administration of Governor Adlai Stevenson. At the time, Illinois had no more revered member of the bench or bar. Stevenson had placed Wally Schaefer, as he was known, on the state high court in 1951. He subsequently won election and sat on the court until 1976, when he joined Judge Stevens's former law firm. Stevens's former partner Edward Rothschild had managed his campaign to secure the Illinois Supreme Court seat. In 1962, President Kennedy had considered Schaefer for the Supreme Court of the United States, a seat Kennedy eventually awarded to Justice Byron White.

Nonetheless, there were signs by the late 1960s that Schaefer was resting on his laurels, according to Abner Mikva, who had been in the Illinois General Assembly from 1956 to 1966. "He was a big disappointment to a lot of us," Mikva said. "When he went to the court he showed no courage."[13] Another Illinois political reformer, Chicago lawyer Michael L. Shakman, who clerked for Justice Schaefer at the Illinois Supreme Court, recalled: "He was a friend of Richard J. Daley. He'd been a collaborator of Daley's when Daley was down in Springfield, and he would go over when I clerked for him and see Daley. He was anything but anti-Daley."[14]

Stevens's probe of the Solfisburg/Klingbiel affair, as told by Kenneth Manaster in his 2001 book, *Illinois Justice: The Scandal of 1969 and the Rise of John Paul Stevens*, uncovered disturbing evidence. It seemed that Justice Schaefer was unduly concerned about protecting the public image of the Illinois Supreme Court as the bribery charge against two of its members emerged in the press. In a 1999 letter to author Manaster, Greenberg Commission vice chairman Henry L. Pitts said, "I was always confident that Walter Schaefer and others then on the court fully expected that the Special Commission would pull their chestnuts out of the fire with a perfunctory and bland report."[15]

The Stevens probe and Manaster's subsequent inquiries revealed that Schaefer had engaged in improper, off-the-record conversations with a personal friend, Roy M. Fisher, editor of the *Chicago Daily News*, about the court's secret deliberations in the *People v. Isaacs* case. No one knew at the time where the *Daily News* was getting its scoops. "The testimony of other justices would soon show that some of them were none too pleased with this breach, but also that neither they, nor anyone else, realized that Schaefer, the court's most revered member, was the source," Manaster wrote.[16] One of the justices, Byron O. House, said in his deposition, "I was literally astounded . . . but we don't know yet where that [leak] came from. It is a monumental thing to me."[17] Manaster added, "Evidently it was not a monumental thing to Schaefer."[18]

In Schaefer's deposition to Stevens, Schaefer told of receiving a call from Fisher and discussing the controversy with him and, later, telephoning Fisher to ask him to quash a story about the scandal until Klingbiel returned from a trip. "I . . . called Mr. Fisher at home and woke him up . . . and he told me in considerable detail of the newspaper's investigation of the situation. . . . I asked him to with-hold publication until Justice Klingbiel came back. . . . He said he would consider my request, which I put to him as a request of the Court in fairness to Mr. Justice Klingbiel."[19]

In his final report, Stevens avoided comment on Schaefer's questionable sub-rosa dealings with a newspaper editor. He zeroed in on Schaefer's decision not to publish his dissent in the *People v. Isaacs* case. Stevens established that the Illinois Supreme Court's handling of dissenting views was lax compared to the procedure at the U.S. Supreme Court.

In Illinois, dissenting opinions, if reduced to writing at all, were often not published or were attached well after the cases were decided. In his deposition, Schaefer said he did not share his draft with his colleagues, even with Justice Robert C. Underwood, who like Schaefer had voted against the *Isaacs* decision. He said he did not know until Sherman Skolnick's charges erupted that Underwood also had prepared his own dissent:

[Stevens]—Is it fair to summarize at least a part of the point that you are making to be that for you to have prepared the kind of opinion you would have wanted to publish would have required more time and you may not have wished to hold up the handing down of the decision?

[Schaefer]—That is correct. The decision had come down. . . . The notation in the upper right-hand corner, 'No dissent filed,' is my handwriting.[20]

At the U.S. Supreme Court, drafts of dissenting opinions routinely circulate among the chambers during the opinion-writing process, and final versions commonly are published at the same time as the ruling opinion. Often, dissenters in the drafting phase influence the result, even to the point of reversing an initial vote. A draft dissent may thus become a majority opinion for the Court, with the former majority opinion published as a dissent. Stevens's report to the Greenberg Commission stated, "It is not uncommon for Justices of the Illinois Supreme Court to fail to note their dissent to opinions against which they voted. The impression is thus given to the Bar and the public that an opinion was unanimous when in fact it may have been adopted by a divided court."[21]

In his 2001 foreword to *Illinois Justice*, Justice Stevens extended this point and, thereby, described a key element of his judicial philosophy as one of the Supreme Court's most prolific dissenters:

> I do clutter up the U.S. reports with more separate writing than most lawyers have either time or inclination to read. For many years before the *Isaacs* case was decided, most appellate judges refrained from expressing their disagreement with the views of the majority except in exceptional circumstances. Some of our greatest jurists wrote dissenting opinions that were never published. Dissents were often viewed as a threat to the collegiality of the appellate court. Moreover, they tended to undermine the illusion that the law is a seamless web of certain, definite and harmonious rules. Even today in most European tribunals, dissenting opinions are gauche, if not verboten. I am sure that prevailing view explains why Justice Schaefer—one of the finest judges who ever served on the Illinois Supreme Court or, indeed, any court in the country—decided not to publish his dissent in the *Isaacs* case. When I learned in the course of our investigation that he had in fact dissented from the majority's decision, my immediate and strong reaction was that the public should have been informed of that fact when the decision was announced. If there is disagreement within an appellate court about how a case should be resolved, I firmly believe that the law will be best served by an open disclosure of that fact, not only to the litigants and their lawyers, but to the public as well.[22]

During Stevens's five years on the Seventh Circuit, the court developed a reputation as a liberal bastion, contrary to President Nixon's pledge to shift the federal judiciary in a conservative, law-and-order direction. "The Seventh Circuit Court of Appeals has a deserved reputation as being receptive to civil liberties and civil rights claims," the *Chicago-Kent Law Review* wrote in its first annual review of Seventh Circuit decisions, published in 1974. "In large measure, civil libertarians and civil rights proponents cannot fault the court for its rulings. Most of the decisions reflect a welcome empathy and responsiveness to deprivations of constitutional and statutory rights."[23]

Most of the judges had been appointed by Democrats. One of them, former Governor Otto Kerner, picked by President Johnson in 1968, infuriated Nixon and Attorney General Mitchell by continuing to speak out on the liberal findings and recommendations of the Kerner Commission Report on urban riots in the mid-1960s. A few months after Stevens joined the bench, Nixon and Mitchell engaged in one of their frequent Oval Office tirades, captured on the Nixon White House Tapes. This time, they aimed their venom at Kerner and the Seventh Circuit court.

[Nixon]—What's the situation on Daley and his people—Kerner. Are you going to do anything out there?

[Mitchell]—I believe there will be, we've had some indictments.

[Nixon]—I don't want to do anything to him [Daley]; you know what I'm saying, but—

[Mitchell]—No, but I think that—

[Nixon]—Maybe Kerner?

[Mitchell]—Kerner and so forth, because—

[Nixon]—I'd like to see you get him.

[Mitchell]—Yeah, I would, too, for a number of reasons. One, I don't like to see these bastards sitting on these courts, because they have just killed us, this political court out there in the Seventh Circuit.

[Nixon]—Is that right?

[Mitchell]—Oh, they've just killed us.[24]

At the end of 1971, a federal grand jury indicted Kerner for mail fraud and tax evasion relating to his tenure as governor. He was convicted and imprisoned.

Even the Republicans on the Seventh Circuit disappointed Nixon. Not only did Nixon appointee Judge Pell, regarded as the most conservative member, vote to reverse the *U.S. v. Dellinger* Chicago Seven convictions, but he also filed a lone dissent that went beyond the majority opinion, declaring that the law under which the protesters had been indicted was an unconstitutional infringement of free speech.

As for Stevens, his civil liberties sympathies dated back at least to his clerkship with Justice Rutledge and his friendship with Northwestern University law professor Nathaniel Nathanson. Through Nathanson, Stevens in 1954 represented an indigent defendant, Arthur La Frana, who was serving a life sentence for the gunshot murder of a female theater ticket booth operator in 1937. On orders of the U.S. Supreme Court, the case had been revived and appealed to the Illinois Supreme Court, with Stevens representing La Frana. The opinion by Justice Walter Schaefer upheld Stevens's claim, based in part on his discovery of an unpublished newspaper photograph of La Frana, that his client's confession had been beaten out of him. As a judge, Stevens became a guardian of legal procedures available to prisoners for post-conviction appeals.

Nonetheless, analyses by numerous legal scholars of Stevens's five-year tenure on the Seventh Circuit, during which he participated in 542 decisions and wrote 289 opinions, dissents, or concurrences, did not prompt academics and interest groups to classify Stevens as a liberal judge. Words prevailing in summations of his Seventh Circuit output were "moderate," "centrist," "balanced," "generally conservative," and "careful craftsman."

A *New York Times* analysis, written in December 1975 while Stevens was under consideration for the Supreme Court, found his Seventh Circuit opinions "followed established procedures rather than a political or legal ideology." More specifically, the *Times* review said Stevens tended to obey legal precedents, favor judicial restraint, trust in the legal system and defend economic competition against government intervention. On the other hand, the *Times* concluded, Stevens stood firmly for litigants denied basic individual or property rights who could demonstrate that government agencies had failed to follow established procedures and precedents. "The result is some of Judge Stevens's opinions would be called conservative by civil libertarians and others would displease the law-and-order advocates," *Times* reporter Lesley Oelsner wrote.[25]

A federal circuit court of appeals has limited opportunities, given its subsidiary role to the Supreme Court, to innovate in the process of law. But as a new judge, Stevens had no apparent interest in doing so. He saw his job as one of society's many decision makers, along with legislators, government agency chiefs, business managers, juries, lower court judges, school authorities, and others. There was no reason to believe, he often said, that his court's opinion of a controversy necessarily held any more wisdom or integrity than the opinions of others who touched the dispute before it arrived on appeal at the Dirksen Courthouse.

Stevens mused about his task in a 1973 speech to Northwestern law school alums, which he titled "The Education of a Judge": "In the flow of cases that our court processes I have been surprised to note how often the outcome depends, not on our appraisal of the merits, but rather on our identification of the proper decision maker. . . . Every decision maker—whether he be an umpire in the World Series, a legislator, a corporate manager, a member of a school board, or a federal judge—is fallible. But if he has earned the right to make decisions through an acceptable selection process, it is safe to predict that most of his decisions will be acceptable."[26] Stevens entertained his audience by noting that he recently had voted in favor of a political appointee who had sued Illinois's governor to get his job back but, in a subsequent ruling in the case, had voted in favor of the governor who had fired the employee [*Adams v. Walker*, 1974].

Judge Pell demonstrated in his dissent [from the second ruling] my votes were logically inconsistent and could only be explained by the fact that I had changed my mind. In a matter of weeks I had become an older and wiser judge. Of course, . . . since I voted on both sides of the same issue, I can await Supreme Court review with complete equanimity because the Court will surely agree with at least one of my votes. . . . I have learned how the security of life tenure enables a federal judge . . . to feel completely free to vote either way—indeed, even both ways—whenever a new issue confronts him.[27]

Judge Frank M. Coffin, former chief judge of the First U.S. Circuit Court of Appeals in Boston and author of the memoir *The Ways of a Judge: Reflections From the Federal Appellate Bench,* could have been describing Stevens when he depicted the introverted nature of the job: "One of the paradoxes about appellate courts is that there can co-exist the kind of intimate collegiality . . . and a profound, almost antique individualism. . . . In the supertechnical, industrialized, computerized, organized age, appellate courts are among the last redoubts of individual work."[28]

Although he was permitted to hire two law clerks per year, Stevens preferred a single clerk, known as an "elbow clerk," who worked at the elbow of his boss for a one-year assignment. Stevens donated the salary of his second clerk to employ a clerk for the court as a whole. He and his elbow clerk worked like a small, independent law firm. "My relationship with him was very much like the relationship of an associate to a senior partner in a law firm," said former Seventh Circuit clerk James S. Whitehead. "There was a tremendous amount of cordiality, of mutual professional respect, of openness, but there wasn't a lot of closeness. We each sort of did our jobs. He wasn't a pal. I don't think we ever went to lunch together."[29] "I thought there was going to be a lot of writing involved, bench memos and so on," recalled former clerk Robert A. Garrett. (A bench memo is a summary of a case prepared by a law clerk for an appellate judge before the judge sits at the bench to hear oral arguments by advocates in the case.) "It was much more of a speaking clerkship. We would talk through a lot of things. I would find him developing his thoughts and his arguments by that give and take."

But Stevens was learning to judge, not to debate. Clerks were unlikely to change his mind once he had read the facts of a case and the relevant law. "He was a very challenging person to have to debate on issues," Garrett recalled. "I argued a case in the Supreme Court a few years ago, and my greatest worry was that I was going to have to answer questions from Stevens. Most people worry about [Justice Antonin] Scalia; I worried about Stevens. I could never in the time that I clerked for him, at least to my own satisfaction, answer things well enough to persuade him in an argument."[30]

H. Douglas Laycock, a clerk for Seventh Circuit Judge Walter J. Cummings during Stevens's tenure, recalled that, to maintain friendly relations and clear the docket, two of the three judges hearing a case typically deferred to the text of the third member who had been assigned to write the opinion. Backseat editing was kept to a minimum. "The other two members of the panel would approve almost anything he said so long as it did not change the result agreed upon in conference," Laycock said. "Judge Stevens would not; if he disagreed with a passage in an opinion, he would call the opinion writer and try to work out mutually acceptable language; if that failed, he would file a separate opinion. Indeed this is how I came to know Judge Stevens so well; on some cases I worked as closely with him as I did with Judge Cummings."[31]

Stevens's first law clerk, Gary Senner, was emblematic of his approach to the job. Unlike most clerks to judges, Senner was not a freshly minted law school graduate but a former litigator in the Justice Department's antitrust division who had joined Stevens's law firm, as it happened, on the day Stevens was nominated to the bench. He had applied to the firm because of Stevens's reputation and was pleased to follow him to the bench. "My year there he was learning to be a judge," Senner said. "He was very conscious that intellectually there was a transition that you had to make" from the private practice of law. But Stevens wanted to "hit the ground running," Senner recalled. "He was looking for somebody as a sounding board who had a little more experience." For one thing, Stevens was a stickler about correct writing, Senner recalled. "He was very proud and confident of his writing skills," Senner said. "He was an English major. He would lecture me about things like not using 'very' and other adverbs and adjectives—no exaggeration."[32] Stevens would not sign even routine opinions for the court that he felt he had not contributed to sufficiently, Garrett said.[33]

Pride of authorship was only part of the story. As Judge Coffin wrote in his memoir, "to the extent that we do our job well, using the disciplines of our guild well, we move from mere job-bist to craftsman and occasionally to master craftsman when we write an opinion that marshals facts and precedents, logic and analogy, and the broad policy implications of the decision in contemporary society so that the result is seen as fair, expectable, and perhaps even inevitable."[34] Stevens seemed to be striving for Coffin's ideal. But "as a very junior judge, he wasn't seeing neces-sarily the best cases to write on," said Senner. "So, when he got a case that involved an opportunity to think about an issue that had broader implications—fairness of the legal process—then he probably dealt with it with more interest than somebody who'd been sitting on the bench for twenty years. It was an opportunity to start fashioning his view of judging."[35]

His first opportunity to flex his judicial and rhetorical muscles came, it should be no surprise, in dissent. In 1969, the Wisconsin Assembly cited a Catholic priest, Father James Groppi, for contempt and ordered him jailed summarily for leading a parade of protesters to disrupt a legislative session. Groppi was a well-known activist on behalf of the poor in Milwaukee. The story received national attention. *The New York Times* headline read, "Groppi Arrested in Church, Refuses $50 Bond." A White House daily news summary prepared for President Nixon at the time reported the incident and informed Nixon that the Wisconsin assembly had used "an obscure 1848 law" for the "unprecedented action" on a 71-to-24 vote. In the margin, Nixon scribbled "good!" and underlined the word.[36]

A federal judge in Wisconsin blocked the assembly's action, saying that the legislators failed to grant Groppi his basic consti-tutional right to respond to the charges against him. But when the lawmakers appealed to the Seventh Circuit, Judge Wilbur Pell sided with them. In an apparent reference to the unruly Chicago Seven trial, Pell wrote (*Groppi v. Leslie,* 1970): "We cannot be unmindful of recent relatively unprecedented illegal disruptions of the proceedings in courts in our country." The Groppi case "assumes in our judgment critically significant proportions as to the ability of deliberative legislative bodies to carry on their governmental functions."

Pell ruled that permitting a public trial on the charges against Groppi "could easily become a favorite tool in the politics of confrontation and obstruction, and representative government (whatever its present faults) would grind to a halt." Groppi lost again, in a second opinion by Pell, when the full Seventh Circuit bench, including Stevens, reheard the case.

The majority decision was "consistent with the 'law and order' approach to the work of federal judges then being espoused by President Nixon and the Justice Department," Stevens said. He remembered Senator Percy's suggestion that the Seventh Circuit might be a stepping stone to the Supreme Court. "At the time of our conversation I did not place any weight on that suggestion, but when the Groppi case confronted me, I knew that a published dissent would definitely foreclose any such possibility. The collateral benefit of that dissent for its author was immunity from the risk that thoughts about future advancement might subconsciously affect my work on the bench."[37] Later, he said of the Groppi case, "It was sort of my declaration of independence. I was free to go about my work."[38]

Stevens's cordial relations with Pell, a fairly stuffy and tightfisted jurist who hailed from Shelbyville, Indiana, included their banter over Pell's use of large, obscure words in judicial opinions. Even after he left the Seventh Circuit to join the Supreme Court, Justice Stevens continued to kid Judge Pell about his five-dollar words.

Near the end of the Court's 1977–1978 term, Stevens wrote one of his first nationally controversial opinions. It concerned a radio broadcast of comedian George Carlin's monologue about "seven dirty words" [*F.C.C. v. Pacifica Foundation*]. The ruling, which limited First Amendment free speech rights, drew a sharp dissent by liberal Justice William Brennan and was approved barely by a five-to-four majority. In a letter to Pell during this time, Stevens applauded Pell's use of the word "quidnuncish," which means wanting to know gossip. "That's how I feel now," he wrote from inside the Marble Palace.[39] The next year, Stevens wrote a formal letter to Daniel J. Boorstin, the Librarian of Congress, with a copy to Pell, requesting a copy of the "Shelbyville Edition of the Oxford English Dictionary" from the Library of Congress so that he could better perform his duty to oversee the Seventh Circuit.[40]

Pell used no outsized words in his Groppi opinions. In his dissent, Stevens supported Groppi's demand for a hearing and dismantled, with abundant verbiage, Pell's concern about the preservation of order in civic institutions: "In my opinion the preservation of order in our communities will be best ensured by adherence to established and respected procedures." To support that succinct opinion, he deployed his clerk, Gary Senner, to the Dirksen Courthouse law library. In eighteen footnotes that exceeded the word count of his main text, Stevens cited several dozen cases and historical references dating back to 1795, including the 1832 arrest of Sam Houston by the U.S. House of Representatives. "He liked to put things in the footnotes that were very scholarly and of historical interest," Senner said.[41] He inserted citations from judicial heroes Justices Oliver Wendell Holmes, Louis Brandeis, and Felix Frankfurter.

Such an outpouring of scholarship did not inflate all of Stevens's opinions. But in this early effort as a dissenter, he swung for the fences like a rookie baseball slugger. Attempting to give the Wisconsin legislature's appeal its due, he wrote, "the closest case I have found" was a Supreme Court decision from 1888 concerning a lawyer accused of assaulting a U.S. marshal in open court.

A year later, the Supreme Court, in a unanimous opinion written by conservative Chief Justice Warren E. Burger, reversed Pell's decision in no uncertain words. But Stevens's sense of accomplishment did not extend to congratulations for Groppi. Indeed in a 2001 speech he used the kind of word that made Pell beam, "contumacious," to describe Groppi's act of civil disobedience.[42] "Father Groppi was not a hero to him in any way," said Lawrence Rosenthal, a former Stevens clerk.[43]

The Groppi case centered on legal procedure, a special purview for judges. The merit of Groppi's agitation on behalf of the poor and disadvantaged did not matter. "I believe judges are qualified by experience and training to evaluate procedural fairness and to interpret and apply guidelines established by others," Stevens wrote in one of his many Seventh Circuit dissents (*Shirck v. Thomas,* 1971). "I do not believe they have any special competence to make the kind of policy judgment that this case implicitly authorizes." Still, law scholars and other critics often claim that a judge's decisions on procedural questions reflect his or her beliefs about underlying policy issues.

In an effort to indentify liberal tendencies in Stevens's work on the Seventh Circuit, a 1976 *San Diego Law Review* article compared his opinions in prisoner rights cases with those arising from discrimination complaints by women. Stevens's procedural zeal in civil rights cases varied, according to authors Brandon Becker and Michael F. Walsh.[44] They suggested that Stevens was more comfortable in enforcing rights for convicts than for women:

> A consideration of his due process decisions, particularly those involving state action, procedural and substantive fairness, gender discrimination, and prisoners' rights, provides a representative model for analyzing his approach to constitutional decisionmaking. These cases are particularly appropriate, for the questions of law they involved were in flux when Judge Stevens sat on the Seventh Circuit Court of Appeals. Because at that time Supreme Court precedent was sparse or unclear, Judge Stevens had a certain freedom of decision.[45]

As a law clerk in the late 1940s and pro-bono lawyer in the 1950s, Stevens had been engaged in post-conviction prisoner rights issues. The La Frana case made a lasting impression. At that time, Illinois had one of the worst records in the nation in recognizing constitutional rights of prisoners. Nationally, the right of prisoners to due process under the Fourteenth Amendment ("nor shall any State deprive any person of life, liberty, or property, without due process of law") had been debated for decades by legislators, governors, prison wardens, and other decision makers.

"Justice Stevens is proud of his contributions [to constitutional rights for prisoners] and has demonstrated a marked sensitivity to the tragedy of the United States correctional system," the San Diego authors wrote. "For Justice Stevens the tension between the constitutional rights of prisoners, the need for prison security, and the discretion which must be allowed prison officials is an intense reality."[46] For example, in *U.S. ex rel. Miller v. Twomey,* 1973, Stevens ruled that prisoners should have "minimum requirements for due process" before they could be denied so-called good time credits reducing their sentences or be subjected to extraordinary discipline. "Liberty protected by the due process clause may— indeed must to some extent—coexist with legal custody pursuant to conviction," he wrote. "The deprivation of liberty following an adjudication of guilt is partial, not total. A residuum of constitutionally protected rights remains," including in this case advance notice of disciplinary action, "a dignified hearing in which the accused may be heard," the ability to question witnesses, and "an impartial decision maker."

The prisoner rights saga was moving slowly in a more liberal direction when Stevens joined the court, but the newer arena of civil rights was just emerging: gender discrimination under Title VII of the 1964 Civil Rights Act. This area of law lacked a track record of definition or enforcement by judges as well as the U.S. Equal Employment Opportunity Commission, employers, public agencies, or other decision makers. The burgeoning women's movement, building on past victories by African Americans in the federal courts, encouraged experiments in litigation to broaden the definition of gender discrimination under Title VII and to strengthen enforcement procedures. Women's rights advocates, like advocates of rights for African Americans, saw courtrooms as a field of battle that could be more productive than legislative chambers or voting booths.

In 1966, airline stewardess Mary Burke Sprogis sued her employer, United Air Lines, Inc., under Title VII for gender discrimination. Like other airlines at the time, United would not hire a married

woman to be a "stewardess," which was an official job classifica-
tion. If a stewardess married while on the job, she could be and
probably would be dismissed. Sprogis was discharged by United in
1966. But in 1968 the airline, amid considerable public controversy
and a new ruling by the EEOC, revoked its policy regarding stewardess marriages and rehired Sprogis. In 1986, United agreed to pay
$37 million to settle a class-action suit by 1,725 flight attendants,
formerly stewardesses, who had been dismissed under the old rule.

Writing for a majority of the three-judge panel of Walter Cummings, Otto Kerner, and Stevens, Cummings ruled in favor of
Sprogis, affirming the district court's summary judgment (without a
trial) against United Air Lines (*Sprogis v. United Air Lines, Inc.,* 1971).
Nothing in the job of stewardess bore any legitimate relation to their
marital status, Cummings wrote. "The marital status of a stewardess
cannot be said to affect the individual woman's ability to create
the proper psychological climate of comfort, safety, and security for
passengers," he said. "Nor does any passenger preference for single
stewardesses provide a valid reason for invoking the rule."

Stevens dissented. He conceded: "I . . . consider it most doubtful that a job related justification for the no marriage rule can be
proved. . . . As a matter of policy, the majority's view may not only
be contemporary but also wise." But his reading of Title VII found
that United had not discriminated against women under the law.
On the contrary, he pointed out, males, including Sprogis's husband, were not eligible for the job Sprogis had obtained. He added
that Mary Burke Sprogis had been offered another job at United.
He rejected the idea that federal judges were qualified in this case
to embellish the intention of Congress, which sought simply to
end unjust discrimination between men and women. Congress
wrote no law differentiating between "irrational stereotypes and
reasonable requirements" of a job category available exclusively to
women, he noted.

This narrow interpretation helped prompt women's rights activists to charge that Stevens was out of touch when he was nominated
for the Supreme Court. "His rulings—particularly in the case of
Sprogis v. United Airlines—raises [sic] some questions as to whether
he would, as a member of the Supreme Court, be able to provide

equal justice for women," the National Women's Political Caucus wrote to the Senate Judiciary Committee shortly after President Gerald Ford made his selection in 1975.[47]

The claim by women activists that Stevens didn't get it gained traction near the end of his Seventh Circuit tenure. This time, the law in question was not a civil rights statute enacted by Congress but recent Supreme Court decisions concerning reproductive rights, especially *Roe v. Wade*, 1973. Nine couples in northwest Indiana, led by Evelyn Fitzgerald, had sued a local hospital under four civil rights amendments to the Constitution, including the Fourteenth Amendment, for refusing to admit husbands into the hospital's delivery room. The couples had taken classes in the Lamaze child-birth method, a program first popularized in the United States in the 1960s that emphasizes active participation by prospective fathers throughout the birth process. A district judge in Indiana had thrown out the complaint.

On appeal (*Fitzgerald v. Porter Memorial Hospital*, 1975), the case brought some real-world elements to the Seventh Circuit monastery. James Whitehead, Stevens's clerk at the time, and his pregnant wife were Lamaze students. One day, while Stevens was mulling the case, Whitehead told his boss, "time to scoot."[48] He drove to the University of Chicago Hospital to witness his son's birth. The private teaching hospital welcomed both parents in the delivery room. More to the point, one of the university's professors of obstetrics and gynecology had submitted an affidavit for the Indiana couples. The doctor said he had delivered about 1,000 babies in the previous four years with fathers in his delivery room. The presence of the husband contributed to safer, shorter deliveries with no imposition on the hospital or its staff, he said.[49]

In a step to bring more outside participation into the case, Stevens permitted two female law students enrolled in a new federal courts clinic at Indiana's Valparaiso University Law School to argue the case for the plaintiffs. "My parents were both factory workers," recalled Marcia K. Sowles. "My mother worked some overtime and got some extra money and bought me a briefcase."[50] The parents of Linda A.M. Georgeson's husband bought her a suit for the occasion. She was struck by "how far away the judges were" from her. "I remember Judge Stevens being extremely patient and courtly and, I thought, very kind to a law student, because I certainly felt like I was walking into a den of lions and I was going to be attacked."[51] In a few months, Georgeson recalled, she would be able to list on her resume that she had argued before a future Supreme Court justice. But her side lost.

In *Fitzgerald v. Porter Memorial Hospital,* Stevens ruled for a two-to-one majority that couples could not, as a matter of a constitutional right, force public hospitals to allow husbands to attend the birth of a child, even with the consent of their physicians. At the time, Supreme Court findings, citing a right of personal privacy, had outlawed state bans on the use of contraceptives [*Griswold v. Connecticut,* 1965] and upheld the right of a woman to seek an abortion [*Roe v. Wade,* 1973]. The couples in *Fitzgerald* tried to build on the Court's recognition of a right to privacy. But the interest of a wife and husband in having the husband in a delivery room did not rise to the significance required for constitutional adjudication, Stevens ruled: ". . . The dispute within the medical profession as to the propriety and safety of permitting the husband to be present during the routine birth is not one that should be resolved by substituting our judgment for the professional judgment of the defendant hospital. We hold that the so-called right of marital privacy does not include the right of either spouse to have the husband present in the delivery room."

His ruling so angered one Indiana couple that they handcuffed themselves together when they arrived at the Porter hospital, forcing staff members to obtain a hacksaw and separate them before delivering their child, with the husband in another room. In the years immediately after Stevens's ruling, hundreds of public hospitals complied with demands by couples and their physicians to permit expectant fathers in delivery rooms.

Judge Robert A. Sprecher, another Charles Percy judicial candidate on the Seventh Circuit, filed a stern dissent. Sprecher had joined the court in May 1971 as a moderate Republican and was Stevens's neighbor on the twenty-sixth floor of the Dirksen Center. "I dissent completely from [Stevens's] conclusion that the right to privacy does not include the right of expectant parents to have the male present with the female in the delivery room of a public hospital in cases where the attending physician has consented to that procedure," he wrote. ". . . To deny the right of her mate's presence when she desires it at a critical time is unnecessarily, and I believe unconstitutionally, cruel to the expectant mother."

Legal scholars at Vanderbilt Law School, in a 1976 review of Justice Stevens's Seventh Circuit decisions, agreed: ". . . His characterization of the . . . plaintiffs' claim as merely a choice of procedural technique displays a lack of sensitivity to the psychological and emotional importance of the moment of childbirth to the mother and father. . . . Stevens thus suggests a means for limiting all aspects of the protection afforded by the right of privacy."[52]

In their review for the *San Diego Law Review,* Becker and Walsh criticized what they saw as Stevens's greater interest in protecting prisoners' rights compared to women's rights: "With all due respect to the Justice, we hazard a criticism of his technique of narrow construction. In the gender discrimination and prisoners' rights cases, Justice Stevens's technique of constitutional adjudication was substantially similar; only the context changed. Therefore, we believe these two lines of cases can be reconciled only by assuming unstated premises which Justice Stevens has not articulated in his decisions."[53]

In his confirmation hearing for the Supreme Court, Stevens gave Senator Edward M. Kennedy a one-word answer, "yes," and declined to elaborate when Kennedy asked if he would use the same standard of judicial oversight that has been employed by courts "for securing greater opportunities for blacks" on behalf of women's rights as well.[54] At a continuation of the hearing the next day, however, he told Senator Charles M. Mathias, Jr., that he had thought about Kennedy's question overnight and had concluded "I am not sure. . . . The standard of review [for sex discrimination complaints] may or may not be the same as in racial discrimination areas."[55]

Stevens appeared to be looking for guidance and was not willing on his own to create greater protections for women against discrimination, given the fact that gender, unlike "race, color [and] previous condition of servitude," was not mentioned in the Constitution. During his confirmation hearings, he suggested that the proposed

Equal Rights Amendment to the Constitution, adopted by Congress in 1972 and then under consideration by the states, "might provide a standard of review" for gender discrimination.[56]

But that remark merely annoyed women activists further, because Stevens had authored a Seventh Circuit opinion that, in the name of state sovereignty, effectively blocked passage of the amendment by the Illinois legislature [*Dyer v. Blair,* 1974] and mortally wounded the national ERA campaign. He also stated at his confirmation hearing that the proposed amendment probably was unnecessary to advance women's causes. In short, Stevens's tenure on the Seventh Circuit scored poorly with the women's movement, which became the chief organized opposition to his confirmation for the Supreme Court.

In terms of "unstated premises," as Becker and Walsh put it, two possible motivations, which Stevens often has discussed, come to mind. First, he had an interest in avoiding docket creep in appellate courts. The momentum of civil rights litigation that began in the 1960s on behalf of women, racial minorities, and prisoners, whatever its positive value for society, enlarged the caseloads of courts of review throughout the nation. The problem was not just utilitarian—an increased demand for judicial review versus the supply of appellate judges. More important, the trend threatened to increase the number of errors judges made and to jeopardize the independence of the third branch of government by embroiling judges in essentially political issues that had been thrown into the courts by political combatants. Like Father Groppi's march on the Wisconsin legislature, women's march into the courtroom to achieve political aims abused democratic institutions, according to this theory.

But on a much different and more strategic level, Stevens's restraint in *Fitzgerald* helped assure that fundamental liberties for men and women were not diluted by secondary, court-imposed "rights," such as a husband in a delivery room. Although he did not say so directly, he hinted in *Fitzgerald v. Porter Memorial Hospital* that the Supreme Court's *Roe v. Wade* decision would better survive the coming political firestorm if federal courts could not be accused of expanding the right to privacy doctrine that Justice Harry Blackmun had used to affirm a woman's right to have an abortion.

"It is somewhat unfortunate that claims of this kind tend to be classified as assertions of a right to privacy," Stevens wrote in *Fitzgerald*. To the adjective "unfortunate," he might have added "unnecessary" and "risky." From its founding, he wrote, the United States has a long tradition of respecting "the American heritage of freedom—the abiding interest in individual liberty that makes certain state intrusions on a citizen's right to decide how he will live his own life intolerable. Guided by history, our tradition of respect for the dignity of individual choice in matters of conscience and the restraints implicit in the federal system, federal judges have accepted the responsibility for recognition and protection of these rights in appropriate cases. But can it fairly be said that [*Fitzgerald v. Porter Memorial Hospital*] is such a case?" His answer was no.

Using this logic, Justice Stevens quoted his own words from *Fitzgerald* to recognize several basic individual liberties in landmark Supreme Court cases about abortion (*Thornburgh v. American College of Obstetrics and Gynecology*, 1986), homosexual conduct (*Bowers v. Hardwick*, 1986), and assisted suicide (*Vacco v. Attorney General of New York*, 1997). On these occasions, his answer was yes. By having ruled conservatively that a preference for a husband in the delivery room did not merit action by federal judges, under either the Constitution or understandings of personal liberty that pre-date the Constitution, he could more persuasively support—with or without a right to privacy rationale—the liberty of individuals to make more essential decisions, such as abortion, homosexual behavior, and assisted suicide.

"The Court has emphasized the individual interest in privacy, but its decisions have actually been animated by an even more fundamental concern," he wrote in his *Bowers v. Hardwick* dissent. Abortion rights advocacy group NARAL Pro-Choice America, in its 2008 biographies of Supreme Court justices, declared, "Justice Stevens is now the strongest supporter of the right to choose on the Supreme Court."[57]

CHAPTER EIGHT

The President

Picking justices for the Supreme Court has become a minor industry in American politics, with competition among well-funded advocacy groups on the left and right, as well as extensive media exposure for talking heads. Justice Stevens wistfully remembers his nomination to the Court as a watershed moment in at least one respect. His confirmation hearings before the Senate Judiciary Committee in December 1975 were the last not to be televised.

But there were more distinctions. Stevens's nomination to the Court was the first since the 1973 *Roe v. Wade* decision on abortion. Although *Roe* had been the law of the land for nearly three years, political operatives had not yet begun to exploit the subject. Stevens was asked about capital punishment, discrimination against women, and a few other issues, but not abortion.

Stevens's nomination represented the end of an era in other ways, according to research by political scientist John Anthony Maltese, who analyzed nominations through the administration of President Bill Clinton.[1] Between the end of World War II and Stevens's nomination by President Gerald R. Ford, twenty sets of judiciary committee confirmation hearings for Supreme Court nominees were staged. The average length of the resulting transcripts was 232 pages. The Stevens transcript numbered an average 229 pages, thanks in part to the inclusion of lengthy and unsubstantiated harangues against the nominee by two disgruntled private individuals. But for the eight nominations afterward, through Justice Ruth Ginsburg in 1993, the average was 1,845 pages. Likewise, Maltese counted just three special-interest groups participating in Stevens's hearings, average for the postwar period until then. In the eight hearings afterward, the average was eighteen, including forty-three groups weighing in for the 1991 hearings for Justice Clarence Thomas.

Future nominees for the Court might feel a sense of longing for Stevens's low-key confirmation, conducted without live television coverage or sophisticated Internet propaganda campaigns, and concluded after just three days with a unanimous vote by the full Senate. But Stevens was one candidate for whom greater scrutiny might have been justified. As the 101st justice, he is the only justice nominated by a president who was not chosen by voters in a national election. The notion endorsed by the Founding Fathers that Americans would indirectly select federal judges as they chose their presidents did not apply. Ford became vice president by Nixon's appointment after Spiro T. Agnew resigned and President Nixon was forced to tender his own resignation. This unique circumstance, compounded by the controversy of Ford's pardon of Nixon, might well have prompted greater public inquiry into Stevens's judicial ideology and skill. Margaret Drachsler of the National Organization for Women pointed out the problem at Stevens's confirmation hearing: "This appointment was made by a president who has not been elected to the presidency and who has never been elected to any office by a constituency larger than a congressional district."[2]

But a more urgent historical circumstance overshadowed the Stevens confirmation process. His appointment to the Supreme Court played out against national disgust in the judicial system under President Nixon. In the immediate wake of the abuse of power by the Nixon justice department, Ford decided to place independence and professionalism over pandering and gamesmanship as a winning political strategy for filling a vacancy on the Supreme Court.

This was the second time that an overarching public concern kept Stevens in the background as he was being measured for black robes. Five years earlier—during which time an aide to the state's leading Republican contemplated elevating a federal judge with a serious drinking problem and two state supreme court justices resigned in a bribery scandal—the disreputable Illinois judiciary had put judicial selection in a bad light and opened the door to a virtually unknown judicial candidate with no political or ideological pedigree. As a result, no questions were asked when Stevens's name finally emerged as Senator Percy's candidate for the Seventh Circuit.

When President Ford was asked to name the individual who was most influential in his decision to nominate John Paul Stevens for the Supreme Court, his answer was, surprisingly, Donald Rumsfeld. "Don was my chief of staff," Ford said. "The department of justice had fallen into disrepute over the Watergate problem and so forth. Don came to me and said we have to find somebody who is impeccably honest and is first class in the legal profession" to be attorney general.[3]

But Rumsfeld was thinking of more than just a clean new face at the U.S. Justice Department. He was thinking of the institutional power of the presidency. Senator Sam J. Ervin, Jr., of North Carolina, who had become a national hero for his role in the Senate Watergate hearings, had introduced legislation at the end of 1973 to sever the justice department from the executive branch and make the attorney general an independent federal officer. Citing political abuse of the department under former Attorney General John Mitchell, who was also Nixon's 1972 campaign manager, Ervin proposed that the president be allowed to appoint an attorney general but to a six-year term, in theory placing the individual outside the four-year presidential election cycle. Moreover, the post would not be part of the president's cabinet. The Ervin bill was the subject of Senate hearings in 1974. "There were theories floating around to try to make the department of justice independent of the executive branch of the federal government, which I thought was a very poor idea," Rumsfeld recalled. "I still do. It struck me that the way to avoid that idea was for President Ford to nominate an individual who was widely respected."[4]

"He recommended for attorney general Ed Levi," Ford said. "He had a superb reputation, and I said fine."[5] At the time, Edward

H. Levi was president of the University of Chicago, having been dean of the university's law school and provost. He was more than a distinguished academic confined to the ivory tower. He came from the Robert Maynard Hutchins mold of spirited academic activism. As his law students and faculty knew, Levi was a tough, activist intellectual. University of Chicago sources, speaking anonymously to *The New York Times* after his appointment by Ford in January 1975, provided a spectrum of adjectives: compassionate, exhilarating, cold, calculating, impersonal, and downright nasty.[6] Robert H. Bork, who studied law under Levi, said: "There was a certain amount of pain associated with the class. Levi did not tolerate slow responses, silly answers, or opinions held on sentimental rather than intellectual grounds. . . . I do not wish to convey a sense of bluntness, much less brutality, but there was a price to be paid for sloppy thought."[7]

Rumsfeld knew Levi's reputation as an administrator. In early 1969, Levi had directed a successful standoff by the university against a group of students who had taken over the campus administration building and damaged Levi's Hyde Park home. Levi kept police away from the two-week sit-in. (Privately, he told Charles Percy, who was a trustee of the university, that he "would resign if he had to bring in the police."[8]) The demonstrators admitted defeat and retreated without incident. But they protested anew that spring after Levi expelled several dozen students, more than had been kicked out after more aggressive sit-ins at Columbia University and the University of California at Berkeley.

In a 2002 tribute to economist Milton Friedman, the University of Chicago's best-known Nobel Prize winner, Rumsfeld, then the secretary of defense under President George W. Bush, recalled: "As a young congressman in the 1960s, I used to go to seminars at the University of Chicago. Bob Goldwin was the director of the Center for Continuing Education there. He would gather a cluster of geniuses and then allow a few young pups to come and learn at their feet. As a then young pup, I was so privileged and participated in a number of discussions."[9] Robert A. Goldwin later signed on as an aide to Rumsfeld when Rumsfeld became chief of staff in the Gerald Ford White House.

Levi, who looked professorial in his glasses and ever-present pipe, staked out his independence in his confirmation hearing and swearing-in ceremony. When he took the oath of office in February 1975 as the fifth attorney general in six years, he said, "We have lived in a time of change and corrosive cynicism concerning the administration of justice. Nothing can more weaken the quality of life or more imperil the realization of the goals we all hold dear than our failure to make clear by word and deed that our law is not an instrument for partisan purposes."[10]

Politically, Levi was an enigma. Some members of Congress thought he was a conservative Republican. His father was a Republican. Levi had been involved in Percy's brief presidential exploratory effort. But Mayor Daley convinced Senator Kennedy that Levi was acceptable to Democrats. Others had heard he was a liberal Democrat. The White House mistakenly allowed such speculation to fester by not immediately securing the approval of the nomination by Mississippi Democratic Senator James O. Eastland, chairman of the judiciary committee. As a result, Ford's staff vowed not to tarry in locking up a Supreme Court appointment.

Levi did not become an intimate presidential counselor. For that role, Ford had his University of Michigan fraternity brother and early law partner, Philip W. Buchen. Faced with the Watergate legacy and ongoing disclosures about the misuse of intelligence gathering by the Federal Bureau of Investigation, Levi entered the administration with a reform mission to correct "the continuing disaffection of the American public and disbelief in the system of justice," recalled Jack Fuller, former editor and publisher of the *Chicago Tribune,* who worked with Levi at that time. "The second thing is he had Gerald Ford behind him," Fuller said. But "Edward was not popular around the White House."[11] For example, Fuller recalled, "Edward persuaded President Ford to propose a gun control bill that the political people at the White House resisted."[12] Levi wanted to restrict handguns in metropolitan areas, but the idea went nowhere. Then Levi offered reforms to national security surveillance authorization that annoyed the intelligence community and, at the same time, sparked criticism among civil libertarians in Congress. During the 1976 election year, Fuller added, Levi authorized an investigation into possible campaign finance abuse by President Ford.[13] No charges were filed.

Nonetheless, Levi was, from the start, in charge of the process of selecting a Supreme Court nominee. No one else in Ford's universe had the stature for the job. Levi had been considered for the Court during the Nixon years—even though Nixon recoiled at the idea of putting a Jew on the Court—and continued to have supporters for the post, including Mayor Daley and Senator Percy, despite Percy's fingers-crossed hint to Stevens in 1970. But there was no way that Ford could propose his attorney general for the Court without facing a charge of Nixon-like cronyism. Instead, Ford's strategy of detaching himself from the nomination process, in recognition of the Watergate legacy, strengthened Levi's hand as an independent source of potential nominees.

Justice William Douglas's deteriorating health was well known as the Court went on its summer recess in 1975. Two days before Douglas submitted his resignation on November 12, two memoranda for Ford on the subject of a Supreme Court appointment were written by Levi and Chief Justice Warren Burger.

Burger, who used to chitchat with Nixon in the White House, instead wrote formally to Ford. He lamented the Court's workload under Douglas's repeated absences. "We need nine justices without delay," he said, recommending "a nominee with substantial judicial experience" who knew the routine of appellate review and who ideally would already be removed from politics.[14] Levi's memo listed eighteen names and then pared the list down to nine, including Stevens. Among those missing the cut were Antonin Scalia, an assistant to Levi in the justice department, and Philip W. Tone, a former Jenner & Block partner who was on the Seventh Circuit court with Stevens. At the end of his memo, Levi advised Ford, "looking at the top of the list which I am submitting, I would place the greatest emphasis on Dallin Oaks, Judge John Paul Stevens, and Robert Bork. After these three, I would place Judge Arlin Adams and Vincent McKusick."[15]

Dallin H. Oaks was president of Brigham Young University. More to the point, he had been a top-rated law student and professor at the University of Chicago and was well known to Levi. Bork, another University of Chicago alum, was Levi's solicitor general. Vincent L. McKusick was a private lawyer in Portland, Maine, and a former star pupil at the Harvard Law School who had clerked for renowned appellate judge Billings Learned Hand and Justice Felix Frankfurter; Arlin Adams was a graduate of the University of Pennsylvania Law School and a judge of the Third Circuit U.S. Court of Appeals in Philadelphia.

Meanwhile, the new White House chief of staff, Richard B. Cheney, with the encouragement of White House Personnel Director Douglas P. Bennett, mulled over setting up his own, parallel candidate review process, separate from Levi. Cheney's list, prepared immediately after Douglas's resignation, mentioned five names that also appeared in Levi's first cut, including Adams and Bork. Oaks, Stevens, and McKusick were not on the Cheney list.

Bennett advised Cheney that he "should maintain total control over the selection and processing of this appointment." Cheney, Bennett cautioned, should keep his list, which he called "the President's list," secret and advised that "we should let the press speculate on the Attorney General's list."[16] A review of the press coverage, which featured Bork and Adams but not Stevens, Oaks, or McKusick, suggests that Cheney did not implement Bennett's proposal or that it did not work.

Levi said later that there is a Russian roulette aspect to the naming of Supreme Court nominees.[17] Others have used the term "lottery," also suggesting a game of chance. Such remarks may be proper protocol to assuage the losers, but the White House memo traffic at the time suggests that Levi was in command and preferred Stevens from the start.

Ford was unlikely to name Bork. He was an arch conservative who had done Nixon's bidding as solicitor general during the infamous Saturday Night Massacre, when he fired Archibald Cox, the special prosecutor investigating the Watergate affair. With Democrats in control of the Senate, Levi advised Ford, "There would be . . . little doubt that, on the Court, Mr. Bork would provide strong reinforcement to the Court's most conservative wing."[18] In a subsequent interview with law scholar Victor H. Kramer, Levi said he did not recall Bork being high on the list, although his name had appeared prominently in newspaper stories at the time.[19]

Oaks, despite his close link to Levi, was a Mormon and "would have faced difficulties in view of the then prevailing racial attitude of the Church of Latter Day Saints," Kramer wrote in his analysis of the selection process.[20] On his own handicapping sheet, Ford wrote that he wanted "no Mormon problem confirmation fight."[21] Bork's and Oaks's political liabilities would have been evident to Levi, as they were to Ford, leaving Stevens as the only one of the three names he had assigned "the greatest emphasis."

After initial lists of names appeared in the press, a firestorm erupted. Neither list from Levi or Cheney nor a list of eleven names Ford later sent for review by the American Bar Association contained a woman's name. This blind spot is hard to explain, especially considering the fact that the president's wife, Betty, strongly favored a woman, notably Carla A. Hills, Ford's secretary of housing and urban development. Gerald Ford had elevated Hills from a post as head of the civil division of the justice department. She was just the third woman to serve in a president's cabinet.

"Betty was at that time pressing me to recognize women in whatever appointments I made," Ford said.[22] Someone in the White House was not as clueless on this topic as Ford's chief of staff and attorney general. On the day after Douglas resigned, *The New York Times* reported that "Ford is 'actively' considering appointing a woman to succeed Justice William O. Douglas on the Supreme Court, according to highly placed administration sources. These sources said that an 'important factor' was that Betty Ford has long urged her husband to appoint the first woman justice should a vacancy occur during Mr. Ford's term."[23]

Patricia H. Lindh, Ford's special assistant for women, along with several women's rights organizations, presented names of female judges, academics, and lawyers, including Sandra O'Connor and Ruth Ginsburg. Members of Congress proposed male and female candidates from their states. One of the most aggressive male contenders for the job was Senator Robert P. Griffin, of Ford's home state. Newspaper coverage of the imagined horse race never placed Stevens anywhere near the lead.

Ford wanted to fill Douglas's seat before Congress left for its Christmas holiday and returned for the 1976 election year. Part of his haste may have been Senator Kennedy's last-minute attempt, which was killed by Senate Republicans, to give the judiciary committee the power to screen the White House's list of candidates before a nomination formally was made, just as Ford had given the American Bar Association an implied right of first refusal. In the end, four names were under serious consideration: Stevens, McKusick, Adams, and Tone. Tone, a popular federal judge in Chicago, was being pushed by Rumsfeld's man in the White House, Robert Goldwin. Levi virtually had written him off, but near the end of the search Tone surged toward the top of Ford's private list.

The race came down to Stevens versus Adams, Ford said. Adams had strong backing from Pennsylvania Republicans, led by Senator Hugh Scott. But Levi, in comparing the opinion-writing records of the two in his initial memo to Ford on Supreme Court appointments, deftly gave higher marks to Stevens: "Judge Stevens has proven to be a judge of the first rank, highly intelligent, careful and energetic. He is generally a moderate conservative in his approach to judicial problems, and in cases involving the attempted expansion of constitutional rights and remedies. He has shown particular ability in antitrust and other matters of federal economic regulation and would add strength to the Court in this area. Overall, he is a superb, careful craftsman. His opinions lack the verve of Judge Adams but are more to the point and reflect more discipline and self restraint."[24]

Levi damned Adams with faint praise: "His opinions have considerable flair and reach, which give them interest and can suggest an influential member of the Court, but revealing a certain weakness, not so much in analytical skills—which he has—but in being willing to sometimes by-pass or go beyond the most careful analysis. This is the ultimate question about a judge, of course, but my guess is he has the potential to be a strong and good appointment."[25]

Politically speaking, Adams's "sell-by" date had come and gone. Ford, a veteran of congressional leadership, undoubtedly knew that Senator Scott had pushed Adams during the Supreme Court nomination debates in the Nixon administration to the point that Nixon grew tired of hearing the name. In October 1971, while Nixon was trying to find replacements for retiring Justices Hugo L. Black and

John M. Harlan II, he asked his domestic affairs adviser, John D. Ehrlichman, "Who in the world floated the name of Arlin Adams? We had a hell of a time getting him approved by the bar for the [circuit] court, didn't we?" Ehrlichman responded that Scott had been leaking Adams's name to the press. "I nearly choked when Arlin Adams was mentioned," Nixon said. Ehrlichman went on, Scott "manufactured this big PR thing and put it all over town that the president was seriously considering Arlin Adams."[26]

For his part, Adams claimed that he was "a close associate" of Nixon during his 1968 presidential campaign and soon after was rewarded with a seat on the Third Circuit U.S. Court of Appeals. "There had been two or three times when I was seriously considered for the Supreme Court," he said, suggesting he had grown weary of being so popular. He said he didn't appreciate the FBI questioning his mother "and everybody in the nursing home."[27]

The only champion in Washington Stevens had was Levi. Percy, who had publicly endorsed Levi for the Court, played no role. Levi and Stevens were natives of Chicago's Hyde Park neighborhood. Both had attended the University of Chicago Laboratory Schools. Both had studied English literature as Chicago undergraduates. In law, both specialized in antitrust. Stevens had taught the groundbreaking antitrust course designed by Levi and Aaron Director. In his resume as a nominee for the Seventh Circuit, Stevens had listed Levi as a reference. But Levi was nine years older than Stevens. His relationship with Stevens was intellectual and professional, not social. Levi later warned Victor Kramer that a draft of Kramer's article about the Stevens appointment "gives the impression that he [Levi] knew Stevens better than he, in fact, did know Stevens."[28]

The clincher for Stevens was the American Bar Association. Warren M. Christopher, a veteran Washington insider, headed the ABA's Standing Committee on the Federal Judiciary. He enthusiastically endorsed Stevens as a judicial moderate: "You can line up a number of opinions which seem to indicate he is a conservative. But then you can find an equal number . . . which seem to go the other way."[29] The ABA's desire to regain its influence in the selection of federal judges, after being rebuffed by Nixon, matched Ford's intent to keep the appointment of

Justice Douglas's successor on a nonpolitical plane. But the ABA's credibility and political sway was under assault. Women's groups noted that there were no women on Christopher's committee. The ABA's reputation as a conservative white male bastion persisted well beyond the protest era of the 1960s.

Even Senator Percy, who, like Ford, found bar associations a useful tool in presenting judicial appointments as nonpolitical, was beginning to have doubts: "It is entirely proper for the Senate to debate whether the ABA should have veto power over judicial nominations," he declared in a Senate floor speech in April 1975. "I have been helped greatly by the ABA in many areas, including judicial selection, but I have serious questions about some aspects of the ABA's criteria for judicial service."[30]

Still, Ford and Levi were wedded to the ABA seal of approval. Ironically, Nixon's tiff with the organization may have boosted its value to Ford. In reviewing the Stevens appointment, Levi told Justice Lewis Powell: "One of the significant things about the process . . . was the role which the ABA played. . . . It was not just a question of giving the highest recommendation."[31] It didn't hurt Stevens that the incoming president of the organization at the end of 1975 was Justin Stanley, the Chicago lawyer whose friendship with Percy had helped instigate judicial reform in Illinois.

Four days before revealing his selection, Ford held a White House dinner for federal judges from all over the nation. Among the 118 persons in attendance were Stevens and Adams. Betty Ford recalled in her memoir: "Jerry had been close mouthed about his intention, but while we were dressing he slipped, and said, 'Well, the man I'm going to appoint will be at the dinner tonight,' and my heart sank. It was the first inkling I'd had that he wasn't going to name a woman."[32]

"At the White House dinner, I naturally wondered whether there might be some discussion of the vacancy, but I recall no such discussion," Stevens said. "After the dinner, he [Ford] visited our table and chatted with me for about fifteen minutes. As I recall the conversation, most of it related to the status of negotiations with

New York City, which at the time was on the verge of bankruptcy and seeking financial aid from the federal government." According to Stevens, the two men connected as one lawyer talking to another about a case—the case of New York City's financial plight—not as a president talking to a federal judge about a promotion.[33]

Ford announced his choice on the day after Thanksgiving. That morning, a last-minute White House staff meeting aired some final concerns, starting with Stevens's health. The prolonged illnesses of Justices Douglas and Marshall had hobbled the Court, guaranteeing that a nominee's health would be an issue at any confirmation hearing. In August 1971, doctors in California performed a heart bypass on Stevens after he complained to his family doctor about chest pain. One of the consulting physicians was his boyhood chum Dr. Robert W. Jamplis, who later would attend Stevens's installation to the Court. Jamplis and three other doctors gave him a clean bill of health following the surgery.

Stevens's adopted son, John Joseph, was mentioned in the final meeting as "a stepson" who had had "lots of trouble" with the police, according to notes by White House lawyer Edward C. Schmults. Stevens's proposal to have the Chicago Bar Association investigate the conduct of Judge Julius Hoffman came up for discussion. Hoffman was still a hero among Republican conservatives. He privately had registered his opposition to Stevens. So had Chicago attorney Charles Bane, whose tax problems forced him to withdraw from consideration for the Seventh Circuit post Stevens had obtained. The Schmults memo recorded that there was "no real civil rights or religious opposition" to Stevens, because he was unknown to leaders of either constituency.[34]

One of Stevens's law clerks, Sharon Baldwin, took the call shortly after noon from the White House. The Dirksen building in Chicago was nearly empty on the day after Thanksgiving and the office secretary had the day off. "He'll take it; hold on," she said.[35] "I don't remember my exact words, but I know that my answer was prompt and unambiguous," Stevens recalled.[36]

Stevens told Ford that he wanted to inform his Seventh Circuit colleague Philip Tone immediately, as the two contenders had an agreement between themselves. Their relationship dated to 1948, when Tone took Stevens's desk in the Wiley Rutledge chambers and moved with his wife into the apartment that Betty and John had occupied on 16th Street. Later, John told Phil about an opening at the Popenhusen law firm in Chicago. Phil followed John onto the Seventh Circuit court. Ford asked Stevens to stay mum until his press conference later in the afternoon. A few minutes before the press conference, the White House called Stevens and said it was permissible to leak the news to Tone. But "before I could call Phil, he walked in the office and congratulated me," Stevens recalled.[37]

The White House staff, led by Philip Buchen and Stevens's former law partner Edward Rothschild, began a rapid-fire confirmation campaign. It was Stevens's one and only bid for "elective" office, requiring a majority vote of the Senate, after the pro forma Senate confirmation for his Seventh Circuit seat. Their candidate made courtesy calls to senators and prepared for the confirmation hearing. A White House memo, reflecting regret over delays in the Levi confirmation, spoke of "the delicacy of 'urgency.'"[38] Rothschild cautioned Stevens that many things could go wrong before he would be called to Washington for a fourth time. He advised Stevens not to pack his bags just yet.

But the press and political reaction to Stevens's nomination was predictable, benign, and in some cases amusing. Senator Hugh Scott thought he saw the influence of Donald Rumsfeld and, perhaps, the GOP Princeton mafia on Chicago's suburban North Shore: "Probably a fraternity brother of Don's." Congressman Thomas P. ("Tip") O'Neill, a Democrat from Massachusetts, said, "Who?" Senator James G. Abourezk, a Democrat from South Dakota, when informed by the White House, said, "Thanks, but what happened to the plans to name a woman? Too bad for you guys that Nancy Reagan isn't an attorney."[39] A reporter asked White House Press Secretary Ron Nessen: "Ron, an awful lot of Chicago judges have been investigated [by the government] and private citizens and other groups out there—making sort of a profession of investigating Chicago judges. Has this judge figured in any of those investigations that you know of?" Nessen answered, "No." Another reporter asked, "What is his religion and party, please?" Nessen responded, "As far as I know, we don't know what his religion or party is and neither one of those were a subject of consideration when the various candidates were considered, and you will have to ask Judge Stevens, because I don't have it."[40] William F. Buckley, the leading conservative voice, correctly predicted the future perception of Justice Stevens and, in particular, forecast Steven's firm view on the separation of church and state: "If Stevens is a 'conservative,' the reasonable expectation is that he will 'conserve' liberal interests, by and large. . . . Let us pray. As long as we are not standing on public school property."[41]

In the next few days, commentary from left and right was muted. Conservative columnist George Will, writing in the *National Review,* remarked on Ford's choice well into a broader column about the president's political weakness ahead of the 1976 election. "That Mr. Ford is aware of his limited freedom is apparent in his nomination of John Paul Stevens to succeed Justice William Douglas. The choice of Mr. Stevens is eminently defensible. It is also very timid. . . . But there were other potential nominees— Solicitor General Robert Bork, for one—who are not brilliantly uncharacterizable; who are, rather, well known for their sharply defined views."[42]

From the left, *The Nation* praised Stevens as part of Charles Percy's "fine record for excellent nominations for law-enforcement and judicial posts" but struck the same note about the political constraints that Ford faced: "The dictates of politics do have occasional windfall benefits. President Ford felt compelled, for purely tactical political reasons, to nominate as Justice Douglas's successor a man he might not otherwise have selected. If he had felt free to indulge personal preferences, he probably would have named a right-wing conservative. . . . Judge Stevens is a much better nominee than might have been expected."[43]

Syndicated political columnists Rowland Evans and Robert Novak, who wrote a joint column, insightfully expressed a concern that was voiced—then and later—by some on the left and right: "Mr. Ford furthered a trend toward capture of the nation's highest court by the organized legal profession that could convert it into a body of legal mechanics rather than law givers. . . . Selecting Stevens not only means that five of the court's nine members now will be alumni of federal appellate courts but strengthen[s] the new role in shaping the court exercised by the ABA." They warned of "subtle risks of encapsulating the Supreme Court in blandness never intended for it."[44]

Neither Ford nor Levi said much to clarify the judicial philosophy of their man. Levi gave one hint in an interview by CBS reporter Fred Graham on the CBS Sunday news program *Face the Nation*. Graham remarked that Stevens could be the "swing" vote as the Court considered whether to reinstate the death penalty.

[Graham]—What do you think he's going to do?

[Levi]—I haven't the slightest idea what he's going to do. I didn't read his remarks at his confirmation hearing.

[Graham]—He ducked it.

[Levi]—Of course, I think he'd probably do what I would do, but that's because I think he's a very sound fellow.

[Graham]—What would he do?

[Levi]—I think if one conceded it's going to be equitably used and that there are proper standards, I happen to think that the death penalty would be constitutional. But you have to make sure of that.[45]

Levi was correct, although over time Stevens narrowed the circumstances in which he endorsed capital punishment.

Ford provided no insight into the views of his Supreme Court choice. At a New Year's Eve press briefing in 1975, Ford made no comment about Stevens's style of judging and, more noteworthy still, no reporter asked the question. Instead, like the former college athlete he was, Ford in an opening statement gave the score of the confirmation process: "I can't positively say that this nomination and confirmation was a record, but it is pretty close to it. We did a good job in checking all of the potentials and the net result was in a very, very short period of time we ended up with a man who was confirmed ninety-eight to nothing. That is a pretty good batting average by any criteria."[46]

But an assessment of Ford as merely an expedient political calculator is contradicted by his appearance before the eight remaining justices at their bench at 10 a.m. on December 19, 1975. Ford wore formal morning clothes (long-tailed cutaway coat, striped pants, dark vest, black-and-white striped tie) and sat at the government's counsel table along with two other lawyers, Attorney General Levi and Solicitor General Bork. Ford was the first president to play such an official and deferential role in a swearing-in ceremony at the Court. As he rose, Ford said, "Mr. Chief Justice, and may it please the Court, I appear this morning as a member of the bar of this Court to officially inform the Court that the nomination of Circuit Judge John Paul Stevens to be an associate justice of the Supreme Court of the United States has been consented to by the United States Senate. Judge Stevens is present in the courtroom, ready to take his oath. I request that the attorney general present the commission to the Court."[47] "So far as I can find out," Burger later informed Ford, "it is the first occasion where the president appeared to move the seating of his nominee."[48]

The symbolism of Ford's "request" to the third branch of government was not lost on Stevens. "Despite the critical role played by the executive and the legislative branches in the appointment process, the fact that the conclusion of the process [took] place in a judicial proceeding symbolizes the independence of the judiciary," he said. "I was particularly moved . . . when President Ford, who was a member of the Supreme Court Bar, appeared in Court to introduce Attorney General Levi, who in turn delivered my commission to the clerk of the Court."[49]

CHAPTER NINE

The Newcomer

Stevens joined the Supreme Court on the eve of the nation's bicentennial celebration. Court watchers noted a more particular milestone. With Stevens aboard, the veterans of the Warren Court, with its legacy of liberal judicial activism in the 1950s and 1960s, moved into the minority.

Justices William Brennan, Thurgood Marshall, Potter Stewart, and Byron White hardly represented a left-wing voting block of Warren Court holdovers. Brennan and Marshall comprised a liberal core, to be sure. But Stewart and White often voted with Nixon appointees Warren Burger, William Rehnquist, Harry Blackmun, and Lewis Powell. Still, the "liberal Warren Court," which is the phrase many Americans thought of when they thought of the Supreme Court, was over. The range of judicial philosophies in 1975 looked like a barbell. Two conventionally defined liberals, Brennan and Marshall, balanced two predictable conservatives, Burger and Rehnquist. The four justices in the middle had avoided simple stereotypes. But across the spectrum, the Warren Court brethren were known quantities. In this sense, the Court was settled, with few surprises.

Anyone who cared to inquire knew what to expect from Justice Douglas, the longest-serving member of the Court. Douglas was appointed by President Roosevelt in 1939, when Stevens was an undergraduate. His liberal credentials on issues such as free speech and race relations were firmly established, as was the style of his opinion-writing and his irascible personality. "Justice Douglas was very liberal, more liberal than Justice Brennan," said George A. Rutherglen, a Douglas law clerk who joined Stevens's chambers at the end of 1975. "Many of the positions [Douglas] took he took by himself, but they were clearly identifiable positions, because he had been on the Court since 1939. Everybody knew where Justice Douglas stood. The liberals lost a reliable judge. There was some anxiety that Justice Stevens would pull the Court on crucial issues to the right."[1]

Douglas's retirement sparked regret on the left and anticipation on the right. Stevens, most Court watchers assumed, would join the middle group, creating what some critics saw as a five-to-four majority in favor of blandness. In this context, Stevens was less of a "maverick" than a "newbie." But Stevens did not blend in as expected. He remained the Court's junior member for six years and was always an object of curiosity. Stevens was hard to handicap in part because his work on the Seventh Circuit had not touched many of the controversies the Supreme Court faced. In one of his first Supreme Court cases, for example, he weighed a dispute from the West about water rights and Native Americans. He certainly had no track record on this matter. And he soon faced a more profound issue that had not confronted the appellate judges in the Dirksen Courthouse during his tenure—capital punishment. On matters the Seventh Circuit had considered, Stevens was hard to pigeonhole, as the ABA's Warren Christopher had noted during Stevens's confirmation.

Compounding speculation inside and outside the Court about Stevens's leanings was the fact that he did nothing to resolve the doubts and, in effect, refused to play the game. He had worked in the Marble Palace before, during the far more contentious era of the Vinson Court. He had assisted Justice Wiley Rutledge in accomplishing his work and remaining upbeat amid the personal acrimony among other justices. In some respects, Stevens was the reincarnation of his former boss, who served only six years before he died of a stroke at age fifty-five, the age at which Stevens joined the Court.

Now with his own seat, Stevens transferred in two clerks and a secretary from the Seventh Circuit and set up shop "in the judging business," as he called it.[2] Secretary Nellie A. Pitts, who had been secretary to Judge Robert Sprecher at the Seventh Circuit, became the den mother and master sergeant. Arriving in mid-term wasn't easy, she recalled. The pace of work accelerated, and the sources of paper tripled from the three-judge panels at the Seventh Circuit. "The flow of work was from nine different locations instead of three," she said. "It was night and day."[3]

Stevens installed a black leather chair in the clerks' room in his chambers, where, as he had at the Seventh Circuit, he sat and talked through cases with his clerks. Before the advent of computerized word processing software, he scrawled drafts of opinions in barely legible handwriting on yellow legal pads until Pitts convinced him to use a Dictaphone. He retained his chambers in Chicago for several months at the beginning of 1976, enabling him to work there while he readied his family to move to a home in McLean, Virginia.

"I don't think Justice Stevens had any trouble getting up to speed on the backlog of cases," said Rutherglen. "I can't remember any transitional issues."[4] In a 2007 interview, Stevens said: "Frankly, I felt comfortable pretty promptly. I wasn't a stranger there, and I did feel that my background and memories as a clerk brought a lot of practices and customs of the Court back to mind."[5] Like Douglas, who had been a legendary loner on the Court, Stevens refused to join the so-called cert pool, whereby justices assign their clerks as a unit to sift through certiorari petitions seeking to have cases heard. His insistence on conducting his own cert reviews summoned up the essence of Justice Rutledge and contributed to the impression that the Stevens chambers was a separate law firm inside the Court. Even after more than thirty years on the Court, he was the only justice not to participate in the clerk cert pool.

In his early years, Stevens seemed to be less interested in forming majorities or joining dissenting minorities than in crafting his own opinions, which frequently appeared as lone concurrences or dissents. True to his career as a lawyer, he studied cases with a goal of resolving disputes, one by one, often with a novel answer. He did not have an agenda to move law in one direction or another in concert with like-minded justices. "He was from the very beginning quite independent in his mind and his views," Rutherglen said. This style of granular and solitary workmanship befuddled smug law clerks, Rutherglen recalled. Clerks would ask, "'What new reasoning is Justice Stevens going to come up with?' What they were really saying was, 'Why doesn't he agree with the justice I'm working for?' Everybody was out to get his vote. Because people could not have thought of [Stevens's interpretation of a case], they criticized him for being not predictable."[6] National Public Radio's Nina Totenberg put it this way: "It's like taking camera shots from different angles, and his angle is different than anyone else's."[7]

He was, in shorthand used inside the Court and in the press, a wild card, a loner, a maverick. His name, John, was converted to Jack, as in "jacks are wild." He was called "even Stevens" for writing liberal *and* conservative opinions. Law professor Dennis J. Hutchinson, who had clerked for Justices Douglas and White, told *Time* magazine in 1980, "He seemed prepared in many cases to, if not exactly reinvent the wheel, then at least to reinterpret it. In every major case, he had to have his own little John Paul Stevens theory."[8] The *Time* article called him "gadfly to the brethren."

Hutchinson said that one line repeated around the Court parodied a famous quotation from American naval history: "John Paul Stevens has not yet begun to write." "He is writing almost faster than he's thinking in the first few years. He sees the Court as an intellectual feast," Hutchinson said.[9]

Political science professor Bradley C. Canon cited several negative perceptions of Stevens's independence: "Another characteristic that probably did not endear Stevens to the other justices was his habit of citing himself frequently. Far more than his colleagues, he reprinted or noted his earlier opinions (sometimes even one from his Seventh Circuit days) as if to say he had always known the right answer."[10] In a number of opinions, he quoted past writings by fellow members against themselves, suggesting inconsistency or, at worst, hypocrisy on the part of his peers, Canon said. Such rhetorical jibes are not uncommon in Supreme Court opinions, but they are especially noted by senior justices in the opinions of junior justices. Having seen the swelling docket at the Seventh Circuit, Stevens openly cautioned his brethren, in speeches to law groups, against taking on too many cases and cases unworthy of Supreme Court review.[11]

In a peculiar public comment shortly after his confirmation, Stevens acknowledged the notion that he was detached. To a Chicago audience, he quoted an obscure remark by a British sympathizer during the Revolutionary War. In reply to Thomas Paine's influential pamphlet *Common Sense,* James Chalmers wrote, "Independence and slavery are synonymous terms." Stevens said, "I often think of it. I have the same thought," offering a much different interpretation than Chalmers's. Chalmers warned the colonists that they would enslave themselves if they detached from British rule. Stevens said judges worked hard for modest pay but were compensated in part by the independence granted to them, in the case of federal judges by the Constitution. "The key to the good judge is the independence," he said.[12]

On days of oral argument, Stevens sat next to Powell at the far left of Chief Justice Burger in the center chair. He knew all the justices, especially White and Marshall, from his days as a Rutledge clerk. He admitted to being a bit self-conscious about his height as he stood at the end of the line before the justices entered the courtroom: "I follow Lewis Powell, who is about six feet tall; in front of him is Thurgood Marshall, who is a couple of inches taller; over Thurgood's head I see Bill Rehnquist who is— and appears to be—the father of a star basketball player, and less clearly, up in the front, I see Byron White's massive frame. As I follow them onto the bench, I sometimes think about how appropriate my place in the line of march is."[13]

But his diminutive, five-foot-seven-inch frame carried ample self-confidence and autonomy. Barely six months after Stevens's confirmation, he received solicitations from Senator Charles Percy; White House counseler Kenneth A. Lazarus, who had helped shepherd Stevens through the Senate; and Betty Southard Murphy, chair of the National Labor Relations Board. In separate letters, all three urged him to hire as a law clerk a female lawyer who had been first in her class at a Washington, D.C., law school. "I am hopeful that you are in a position to give every possible consideration to her application," wrote Lazarus. "I commend you to her very highly for the clerkship position," wrote Percy. "It is a genuine pleasure to recommend her to you without qualification," wrote Murphy.[14] He declined. Instead, he hired two graduates of Illinois law schools and a Harvard law graduate, Gregory D. Huffaker, Jr., son of a Lab School chum who had attended his confirmation ceremony.

From the start, Stevens's opinion-writing signaled that he was following his own instincts. The first case for which he wrote the majority opinion (*Hampton v. Mow Sun Wong,* 1976) concerned employment discrimination by the federal government against five resident aliens. With Douglas absent from the case, the Court had been deadlocked on the matter in the previous term. When it was reheard, Stevens provided the fifth and deciding vote. It was hardly a landmark for the Court or a template for Stevens's tenure. Still, the five-to-four decision in favor of the job applicant contained several markers.

First, he captured the votes of the Court's most liberal duo, Justices Brennan and Marshall. Second, in a sign of interpretative nuance to come, Stevens's opinion addressed a slightly different question than the one posed either by the U.S. Civil Service Commission in bringing the case or by the other justices. Justice Rehnquist complained in his dissent that Stevens "enunciates a novel conception . . . quite contrary to the doctrine established by a long and not hitherto questioned line of our decisions." Critiques alleging "novel," meaning "dubious," interpretations by the majority are commonplace in dissents, but they are especially pointed against a junior justice's debut opinion for the Court.

Third, the nine-page opinion contained 49 footnotes, signaling Stevens's pattern of intense elaboration. Justice Blackmun, one of the dissenters in the case and a stickler in opinion-writing generally, soon began to decorate copies of Stevens's opinion drafts with his handwritten disapproval of what he viewed as the freshman's excessive footnotes.

Fourth, Stevens inserted into his opinion one of the simple building blocks of his jurisprudence: "The federal sovereign, like the States, must govern impartially." Fifth, the opinion arose from Stevens's core notion that individuals possess a "liberty interest," which in Stevens's view predates the Constitution. The dissenters disagreed: "There is no general 'liberty' interest in either acquiring federal employment or, in the absence of a statutory tenure, in retaining it, so that the person who is denied employment or who is discharged may insist upon a due process hearing," Rehnquist wrote.

In a dissent later in his first term, also joined by Brennan and Marshall, Stevens elaborated on his concept of "liberty interest," a premise that appears throughout his tenure on the Court and stands as a pillar of his judicial philosophy. The case, *Meacham v. Fano,* 1976, concerned a familiar Stevens issue, the rights of an incarcerated felon:

> Neither the Bill of Rights nor the laws of sovereign States create the liberty which the Due Process Clause protects. The relevant constitutional provisions are limitations on the power of the sovereign to infringe on the liberty of the citizen. The relevant state laws either create property rights, or they curtail the freedom of the citizen who must live in an ordered society. Of course, law is essential to the exercise and enjoyment of individual liberty in a complex society. But it is not the source of liberty, and surely not the exclusive source. . . . I had thought it self-evident that all men were endowed by their Creator with liberty as one of the cardinal unalienable rights. It is that basic freedom which the Due Process Clause protects, rather than the particular rights or privileges conferred by specific laws or regulations.

Law scholars puzzled over what liberties, in Stevens's mind, deserved such existential distinction and ultimate protection. "Justice Stevens's chief failure in his due process opinions has been in not providing a clear rationale for why particular interests are of greater importance than others," wrote Jonathan C. Carlson and Alan D. Smith in an analysis of Justice Stevens's first three years for *The University of Chicago Law Review.* "The Justice's distinctions appear to reflect an emphasis on human dignity as the quality of liberty that demands the heightened protection of the courts. The formulation is not very helpful, however. The concept of dignity is too amorphous and subjective a basis for predictable decisionmaking."[15]

In Stevens's first week of oral arguments, the Court heard eleven cases. He wrote opinions in seven—three for the majority, one concurrence, and three dissents—beginning a prodigious casebook that was notable for its idiosyncrasy as well as its heft. An opinion from his first week on the bench began a long string of Stevens dissents. It was filed separately in the case concerning water rights [*Colorado River Water Conservation District v. United States,* 1976]. Reflecting his preference for judicial restraint and deference toward other decision makers, he maintained that the Tenth U.S. Circuit Court of Appeals in Denver should more thoroughly review the merits of the case before the Supreme Court in Washington considered the matter.

In his first three terms, he was the most prolific writer on the Court, authoring 65 dissents, 35 concurrences, and 36 opinions for the Court. The early years provided plenty of grist but not necessarily much guidance for legal scholars hoping to explain the junior justice to an intensely curious legal community. In one of many statistical portrayals, Professor Russell W. Galloway, Jr., of Santa Clara University School of Law detected "a slight inclination to the right" in Stevens's work in his initial term. On a percentage basis, he disagreed with the two most conservative justices, Burger and Rehnquist, a bit less often than the two most liberal, Brennan and Marshall. But in the October 1976 term, Galloway found Stevens to be "clearly left of center."[16]

A statistical analysis published in 1989 by Professor William D. Popkin of Indiana University School of Law made a remarkable discovery concerning Stevens's independence. Using the annual Supreme Court voting scorecards by the *Harvard Law Review,* Popkin calculated what he called the "variation in the rate of agreement" between Stevens and the eight other justices: "A judge who is as likely to agree with one judge as another will vote with every colleague (whether 'liberal' or 'conservative') in the same percentage of cases" and therefore record a low variation rate, Popkin reasoned. "By contrast, a predictably conservative judge will agree with fellow conservatives most of the time . . . but with liberal judges much less often, thereby exhibiting considerable variation in the rate of agreement."[17]

Through the October 1987 term, Stevens's variation of agreement rate was consistent and by far the lowest on the Court, except for one term in the mid-1980s, when Justice Blackmun scored lower. Stevens's variation in agreement rate ranged from 3.1 percent to 8.8 percent in 1986. The range for conservative Rehnquist was 10.3 percent in 1987 to 22.1 percent in 1985; the range for liberal Marshall was 13.9 percent (average for the five years of 1973 through 1977) to 21.4 percent in 1986. In a related study, there was no sign that Stevens's independent streak faded as he became more comfortable around the Court. His percentage of voting agreement with the majority declined from 77.0 percent in his first term to 63.5 percent ten years later, according to Professor Leslie Bender of Syracuse University College of Law.[18]

Outside the Court, Stevens's performance was monitored closely by lawyers and others in the women's rights movement, which had formed the only organized resistance to his confirmation. In the early years, there were no signs that Stevens's empathy for the sisterhood, as the movement was sometimes called, had increased from his days on the Seventh Circuit.

At the start of the 1976–1977 term, Stevens's first full term, lawyer Ruth Bader Ginsburg appeared to present a case of gender discrimination (*Califano v. Goldfarb,* 1977). Women advocates were rare at Supreme Court oral arguments, and Ginsburg did not get a break from Justice Stevens. "I wanted to duck his question," Justice Ginsburg recalled years later. "We went back and forth."[19] The case concerned a man who was being denied survivor benefits from his deceased wife's Social Security account. At that time, women collected survivor spouse benefits routinely, but men making similar claims had to prove they had received half their income from their wives, even though both had contributed to Social Security on an equal basis. The female spouse in this case was dead, but Ginsburg argued that the law represented discrimination against her, because her work, as measured by Social Security eligibility, was devalued compared to her husband's. The government took the other side, saying the husband was the proper one to make a claim of discrimination. But Ginsburg told the Court, "I don't know any purely male discrimination" in federal statutes. Stevens, in a fairly testy line of questioning, quizzed Ginsburg:

[Stevens]—Pardon me, can I interrupt, just to be sure I understand your point? . . . Is it your view that there is no discrimination against males?

[Ginsburg]—I think there is discrimination against males, yes.

[Stevens] (jumping in before Ginsburg finished her sentence)—If there is such discrimination, is it to be tested by the same or a different standard from discrimination against females?

[Ginsburg]—My response to that, Mr. Justice Stevens, is that almost every discrimination that operates against males operates against females, as well.

[Stevens]—Is that a 'yes' or a 'no' answer? I don't understand. Are you trying to avoid the question?

[Ginsburg]—No, I'm not trying to avoid the question.[20]

When the Court ruled on the case the following March, Stevens joined a five-to-four majority in Ginsburg's favor. But he wrote a separate concurrence that seemed to agree more with the leading dissenter, Justice Rehnquist. In a comment that recalled his Seventh Circuit dissent in *Sprogis v. United Air Lines, Inc.,* Stevens said, "I am convinced that the relevant discrimination in this case is against surviving male spouses, rather than deceased female wage earners."

Like other interest groups, the women's movement found Stevens hard to define. "His performance on the Supreme Court regarding analyses of sex discrimination issues is far stronger than his performance on the Seventh Circuit bench would have indicated," wrote San Francisco lawyer John P. Wagner in an exhaustive 1982 study of Stevens's gender-related opinions. But he concluded, "perhaps the only clear pattern that can be drawn from Stevens's opinions in the area of discrimination against women is that there is no pattern."[21]

Wagner's analysis accurately depicts lawyer and judge Stevens as a puzzle master: "Justice Stevens seems most effective not when advocating a position in and of itself, but when reacting to or acting as 'negotiator' or 'facilitator' between two competing positions." In the opinions Wagner studied, Stevens did not champion fresh public policy in the area of gender discrimination. On the other hand, he did not permit legal technicalities to block progress for women, Wagner found. "While he is not yet a doctrinal 'leader,' he has the potential, the creativity, and the persuasiveness to become a major force in the emerging law of sex discrimination."[22]

For example, in *Craig v. Boren,* 1976, a divided Court in Stevens's first term struck down as unconstitutional an Oklahoma law that barred the sale of so-called 3.2 percent alcohol beer to young people, women under eighteen, and men under twenty-one. The state had defended the different age standards on the basis of traffic safety, saying that alcoholically impaired young male drivers were a greater danger to the public. Women's groups protested the gender distinction on principle.

Stevens joined the plurality opinion, which set a stricter standard for laws that discriminate by gender to meet constitutional muster. But he was unwilling to state flatly that discrimination based on sex, as presented in the facts of *Craig v. Boren,* was simply invalid. Instead, Wagner said, Stevens's brief concurring opinion focused on the process of settling due process claims and suggested that Oklahoma needed to make a better case for preferring one sex over the other. He wrote that the gender-based age distinction for buying 3.2 beer "is not totally irrational." Stevens doubted that Oklahoma could justify separate ages for purchasing 3.2 beer, Wagner noted. But he declined to disallow the attempt. In offering a fine-tuned rationale rather than a broad statement of principle, he left the door open to those who would "smuggle in" excuses for discrimination, Wagner wrote and then concluded: "If so, Justice Rehnquist stands ready to do the smuggling. Justice Stevens, to avoid a move backward, must now provide further conceptual spadework."[23]

Early on, analysts detected that Stevens was implementing the distrust of "glittering generalities" that his Northwestern University law professors had taught him, by attempting to sort through the thicket of case-by-case interpretations of law with an eye toward incremental, ad hoc solutions. In gender discrimination, as in other types of litigation, he was inclined to resolve specific disputes between the litigants but not contribute to the overarching momentum of gender discrimination law and politics. He also declined to engage in the controversy within the Court and among law scholars about creating a template for justices to decide such cases. Critics took him to task for narrow thinking in his early years on the Court. "His penchant for balancing interests often overshadows the principles underlying his opinions," the *University of Chicago Law Review* analysis by Carlson and Smith concluded.[24] Instead of stating his standards of judging for all to see, "Justice Stevens on the surface advocates a nonactivist, nonpolicymaking, essentially adjudicatory role for the Supreme Court," concluded a team of law scholars led by Douglas William Ey, Jr., for the *Vanderbilt* [University] *Law Review*. In his first three terms, Stevens appeared to be searching for "an adequate analytical framework" but hadn't yet found it, they wrote.[25]

Stevens's first writing for the Court on the abortion issue presented this conundrum. As he wrote in *Fitzgerald v. Porter Memorial Hospital* for the Seventh Circuit, Stevens was skeptical of basing the protection of liberty interests on a right to privacy. His concern was common among legal theorists, but to the women's movement this doubt posed a threat to political solidarity that had arisen around Justice Blackmun's privacy rationale for his *Roe v. Wade* ruling. In *Planned Parenthood of Central Missouri v. Danforth,* 1976, the Court retained the essence of the 1973 *Roe v. Wade* decision and disallowed Missouri requirements that women seeking abortions obtain the consent of their spouse and that unmarried women under eighteen obtain the consent of a parent.

Stevens, in a separate opinion that was part concurrence and part dissent, supported the *Roe v. Wade* precedent as "now part of our law," a nod to the principle of stare decisis (respect for previous Court decisions) without additional comment. But he dissented from the Court's ruling barring Missouri's parental consent law for unmarried women under eighteen seeking an abortion. Stevens's willingness to endorse a procedural exception to a woman's right to choose could make matters worse politically for pro-choice forces. "The State's interest in protecting a young person from harm justifies the imposition of restraints on his or her freedom even though comparable restraints on adults would be constitutionally impermissible," he wrote, declining at first to view the issue as a gender issue. "Therefore, the holding in *Roe v. Wade* that the abortion decision is entitled to constitutional protection merely emphasizes the importance of the decision; it does not lead to the conclusion that the state legislature has no power to enact legislation for the purpose of protecting a young pregnant woman from the consequences of an incorrect decision." In a cryptic handwritten note on Stevens's draft concurrence/dissent, Blackmun complained that Stevens and others on the Court failed to understand reality: "Wd drive [young women] to other states & we hv t old routine again. There is another world out there that the Brethren do not appreciate."[26]

Several years later, in a closed-door conference concerning another abortion case, *Thornburgh v. American College of Obstetricians and Gynecologists,* 1986, Stevens told his fellow justices, I "do not know how I would have voted in 1973."[27] The comment seems clear, but isn't. Did Stevens have doubts about permitting women to obtain legal abortions? Did he support a woman's right to choose an abortion but question Blackmun's right-to-privacy justification? Or is the comment merely generic, something Stevens would say about any case he had not directly considered firsthand?

In any event, a Blackmun law clerk advised Blackmun on how to ensure Stevens's critical fifth vote for Blackmun's effort to preserve *Roe* in the *Thornburgh* opinion. Blackmun should strike from his proposed opinion the sentence, "We reaffirm *Roe* not simply because it has been decided but because it is right." The clerk wrote, "The whole thing may be easier for Stevens to swallow if you don't make an express point of not relying on stare decisis."[28] Blackmun deleted the sentence; Stevens gave Blackmun the deciding fifth vote. *Roe v. Wade* remained the law of the land.

But by the time of the *Thornburgh* decision, ten years after *Planned Parenthood of Central Missouri,* Stevens seemed to have moved beyond his concern about the right-to-privacy rationale for permitting abortion. In fact, his concurrence contained language closer to the sweeping statement that Blackmun had removed from his opinion in order to obtain Stevens's vote. It was a not-too-subtle swipe at those who would use religious beliefs as a substitute for secular law in this sensitive area, and it looked a lot like a glittering generality: "In the final analysis, the holding in *Roe v. Wade* presumes that it is far better to permit some individuals to make incorrect decisions than to deny all individuals the right to make decisions that have a profound effect upon their destiny. Arguably a very primitive society would have been protected from evil by a rule against eating apples; a majority familiar with Adam's experience might favor such a rule. But the lawmakers who placed a special premium on the protection of individual liberty have recognized that certain values are more important than the will of a transient majority." Stevens watchers in the legal profession and academia, realizing that he was capable of more than clever resolutions of particular disputes, found themselves asking, what are the "certain values" that deserve special protection as a matter of principle in Stevens's judicial philosophy?

Despite the depiction in the press and law journals of Stevens as a "maverick," a major accomplishment in his first term was a joint effort rare in Supreme Court history. Nearly all published opinions cite a single author, although other justices may join the opinion. But near the end of the October 1975 term, the Court addressed a long-standing dispute about capital punishment with five opinions, each signed by three justices: Potter Stewart, Lewis Powell, and John Paul Stevens. In joining what was called the "writing team" on the death penalty cases, Stevens began a 32-year odyssey that carried him from explicating rationales in the 1970s for capital punishment to nearly deciding in the new millennium that no sufficient rationales existed.

In 1972, the Court (*Furman v. Georgia*) struck down three death penalty decisions in Georgia and Texas and, as a result, halted executions around the nation. The five-vote majority that endorsed the ruling, as well as the four dissenters, each wrote separate opinions, making the decision the longest in the history of the Court at that time. But the single outcome was an effort by the more than thirty death penalty states to enact statutes aimed at satisfying the Court's concern that executions had become random, irrational, and therefore "cruel and unusual" under the Eighth Amendment. The moratorium on executions was in place when Stevens joined the Court.

In 1976, Chief Justice Burger assigned Justice White, who had cast a decisive fifth vote in *Furman,* to draft an opinion for the set of five post-*Furman* capital cases. Burger and White wanted to retain the death penalty and, in doing so, evaluate the new standards that states had legislated in the wake of the *Furman* ruling. In early May, White alerted Burger that he could not hold a majority vote for his approach. Burger, who had dissented from the *Furman* majority's view, was not pleased: "The assignments [of opinions] in this final round are even more difficult than usual," he notified his colleagues as the October 1975 term entered the homestretch. "In the circumstances I suggest we meet at 10 a.m. Wednesday to clear the air."[29]

At the meeting, Burger agreed to take the capital cases from White and assign them to three colleagues: Stewart, the senior member of the troika and a member of the *Furman* majority; Powell, a *Furman* dissenter; and freshman Stevens, who had never written on capital punishment. Stevens never addressed a capital case at the Seventh Circuit. Justice Rutledge, for whom Stevens clerked, often voted to have the Court weigh petitions related to capital punishment and frequently voted in favor of death row inmates in cases involving the wording or administration of state death penalty statutes. But Rutledge never expressed a view on "the constitutionality of capital punishment as such,"[30] according to Rutledge's biographer John M. Ferren.

In the term before Stevens joined the Rutledge chambers, the Court ruled in favor of Louisiana in the most grizzly capital punishment case in its history. In 1945, William Francis, an African American, was sentenced to death at age sixteen for killing a drugstore owner. In May 1946, operators of a portable electric chair failed to deliver a fatal surge of current as Francis screamed in pain. He was returned to prison. The governor of Louisiana issued a new death warrant for six days later. Francis's lawyer appealed, citing double jeopardy and other issues. With Justices Rutledge, Harold Burton, William Douglas, and Frank Murphy dissenting, the Court rejected Francis's plea (*State of Louisiana ex rel, Francis v. Resweber,* 1947). He was put to death on the second try.

During his clerkship, Stevens recommended to Rutledge that the Court decline to take up the appeal of a capital case involving the stabbing murder of a Chinese laundry operator in Washington, D.C. Despite overwhelming evidence against the defendant, his lawyer sought a new trial in part because of a remark by an interpreter employed for the trial. In the hearing of one juror, the interpreter had said, "That son of a bitch is lying and ought to go to the chair." Stevens advised Rutledge, "undoubtedly this was prejudicial," adding that the remark, which the juror failed to report immediately to the judge, "bothers me some." But he noted the strength of the prosecution's evidence and the fact that the jury had taken just eighty minutes to reach a guilty verdict. "I doubt whether the remark affected the result," Stevens said.[31]

During Stevens's confirmation process in 1975, Senator Strom Thurmond of South Carolina began a private conversation with the nominee by saying, "Judge Stevens, I want to talk to you about the death penalty. I'm not going to ask you your views, because that would be highly improper, but I want to tell you how I feel about it."[32] Stevens knew that senators had grilled Justice Blackmun on the death penalty in his 1970 confirmation hearing. For that reason, he and Ed Rothschild strategized about how to handle questions on the subject, but at his hearing no senator asked him directly for his opinion of the constitutionality of the punishment.

Stevens declined to answer Senator Edward Kennedy's related question: "I would like to know your feelings on capital punishment. Do you believe it serves as a deterrent?" Saying he was not prepared to answer, Stevens said, "There have been many times in my experience in the last five years where I found my first reaction to a problem was not the same as the reaction I had when I had the responsibility of decisions."

Kennedy had slightly more luck when he asked about the record of fairness and equity in the application of the death penalty: "Any fair review of its application over any period of time would have to indicate that whether the statute is constitutional or unconstitutional it has been used and generally has been applied more heavily to the poor and to the black people of this country." "Senator, I think that is a fair question," Stevens replied. "I would agree with the thrust of what your question seems to suggest, that we must always be concerned with the impartial administration of the law." But he declined to cite an instance of such impartiality that he had observed: "No such situation comes to mind in the work I have done in the Seventh Circuit."[33]

Powell and Stewart, despite their opposing views in *Furman,* agreed to unite in affirming the basic premise of *Furman*—that state capital punishment laws could be constitutional under certain circumstances, as scrutinized by the Court. The Court needed to assess the new post-*Furman* state laws. Both justices were driven in part by their conviction that one idea—mandatory death sentence laws enacted by certain states to counter *Furman*—was wrong.

Powell and Stewart knew their point of view would carry more weight with a third vote. They took Stevens to lunch at the Monocle restaurant, two blocks from the Court. They were pleased that Stevens's thoughts, especially about the danger of mandatory death sentences, seemed to match their own.[34] The collaboration by Powell, Stewart, and Stevens resulted in a green light for new death penalty statutes in Georgia, Florida, and Texas and rejection of mandatory death penalty laws in Louisiana and North Carolina. The lead decision was *Gregg v. Georgia.* Stevens's assignment was to set out the facts of each of the cases. Powell would explain the overarching premise that the death penalty was not per se unconstitutional. Stewart would explain the reasons for the three-to-two split in their decision covering the five states.

Stevens, who had begun his tenure by speaking his own mind, had reasons to join the group. First, as a novice on the subject of capital punishment and the only justice who had not written on *Furman,* he had no chance of forming a coalition on the capital cases then before the Court. A concurrence or dissent, no matter how well crafted, would be forgotten. By joining Stewart and Powell, Stevens's name would be etched in the law books as a co-author of a milestone capital punishment decision. Indeed, Stevens and Stewart each were listed as having "announced" two of the five opinions, while Powell "announced" the opinion on one case.

Second, the facts of each case as well as state laws applied to them were distinct. For example, in the Texas case, a twenty-two-year-old man was found guilty of raping and murdering a ten-year-old girl; in the North Carolina case, four men were convicted of killing a convenience store clerk. The Texas statute was a bigger stretch to bring into the post-*Furman* death penalty tent than laws under consideration from Georgia and Florida. Setting forth facts and law was an important contribution.

Third, Stevens knew his thinking on the death penalty was unformed. A year later, in *Gardner v. Florida*, 1977, he addressed the magnitude of the problem: ". . . Death is a different kind of punishment from any other which may be imposed in this country. From the point of view of the defendant, it is different both in its severity and its finality. From the point of view of society, the action of the sovereign in taking the life of one of its citizens also differs dramatically from any other state action. It is of vital importance to the defendant and to the community that any decision to impose the death sentence be, and appear to be, based on reason, rather than caprice or emotion."

Yet Stevens realized that "reason" in imposing death was unlike the reasoning process that had brought him into the law and built his reputation. The competition of ideas, gentlemanly disagreements, and the development of pragmatic outcomes may work for an antitrust lawyer with a sophisticated client or a pro bono lawyer defending an indigent prisoner facing a life sentence. But the intellectual process is rubbed raw when one party in a dispute could be killed by the other.

Moreover, in no other area of the law does reasoning, whether conscientious or cynical, so easily lead to unintended consequences. For example, making death mandatory for conviction on certain crimes, as Louisiana and North Carolina had done, seemed to solve the problem of arbitrary sentencing that had prompted the *Furman* moratorium. But juries might be less likely to convict vicious murderers if they were squeamish about death. Acquitting murderers solely because of opposition to the penalty for murder would set justice backward. In the converse, automatic mandatory sentences—without regard to mitigating circumstances—might increase the number of executions, including erroneous killings.

The goal of the Stewart-Powell-Stevens team was to uphold state laws that allowed for discretion by judges and juries in a context of clearly articulated guidelines about aggravating and mitigating circumstances. For example, Georgia's new law allowed the jury to consider—but did not mandate—the death penalty if the murder were accompanied by certain aggravating factors, such as a killing during an armed robbery. Such "guided discretion" was intended to limit the pool of death-eligible defendants and avoid the hazards of mandatory death sentences. Stevens was unprepared to join the abolitionists Brennan and Marshall. They had abandoned nuance in the face of the potential absurdity of seeking ever more rational executions. But over the years the rationalizing approach grew more untenable, as public support for the death penalty faded. Powell rejected capital punishment after he retired in 1987; Blackmun became an abolitionist not long before his retirement in 1994.

The intricacies of the death penalty debate are off-putting to most people, especially those who hold a visceral reaction for or against capital punishment. For example, in *Zant v. Stephens*, 1983, Stevens wrote an opinion from which only Brennan and Marshall dissented that permitted an execution to go forward even though one of the three aggravating factors given the jury by state law had been ruled impermissibly vague by the Supreme Court of Georgia. He thereby reversed the decision of the Fifth U.S. Circuit Court of Appeals, which was not known as being soft on capital punishment. "That was not one of Stevens's better opinions," said Ellen S. Kreitzberg, professor of law and director of the Death Penalty College at Santa Clara University School of Law.[35] In his dissent, Marshall complained: "Even if I accepted the prevailing view that the death penalty may be constitutional under certain circumstances, I could scarcely join in upholding a death sentence based in part upon a statutory aggravating circumstance so vague that its application turns solely on the 'whim' of the jury. . . . There is no way of knowing whether the jury would have sentenced the respondent to death if its attention had not been drawn to the unconstitutional statutory factor." On the other hand, two former Stevens law clerks, James S. Liebman and Lawrence C. Marshall, maintained that Steven's *Zant* decision strengthened the cause of narrowing the pool of death-eligible defendants.[36]

According to Kreitzberg, Stevens's death penalty reasoning began to shift in the 1999 case *Terry Williams v. Taylor* when he ruled in favor of a death row inmate who alleged that his lawyer had failed to introduce significant mitigating evidence that might defeat a death sentence. Earlier, in 1984 (*Strickland v. Washington*) and 1987 (*Burger v. Kemp*), Stevens had disallowed the so-called ineffective counsel defense, but the Strickland case established rules for evaluating ineffective counsel that Stevens used in 1999. By 2002, Stevens was back in his role as a lone dissenter (*Bell v. Cone*), writing in favor of a Vietnam War veteran with a Bronze Star whose death sentence for slaying an elderly couple in a two-day crime spree was issued after a dubious effort by his lawyer.

Noting that the lawyer was himself found to be suffering from mental illness, Stevens cited a report from Illinois by a blue-ribbon commission appointed by Governor George Ryan to study capital punishment. The commission quoted a 2001 national study by the Constitution Project that concluded: "Providing qualified counsel is perhaps the most important safeguard against wrongful conviction, sentencing and execution of capital defendants. It is also a safeguard far too often ignored."[37]

But Stevens's capital punishment jurisprudence did not evolve in a vacuum. Three years after *Bell v. Cone*, Stevens joined a five-to-four majority in *Roper v. Simmons* that disallowed the execution of anyone under eighteen. As the senior judge in the majority, Stevens assigned the case to Justice Anthony M. Kennedy, who switched sides from his stance in *Stanford v. Kentucky,* 1989, which upheld a death sentence for a seventeen-year-old. Kennedy sparked outrage among conservatives in *Roper v. Simmons* not just for changing his mind but also for invoking "international norms" in explaining his decision. In his concurrence, Stevens steered the Court's thinking back to home: "That our understanding of the Constitution does change from time to time has been settled since John Marshall breathed life into its text. If great lawyers of his day—Alexander Hamilton, for example—were sitting with us today, I would expect them to join Justice Kennedy's opinion for the Court." Again in 2002, Stevens found adherents when he wrote the majority opinion in which the Court followed the lead of several states and voided the execution of mentally retarded defendants

(*Atkins v. Virginia*). Five years later, in *Uttecht v. Bowen* (2007), Stevens, in a dissent joined by Justices Souter, Ginsburg, and Breyer, again relied on public opinion to clarify his reasoning on another element of the death penalty debate—jury bias. He denounced the exclusion for cause of a potential juror who said he might not be able to vote for a death sentence. "Millions of Americans oppose the death penalty," Stevens began, adding that there was no basis in law or judicial precedent for excluding jurors based on their doubts about the death penalty, as long as their misgivings would not impair their consideration of death versus life imprisonment.

In 2008 Stevens brought the long journey of his death penalty logic, which had traveled between close-order reasoning and broad principles, up to the abolitionist goal line. In a case testing the constitutionality of Kentucky's protocol for lethal injection (*Baze v. Rees*), Stevens took a big step. To state his new position, he quoted his former colleague Justice Byron White, writing in the 1972 *Furman* decision that halted capital punishment for many years: "The imposition of the death penalty represents 'the pointless and needless extinction of life with only marginal contributions to any discernible social or public purposes. A penalty with such negligible returns to the State would be patently excessive and cruel and unusual punishment violative of the Eighth Amendment.'"

Stevens's choice of Justice White as his model is significant for at least two reasons: First, citing White as the source of his reasoning, like his membership in the post-*Furman* "writing team," counters Stevens's image as a loner who preferred to quote his own past opinions or state a novel approach to an issue. Second, Stevens was the only justice on the Court who had traveled the entire road of the post-*Furman* death penalty jurisprudence. White, a John F. Kennedy appointee who disappointed liberals with the conservative tone of his tenure, was the swing vote in the *Furman* case. The words Stevens quoted were written by White at a time when the nation's capital punishment system needed serious reform, but White was never a death penalty abolitionist. On the contrary, Stevens's two former law clerks James Liebman and Lawrence Marshall argued that White's solution to the unfairness and randomness of death sentences in the early 1970s was to have more of them.[38]

Stevens, citing his own experience with capital punishment, took White's premise in the opposite direction and to the next logical step toward abolition. But he did not go all the way. What he called "the conclusion I have reached with regard to the constitutionality of the death penalty" was a conditional statement, not a declaration: "The risk of executing innocent defendants can be entirely eliminated by treating any penalty more severe than life imprisonment without the possibility of parole as constitutionally excessive."

After 1976, Stevens moved toward the abolitionist side. But, as *New York Times* reporter Linda Greenhouse noted, his *Baze v. Rees* opinion "lacked the ringing declaration of Justice Blackmun's 'From this day forward, I shall no longer tinker with the machinery of death.'"[39] True to his independent streak, Stevens joined the majority in upholding Kentucky's lethal injection program in the last paragraph of his opinion that mostly attacked the concept. He cited deference to state decision makers and respect for precedents, which he knew better than any of his colleagues because he had helped write them for over three decades: "This Court has held that the death penalty is constitutional, and has established a framework for evaluating the constitutionality of particular methods of execution." He had one more step to take—or not.

CHAPTER TEN

The Justice

Four years after joining the Court, Justice Stevens divorced his wife, Betty, and married Maryan Mulholland Simon. The end of John and Betty's 37-year marriage became official on November 13, 1979, three weeks after John's mother died just short of her 98th birthday. In early December, John and Maryan were married in Virginia.

Property records, divorce papers, and interviews with Stevens's daughters indicate that the marital events that peaked in late 1979 had been building for some time. The Stevens and Simon couples had been neighbors and bridge partners in Chicago's Beverly neighborhood for many years. In 1973, the couples moved into adjacent homes in Burr Ridge, an upscale suburb west of Chicago. The oldest Stevens daughter, Kathryn, was away at college during this period, but she remembered, "There was a thing going on with a neighbor. [John and Betty] were going to separate, and then he got appointed to the Court."[1]

Youngest daughter Susan, who was in high school when the family relocated to Virginia, said the marriage breakup came as a shock to her.[2] In the spring of 1979, Stevens moved out of the McLean, Virginia, home that he and Betty had bought in early 1975 and into an apartment not far away in Arlington, to comply with Virginia divorce law. He was the plaintiff in the divorce. Maryan left Ronald Simon in April 1976, a month after the Stevens family moved to McLean. She divorced him in January 1977, claiming mental cruelty under Illinois law. Neither Betty nor Ronald contested their divorces.

Only two justices in Supreme Court history have a divorce on their records—Stevens and his predecessor, Justice William O. Douglas. Douglas's multiple marriages (his fourth wife, Cathy, aided her husband in his final days on the Court) were in the background as Congressman Gerald Ford investigated possible impeachment of Douglas in the late 1960s. Records of Stevens's appointment to the Supreme Court in President Ford's files contain no evidence that Ford or anyone else in the White House was aware of marital problems of the nominee to be Douglas's successor.

On November 14, 1979, Stevens informed his fellow justices, "Although I plan to make no public announcement, I want each of you to know that our divorce decree was entered yesterday. I appreciate your support and understanding during recent months."[3] Unlike press coverage of Douglas's relationships, the story of Stevens's divorce and hasty remarriage received no attention. The transition was accomplished privately, amid a whirlwind of speculation about the Court linked to the publication in December of Bob Woodward's and Scott Armstrong's book *The Brethren*. Dropping a bomb on the staid Supreme Court monastery, Woodward and Armstrong presented an apparently inside look at the machinations of the justices during the era of Chief Justice Warren Burger. Newcomer Stevens was mentioned just briefly in the book. *Time* magazine brought up the Stevens marital story four months later in a brief item titled "Marriage Revealed."[4]

The divorce/remarriage jolted some of Stevens's Washington friends. "My wife and I were quite friendly with [Betty]," said Stanley Temko, who had clerked with Stevens in the Wiley Rutledge chambers in the late 1940s.[5] Temko's wife, Francine, who died in 1998, was an honors graduate of Barnard College and a past editor of the *Columbia Law Review* of the Columbia [University] Law School in New York. Francine, a lawyer in the justice department's civil rights division, also had been chief of staff to a champion of the women's movement, U.S. Representative Bella Abzug of New York.

"Betty was not a great intellectual," Temko said. "She was a very good bridge player, and she was fun, but you wouldn't think of her as being a scholar of the Supreme Court volumes and so forth."

Temko said he was "quite impressed" by Maryan. "She's a very nice woman." But Francine had a "generic reaction" in favor of the first wife, he said.[6] Betty, having moved with John four times to Washington from Chicago, returned to family members and friends in Chicago, where she died in her sleep in 1985.

Among the most curious were Stevens's former colleagues on the Seventh Circuit bench. A judicial conference in Indiana in May 1980 gave several of the judges their first look at Maryan. "We can look forward to the chance to get acquainted with her," Thomas Fairchild, who was chief judge of the circuit at that time, told his colleagues.[7] Shortly before the conference, Judge Wilbur Pell and his wife, Chasey, had dinner with the new couple in Washington. "We were so very pleased to become acquainted with Maryan and to realize what a lovely and appealing person she is."[8]

John and Maryan are inseparable in their private lives and spend most of their time in their home in Fort Lauderdale, Florida. There Stevens is a member of the Coral Ridge Country Club, designed by—and a one-time home of—fabled golf course builder Robert Trent Jones, Sr. Asked about his longevity, Stevens, at age 88, said: "I was asked recently how it was that I managed to maintain my good health. And I came up with an answer that I'm quite proud of. I said you have to marry a beautiful dietician! And that's what I did."[9]

Justice Stevens's accomplishments during his long tenure lie in the more or less exclusive domain of the "scholars of Supreme Court volumes," as Temko put it. Law professor Laura Krugman Ray noted that most of his contributions to the law, like those of his mentor Justice Rutledge, are found in his dissents and concurrences, not in high-profile opinions for the Court.[10]

Still, the time line of Stevens's opinions for the Court majority reveals two overlapping trends in the growth of his judicial philosophy. Both are direct consequences—payoffs, his admirers would say—of his elevation to the bench as a political and judicial independent. He became more liberal, and he became more pragmatic. In both aspects of judging, he changed, aided by an absence of political or doctrinal anchors. As Stevens put it in a 2005 speech to the Fordham [University] Law School, "Learning on the job is essential to the process of judging."[11] Many justices, secure in their lifetime appointments, have altered their views of law during their years on the bench. But Stevens is one of the few who openly designate a willingness to change as a critical element of the job.

When *The Green Bag*, an "entertaining" journal of law, commissioned a bobblehead doll of Justice Stevens in 2003, the artist depicted four of Stevens's better known opinions in which he wrote the majority decision, two from 1984 and two from nearly two decades later.[12] The doll tells much about the eclectic and often arcane work of the Court. But it also shows Stevens in transition. In its left hand the Stevens figure holds a Supreme Court case volume open to his decision in *Chevron USA v. National Resources Defense Council* (1984). The six-to-zero ruling (Justices Thurgood Marshall, William Rehnquist, and Sandra O'Connor did not vote) established rules under which courts and litigants must defer to the discretion of federal regulatory agencies to interpret laws governing their work. In the opinion, Stevens restated a view of judicial restraint that he brought with him to the bench. Expertise and decision making skill do not necessarily reach their pinnacle in the courts, he maintained:

> Judges are not experts in the field, and are not part of either political branch of the Government. Courts must, in some cases, reconcile competing political interests, but not on the basis of the judges' personal policy preferences. In contrast, an agency to which Congress has delegated policymaking responsibilities may, within the limits of that delegation, properly rely upon the incumbent administration's views of wise policy to inform its judgments. While agencies are not directly accountable to the people, the Chief Executive is, and it is entirely appropriate for this political branch of the Government to make such policy choices—resolving the competing interests which Congress itself either inadvertently did not resolve, or intentionally left to be resolved by the agency charged with the administration of the statute in light of everyday realities.

According to the Supreme Court Database created by professor Harold J. Speath of Michigan State University, Stevens's *Chevron* opinion was "conservative."[13] Stevens resolved the case in favor of industry and against environmental interests, although from a different perspective the ruling could be interpreted as a "liberal' assertion of the power of federal regulators.

The Stevens bobblehead figure stands on an outsized Sony Betamax videotape recorder (VTR), representing his five-to-four opinion in another 1984 case, *Sony Corp. v. Universal City Studios, Inc.* The case concerned demands by Universal Studios and Walt Disney Productions to be compensated by Sony for giving consumers using Sony VTRs the ability to copy Universal and Disney movies in violation of the Copyright Act. A federal district court had found in favor of Sony; a court of appeals reversed the decision and favored the producers. Over two terms of the Supreme Court, Stevens single-handedly turned his colleagues around—against an opposing view led by Justice Harry Blackmun—to rule that no violation of the Copyright Act was involved in home use of VTRs. "He completely ripped victory out of the jaws of defeat," recalled National Public Radio's Nina Totenberg.[14] The five-four lineup was unusual, with liberal Justices Marshall and William Brennan and conservative Justices Rehnquist and Burger dividing their normally paired votes. The home entertainment industry was born. The Spaeth database counts Stevens's opinion in *Sony* as "liberal," benefitting consumers over business. But it was not activist. The majority opinion contained no novel policy prescriptions about either the new VTR technology or long-standing copyright law, which dates to Article I of the Constitution. Instead, Stevens called upon his antitrust expertise:

"The Court of Appeals' holding that [Universal and Disney] are entitled to enjoin the distribution of VTR's, to collect royalties on the sale of such equipment, or to obtain other relief, if affirmed, would enlarge the scope of [their] statutory monopolies [under the Copyright Act] to encompass control over an article of commerce that is not the subject of copyright protection. Such an expansion of the copyright privilege is beyond the limits of the grants authorized by Congress. . . . It may well [be] that Congress will take a fresh look at this new [VTR] technology, just as it so often has examined other innovations in the past. But it is not our job to apply laws that have not yet been written."

In 2001, the Supreme Court confronted a law that was just ten years old and had no literal constitutional heritage. The bobblehead doll has Stevens holding a golf club, memorializing his decision in *PGA Tour, Inc. v. Casey Martin.* By a seven-to-two vote, the Court decided that Martin, a handicapped professional golfer, had the right under the Americans with Disabilities Act of 1990 to ride in a golf cart, in violation of a PGA Tour rule. Justice Antonin Scalia, joined by Justice Clarence Thomas, held high the banner of judicial restraint, calling Stevens's ruling "ridiculous" and "silly." "Rules are rules," Scalia declared, saying the Court's interference in the "tradition" of PGA golf was a bizarre extension of the Court's role and an invitation to "lucrative litigation." But in a classic statement of judicial pragmatism, Stevens argued, in effect, that the Americans with Disabilities Act had no value if it didn't open doors to new and untried opportunities for the disabled. Respect for tradition and concern over unintended consequences should not foreclose the intent of Congress to try to make life better for Martin and other disabled persons, he argued:

> What [the ADA mandates] is to allow Martin the chance to qualify for and compete in the athletic events petitioner offers to those members of the public who have the skill and desire to enter. That is exactly what the ADA requires. As a result, Martin's request for a waiver of the walking rule should have been granted. The ADA admittedly imposes some administrative burdens on the operators of places of public accommodation that could be avoided by strictly adhering to general rules and policies that are entirely fair with respect to the able-bodied but that may indiscriminately preclude access by qualified persons with disabilities. But surely, in a case of this kind, Congress intended that an entity like the PGA not only give individualized attention to the handful of requests that it might receive from talented but disabled athletes for a modification or waiver of a rule to allow them access to the competition, but also carefully weigh the purpose, as well as the letter, of the rule before determining that no accommodation would be tolerable.

Here, unlike in the *Sony* opinion, Stevens used his judicial skills to implement a solution that, in Abner Mikva's words, moved forward the ball of social progress. Using creative reasoning that might seem odd to most golfers, Stevens ruled that Martin was a customer of the PGA Tour's service, just like the spectators at PGA Tour events, and that the ADA applied to both. Stevens thereby validated expansive enforcement of the ADA. Scalia, using colorful references to novelists Franz Kafka and Kurt Vonnegut as well as the books *Alice in Wonderland* and *Animal Farm*, denounced the opinion as foolish judicial activism.

The date 8/17/98 is inscribed on the videotape recorder upon which the Stevens bobblehead figure stands, marking the early morning when Daryl Renard Atkins, a mentally impaired man, committed murder. In *Atkins v. Virginia* (2002), Stevens overcame strident opposition of Justices Scalia and Rehnquist to form a six-to-three majority in favor of banning capital punishment for the mentally impaired. The decision, representing old-school liberalism instead of pragmatism, reversed a ruling from just three years earlier, *Penry v. Lynaugh* (1989), which held that mentally impaired persons could be subject to the death penalty. Stevens dissented from the *Penry* judgment with little elaboration. Unlike *Martin*, *Atkins* did not open doors to any new experiments toward the evolution of American society. It simply represented a fresh, liberal interpretation of the Constitution's Eighth Amendment rule against cruel and unusual punishment based on Stevens's findings about how society already had evolved:

> Those mentally retarded persons who meet the law's requirements for criminal responsibility should be tried and punished when they commit crimes. Because of their disabilities in areas of reasoning, judgment, and control of their impulses, however, they do not act with the level of moral culpability that characterizes the most serious adult criminal conduct. Moreover, their impairments can jeopardize the reliability and fairness of capital proceedings against mentally retarded defendants. Presumably for these reasons, in the 13 years since we decided *Penry* v. *Lynaugh*, the American public, legislators, scholars, and judges have deliberated over the question whether

the death penalty should ever be imposed on a mentally retarded criminal. The consensus reflected in those deliberations informs our answer to the question presented by this case: whether such executions are 'cruel and unusual punishments' prohibited by the Eighth Amendment to the Federal Constitution.

Stevens's opinion for the Court in *Atkins* revealed his liberal side in full flower. It was one of a string of cases in which Stevens led the Court to liberal decisions on homosexual rights (*Lawrence v. Texas*, 2003), affirmative action (*Grutter v. Bollinger*, 2003), and habeas corpus rights in the so-called war on terror (*Rasul v. Bush* (2004), *Hamdi v. Rumsfeld* (2004), and *Rumsfeld v. Padilla* (2004)). Summarizing the Court's 2003–2004 term, former Solicitor General Theodore B. Olson told the Federalist Society that change was in the wind: "Conservatives have every reason to weep. . . . Conservatives lost virtually every important controversial case that came before the Court. . . . The Court broke considerable new ground in opening the door to the recognition of new causes of [legal] action, new rights, and the assimilation into American law of perceived norms of international law, the decisions of courts of other nations, and the writings of law professors." Olson went on to give credit, or blame, where he thought it was due: "Justice Stevens led the charge. . . . The crafty and genial hand of Justice Stevens . . . was everywhere evident."[15]

The *Martin* and *Atkins* opinions, both rated "liberal" in the Spaeth database, seem to have little in common. But they typify the output that Olson summarized. The contrast in Stevens's approaches regarding the two disabled men, Martin and Adkins, sums up the twin sides of his judicial liberalism that analysts have observed to be building since the mid-1990s. In *Martin*, Stevens applied a broadly pragmatic interpretation of a federal law, the Americans with Disabilities Act, with an optimistic eye toward the possibilities that might flow from Congress's intent in passing the law.

In *Atkins*, Stevens did not look forward, as pragmatists might. He looked back to a 1958 denationalization opinion by Chief Justice Warren, who declared in *Trop v. Dulles* that the Court must follow "evolving standards of decency that mark the progress of a maturing society" in deciding what was or was not cruel and unusual punishment. Stevens stated what he believed to be the current status of "evolving standards of decency." He had cited no public opinion polls in his forward-looking *Martin* opinion. But in *Atkins*, Stevens sought to take a snapshot of the state of the evolving standards regarding capital punishment by citing public opinion, a source of knowledge that justices, including Stevens, typically are loath to quote in their work. Votes by state legislatures on capital punishment bills, public opinion surveys, interest group studies, and opinion surveys from other countries all pointed to exempting mentally impaired persons from the death penalty, Stevens claimed. Conservatives Rehnquist and Scalia were outraged that Stevens openly exhibited Mr. Dooley's cynical assessment, that the Supreme Court follows the election returns. The weight of this public sentiment had changed since the *Pentry* decision, and Stevens led the Court in following the change of public opinion.

Martin and *Atkins* were two sides of the same coin, a single "glittering generality" that underlies much of Stevens's work as a justice. A central theme of Stevens's jurisprudence is a belief that law must protect individual dignity, even the dignity of the worst criminal offender. On this point, Stevens hasn't changed from his opinions in the mid-1970s for the Seventh Circuit in prisoner rights cases. This belief appears, usually in dissent, in a variety of legal situations, from the right of one of the forty "most dangerous and recalcitrant inmates" in Pennsylvania's penal system to receive daily newspapers (*Beard v. Banks*, 2006) to the right of an accident victim in a vegetative state to have her previously expressed wish not to be kept alive by artificial means honored despite a Missouri law giving the state the power to decide (*Cruzan v. Missouri Department of Health, 1990*). This consistent interpretation explains how Stevens can say his basic principles haven't changed. What has changed since the mid-1990s is his ability to affect outcomes by drawing the votes of his colleagues toward his pragmatic, liberal approach to law.

Not long after Stevens joined the court, some commentators found his style unappealing. In his widely quoted 1983 book *The Burger Court: The Counter-Revolution That Wasn't*, Court scholar

Vincent Blasi criticized Stevens in a brief profile: "As Stevens began his service as a justice, knowledgeable observers expected him to become a leader on the Court by virtue of his powerful intellect and moderate instincts. That has not happened. Instead, Stevens has tended to develop highly original, sometimes idiosyncratic theories that fail to win the endorsement of his brethren. He is a formidable but unconventional legal thinker. With Stevens operating as he has at the center of the Court's divisions, the effect of his independence of mind often has been to fragment potential majorities and leave the state of the law indeterminate."[16]

In one respect, not much changed in Stevens's more than three decades on the Court. Totenberg said Stevens is "80 percent" the judge he was in 1975.[17] *Harvard Law Review* statistics for the October 2008 term show that Stevens was again the leading writer of dissents, with 17 dissents from 78 opinions compared to 13 dissents from 70 opinions the previous term. The number of his concurring opinions dropped to 3 in 78 from 8 in 70. His votes in the 2008 term were most closely aligned with Justice Ginsburg, 81 percent agreement, nearly equal to the Scalia/Thomas alignment of 82 percent. He agreed with Justices Thomas and Samuel A. Alito, Jr., just 36 percent of the time each, the weakest paired alliances on the Court. As in the 2007 term, he was the least likely to join the majority in non-unanimous cases.

But the raw data on Stevens's votes do not adequately reflect the dynamics of voting and opinion writing on the Court. Despite the image of a right-wing Court under Chief Justice John G. Roberts, five of the twelve opinions holding a bare majority of five to four votes in the October 2007 term were written by a Court majority led by Stevens, the senior liberal. In each of the close calls in which Stevens was the senior justice, he assigned the opinion to someone else, including Justice Anthony Kennedy three times and Scalia once. In two other five-to-four cases, Stevens was in the majority, led by Chief Justice Roberts, meaning that liberal Stevens was in the majority in seven of the twelve five-to-four decisions by a conservative Court.[18]

From a political standpoint, the power to assign an opinion may be used strategically by the senior justice on a case to secure the fifth vote, in effect by appealing to a wavering justice's pride of authorship. But Justice Ginsburg says there is a more mundane reason for assigning a case to a justice who is the weakest vote in a five-four majority. If the weak voter changes his or her mind during the opinion-writing process, the case does not have to be reassigned, she noted. "It makes sense," she said. "It's an economic use of time."[19] In either event, Stevens is not known to insist on writing high-profile opinions, and he is rarely a weak vote. Both factors help explain why Stevens seems like an outlier whose name is seldom featured as the author of five-four controversies that draw headlines. Nonetheless, "the account of Justice Stevens as idiosyncratic might have had more validity in his early time on the Court," Ginsburg said. "During the years I've been on the Court, I have not seen Justice Stevens that way."[20]

A justice whose written record emphasizes dissents and separate concurrences seems the very definition of an independent judge. Yet independence does not necessarily suggest disengagement or futility, for two reasons. First, law as interpreted by the Supreme Court encompasses the entire record of opinions in each case. On many occasions, a published dissent or concurrence lives again in subsequent opinions of the Court or in legislative action by the states or Congress. In particular, state courts, legislatures, and administrators often are guided by the reasoning in dissents and concurrences from the Supreme Court.

Transforming a dissent into a majority opinion may take time. In 1990, Stevens filed a lone dissent in a death penalty case (*Walton v. Arizona*). The case centered on the question of how so-called aggravating circumstances (such as extreme cruelty) should be applied by judges and juries to make a defendant eligible for execution. The Court upheld an Arizona law that allowed a judge to make the determination. Stevens, in a dissent that cited legal history and targeted a "reactionary" Justice Scalia on the opposing side, insisted that juries, not a judge, must be the prime source of determining aggravating circumstances, just as juries determine other facts in the trial phase of the case.

In a seven-to-two opinion written by Justice Ginsburg, the Court overruled *Walton v. Arizona* in 2002. As the senior judge in the majority, Stevens assigned the case to Ginsburg and did not write separately. Scalia joined the majority and wrote a concurrence, drawing upon his ever-present belief in "tradition" to concede Stevens's point from *Walton v. Arizona*: "Our people's traditional belief in the right of trial by jury is in perilous decline. That decline is bound to be confirmed, and indeed accelerated, by the repeated spectacle of a man's going to his death because a judge found that an aggravating factor existed. We cannot preserve our veneration for the protection of the jury in criminal cases if we render ourselves callous to the need for that protection by regularly imposing the death penalty without it." "Justice Stevens won out," said former Stevens clerk Edward Siskel. "He is a strategic actor in his role as the senior justice."[21]

Second, dissents and concurrences seldom are written in a political vacuum inside the Court. Usually they are the product of negotiations and a factor in shaping the outcome of a case. The writer of dissenting or concurring drafts, which are circulated among the justices as the case is being resolved, usually wants to influence his or her colleagues. In turn, the majority or plurality tries to gain the support of a justice who plans to write separately. For example, Stevens's draft dissent in *Sony v. Universal City Studios* transformed into a majority opinion, and the initial majority opinion by Blackmun turned into a dissent.

In January 1992, Kathy Moriarity, a Stevens clerk, forwarded a compliment to Stephanie Dangel, a clerk to Justice Blackmun: "I meant to tell you before I forgot. Justice Stevens mentioned that he thought Justice Blackmun (and hence, indirectly, you) did a nice job with Burson [*Burson v. Freeman,* 1992]. He doesn't agree with it, of course, but he thought the opinion was well written."[22] Such courtesy was normal among chambers, even after deeply felt disagreements on cases, but Stevens's nod to Blackmun suggests his political skill as a writer of dissents.

Two months earlier, the Court and all America had been stunned by the confirmation battle surrounding conservative Justice Clarence Thomas to succeed liberal Justice Marshall, both African

Americans. Afterward, the barbell alignment of justices matched a newly enlarged conservative bloc—Justices Rehnquist, Scalia, and Thomas—against two other Republican appointees—Stevens and Harry Blackmun—now identified as the liberal wing. A moderate center—Justices O'Connor, Souter, Kennedy, and White—held sway in several major decisions.

The term that began in October 1991 confronted big controversies—including abortion, school prayer, and free speech—that were familiar to most Americans. When the term ended in July 1992, *The New York Times* called it "a surprising and fascinating Supreme Court term."[23] As usual, most of Stevens's writing appeared in dissents and concurrences, not in opinions for the Court. But memoranda circulated among the chambers and available in Blackmun's papers at the Library of Congress show that Stevens was by no means closeted in his chambers.

After reviewing the Blackmun papers, which were released to the public in 2004, just five years after his death, Linda Greenhouse of *The New York Times* commented: "John Paul Stevens, who seems to be much of a loner, is a very strategic player behind the scenes. That was a very interesting revelation from those documents."[24] Much of this insight is drawn from the October 1991 term, thanks to two exceptionally enthusiastic and chatty law clerks in Blackmun's chambers, Molly McUsic and Stephanie Dangel. Two cases from that term, *Burson v. Freeman* and *Planned Parenthood of Southeastern Pennsylvania v. Casey,* reveal how Stevens shaped results and advanced the left side of the newly constituted ideological split on the Court.

Stevens's activity in that term is particularly notable because in the first half of 1992 he underwent chemotherapy treatments at Georgetown University Hospital for prostate cancer. A prostatic specific antigen (PSA) test followed by a biopsy of his prostate gland revealed a cancerous tumor. "I feel fine and I am not at all concerned about the future," Stevens, age seventy-one, told his colleagues.[25] But Justice Lewis Powell, who had retired not long after a tough bout with prostate cancer, cautioned him: "This could be burdensome after you have been on chemotherapy for a few days. I hope you do not overtax yourself."[26]

Burson v. Freeman was one of dozens of obscure cases that the Court takes up each term in which a seemingly minor dispute (such as protecting the snail darter) presents elemental questions of interpreting law. *Planned Parenthood v. Casey,* on the other hand, needed no introduction. It was nothing less than a milestone opportunity for conservatives to overturn the *Roe v. Wade* decision of 1973.

Burson concerned the power of states to prohibit electioneering within one hundred feet of polling places on election day. Tennessee, like other states, enforced a so-called campaign-free zone outside polling places, a practice derived from voting reforms first implemented in Australia in the 1800s. Mary Rebecca Freeman, a campaign worker and sometime candidate in local elections, sued to outlaw the zone and won in the Tennessee Supreme Court. Tennessee's high court decided that the campaign-free zone was a free-speech restriction that the state had not adequately justified under federal and state constitutional guarantees. When Tennessee appealed to the U.S. Supreme Court, the initial conference among the justices indicated that the Supreme Court would reverse the state court and reinstate the zone.

At the conference on the case, Stevens remarked, "[I] do not feel strongly" but he added that Tennessee had not made a sufficient showing of need for its selective denial of free speech.[27] Chief Justice Rehnquist—who declared during the debate that voting was not an expression protected by the first amendment—disagreed. He assigned the case to Blackmun, the most liberal of those voting his way at the conference. Not coincidentally, Blackmun had been an ally of Stevens on many issues, notably abortion. (Thomas did not participate in the case, which was argued before he arrived.)

Many Americans, as well as the Court's majority in *Burson,* would agree that a campaign-free zone around their polling place is a practical convenience. Still, the facts of the case seemed to foretell another predictable dissent by Stevens on behalf of unrestrained political speech. The Tennessee law appeared likely to be upheld, with Rehnquist and Blackmun in alliance and "maverick" Stevens on the sidelines. But the simple matter turned complex and far more momentous when Justice Scalia's view of the case emerged.

In the conference, Scalia voted with Rehnquist and Blackmun to reverse the Tennessee court. But he declined to follow Rehnquist in joining Blackmun's opinion. Instead, he drafted a solo concurrence and attempted to draw the votes of Kennedy and White to his more radical and sweeping interpretation, against which Stevens and Blackmun felt strongly.

In ideological terms, the ensuing debate, which lasted nearly eight months, pitted Scalia, as a champion of tradition in law— meaning "what is"—against Stevens, as an advocate for pragmatism in law—meaning "what may be." Either approach to the law can spawn activist judges intent on pulling back the law or pushing it forward. Either can fly the banner of "strict construction" of statutory texts and judicial precedents. This divide, more than "liberal" or "conservative" or Republican or Democrat, explains much of internal Supreme Court politics during Stevens's tenure.

The Supreme Court is immersed in tradition, from the black robes of the justices to the ban on television coverage. Such traditions are supposed to serve two purposes: maintain reverence for the Court and law and, just as important, allow justices to focus efficiently, even monastically, on their jobs. Traditional typographical and stylistic forms for lawyer's briefs and justices' opinion drafts, for example, eliminate the need to think about presentational aspects of paperwork and facilitate communication among the nine chambers. Robes relieve justices of worrying about what color to wear during oral arguments and to avoid sartorial statements, intended or not, from the bench. Tradition plays a role in deciding cases, as well. Respect for each phrase of the Constitution is central to American law, whether or not a justice identifies with the so-called originalist view of constitutional interpretation.

But one school of interpreting statutes and the constitution takes the idea of tradition much further. Justice Scalia and other adherents to this theory see the nation's legal, cultural, moral, and institutional traditions as the essential building blocks of democracy. Simply put, the American majority established these traditions and, therefore, the status quo merits great deference by unelected judges. In this view, novel interpretations of law by activist judges (as in *PGA v. Martin*) and the opinions of non-U.S. Courts (as in *Atkins v. Virginia*) corrupt tradition.

The word *tradition* appears throughout Scalia's writings. In his *Burson* concurrence, he used "tradition," "traditions," "traditional," or "traditionally" ten times in four short paragraphs. Court prec- edent requires justices to give their greatest scrutiny to any attempt to limit speech in public forums, such as public parks and side- walks. A one-hundred-foot circumference around polling places often includes such spaces. But "because restrictions of speech around polling places on election day are as venerable a part of the American tradition as the secret ballot, [Tennessee's campaign-free zone law] does not restrict speech in a traditional public forum, and the 'exacting scrutiny' that the plurality [of four justices led by Blackmun] purports to apply is inappropriate," Scalia advised his fellow justices.

In other words, banning electioneering near the polling place is accepted practice, and it should therefore continue to be accepted practice. Seen in the context of abortion, homosexual activity, athe- ism, assisted suicide, and a host of other personal choices at odds with traditional public norms, Scalia's reliance on tradition as the touchstone for Supreme Court review represents a major threat to anyone who believes that law must evolve with society, sometimes with the aid of judges. As any advocate of an idea would, Scalia parses cases of all sorts in search of opportunities to inject his theory into the process of making justice.

Framing the debate in this way, Stevens represented the contrary view: Americans fought the revolution and wrote the Constitution precisely to protect individuals from entrenched institutions and values imposed by a majority.

As they struggled to justify Tennessee's campaign-free zone on the basis of thin historical evidence, Blackmun and clerk Stepha- nie Dangel, whose memos to her boss contained an extraordinary amount of personal musings, wanted Scalia's vote for Blackmun's *Burson* opinion. But they realized the constitutional quicksand that Scalia's concurrence would lead them into. "Who knows, maybe [Scalia] will come to our defense. What a scary thought," Dangel wrote.[28] "I fear that the only general principles that will come from this case are those that will haunt you."[29] She acknowledged the strategic dilemma. At first, she advised a "conciliatory tone that will avoid a counter-attack by Justice Scalia. . . . I do not want to criticize explicitly [Scalia's] concurrence for fear of losing his vote [for a five-vote judgment of the Court]."[30] Nonetheless, by the end of April, Dangel changed her mind: "I recommend that you not give into [Scalia's] demands . . . [because] the loss of his [fifth vote] would limit his use of our opinion in the future."[31] Dangel did not want a Blackmun opinion to become a platform for what she feared would be regressive judgments by the Court against abortion rights or other achievements in personal freedom.

Meanwhile, after several months of research, Dangel failed to find a convincing legal rationale for Tennessee's campaign-free zones, just as John Paul Stevens had suspected. "I am, as I have been from the start, sympathetic to JPS's criticism . . . ," she told her boss. "JPS'[s] final criticism is that we have not put the heavy burden of justification on [Tennessee]. I find this the most difficult criticism to answer, for to a large degree we have shifted the burden of justification from the State to the [Supreme Court] library staff."[32]

Blackmun eventually conceded, in a note to Stevens, that the primary goal of the case had become preventing Scalia from diluting the Court's strict scrutiny of state's attempts to suppress political expression. "I hope we at least can get a majority to agree on the strict scrutiny approach," he told Stevens.[33] He informed Scalia that he would not budge from his opposition to the idea that "a law can pass strict scrutiny 'because history says it does.'"[34]

In his dissent, joined by Justices O'Connor and Souter, Stevens rescued Blackmun from himself. Making justice, he argued, should be based not on tradition but on evidence. No matter what purpose the zones might serve in 1992, research showed that Tennessee and other states initially used the zones to limit voting participation by African Americans and new immigrants, he pointed out. He attacked Blackmun's and, by implication, Scalia's reasoning that election-day tradition was sufficient to save the zones. Other traditions, such as poll taxes, voter residency requirements, and onerous petition requirements, had been outlawed as unconstitutional assaults on individual rights, he noted.

The Blackmun opinion (and Scalia concurrence) "confuses history with necessity and mistakes the traditional for the indispensible," he wrote, in classic pragmatist form. Moreover, the zones tend to favor political "ins" at the expense of "outs," he said. In this instance the practical must give way to the pragmatic: "Candidates with fewer resources, candidates for lower visibility offices, and 'grassroots' candidates benefit disproportionately from last-minute campaigning near the polling place. . . . The hubbub of campaign workers outside the polling place may be a nuisance, but it is also the sound of a vibrant democracy." In a separate note to Blackmun, Stevens was sterner: "Traditions—especially traditions in the law—are as likely to codify the preferences of those in power, as they are to reflect necessity or proven wisdom."[35]

The tradition of campaign-free zones lives on in many states, thanks to the plurality votes of Justices Blackmun, Rehnquist, White, and Kennedy in *Burson v. Freeman*. But Stevens's dissent eliminated the chances that *Burson* would become a wedge for Scalia's theory of law.

Campaign-free zones at polling places were hardly the burning issue before the Court at the start of the 1992 election year. All eyes were on *Planned Parenthood v. Casey*. Blackmun clerk Molly McUsic advised her boss, "The prospect of this case being heard has gripped the attention of the outside world, both pro- and anti-*Roe* groups."[36]

McUsic knew that the *Roe v. Wade* decision, which was the signature of Blackmun's nearly twenty-two years on the Court, effectively would be overturned if the Court upheld the latest Pennsylvania abortion law. The Pennsylvania law eroded the right to abortion asserted by the Supreme Court by imposing a series of restrictions. Upholding Pennsylvania would gut the principal finding of *Roe v. Wade*—that a woman's right to an abortion, like other basic liberties, was protected by the Court's strictest scrutiny against government interference.

Early in the year, political strategists outside the Court and law clerks inside debated whether it would be better to hear the case as soon as possible or postpone it. Holding off might keep a lid on the controversy. There was a chance that a Democrat would be elected president in the fall and appoint liberal justices to replace aging Justice White and infirm Justice Rehnquist, two of the anti-*Roe* votes. The odds for the women's movement could be more favorable in 1993.

On the other hand, "if you believe that there are enough votes on the Court now to overturn *Roe,* it would be better to do it this year before the election and give women the opportunity to voice their outrage," McUsic advised Blackmun." 1991 was a horrific year for women, considering Clarence Thomas [Thomas was confirmed] and the William Kennedy Smith trial [Smith, a nephew of Senator Edward Kennedy, was acquitted of raping a woman], but women indisputably have more power today than they did in 1973."[37]

As this tactical debate was underway, the clerk grapevine picked up fresh intelligence: Republican appointee Justice Souter, in his second year on the Court, was fashioning a new approach that would retain the essential holding in *Roe v. Wade*, that women had a constitutional right to an abortion, on the basis of stare decisis (respect for past Court rulings). It was Souter's first contribution to the debate. Although Souter was known to respect past decisions, his stance was a bit of a surprise. In his first term, 1990–1991, he had sided with the conservatives on other issues. He had proven to be least likely to agree with Stevens, although he told a friend he considered Stevens to be the "smartest" member of the Court.[38]

Sixteen years earlier, freshman Justice Stevens had joined two colleagues in a rare joint opinion affirming the constitutionality of executions and passing judgment on state laws permitting the death penalty. Now, Souter joined Justices O'Connor and Kennedy—as before, all Republican appointees—in another troika. Justice Thomas had replaced Justice Marshall, increasing the Court's anti-*Roe* vote. But the troika plus Stevens and Blackmun meant that there were still five votes to uphold the basic judgment.

Blackmun clerk Stephanie Dangel worried that the troika's moderate approach would "have the effect of removing abortion from the political agenda just long enough to ensure the re-election of Pres. Bush and the appointment of another nominee from whom the Far Right will be sure to extract a promise to overrule *Roe*."[39] Earlier, she had speculated that "once this opinion comes out, there will be no more speculation about a Vice President O'Connor or a Chief Justice Kennedy—and, as [Souter] himself recognized—I suspect Barbara Bush will find herself another most-eligible bachelor to include on her White House invite list."[40]

But the critical factor in determining the impact of *Planned Parenthood v. Casey* was the extent to which Blackmun and Stevens would agree with the troika. As in the capital cases of 1976, states were looking for guidance. Five votes for all or most of the O'Connor-Kennedy-Souter opinion would have more influence than a fractured outcome with partial concurrences or dissents mixed throughout the published opinions.

Stevens took the lead in stating the points of agreement. "While I tend to agree with most of [Stevens's] list, I tend to disagree with him on a few of the sections," Dangel wrote as the troika's draft opinion circulated.[41] Stevens's goal, which the troika endorsed, was to concentrate the points of difference between them and Stevens/Blackmun in a single section late in the troika's text. Stevens also advised the troika to tone down their doubts about the basic rationale of *Roe v. Wade* in order to make the language more comfortable for him and Blackmun. The troika complied. Stevens's tactics enabled Stevens and Blackmun to agree unreservedly with the first three of six sections and the bulk of the overall opinion. The troika presented a five-vote Court majority upholding the essence of *Roe v. Wade*.

In a significant twist, Dangel signaled Blackmun that Stevens wanted to inject a defense of a woman's right to choose that differed from a right to marital privacy. Since his days on the Seventh Circuit, Stevens had seemed to be dubious of justifying abortion on the basis of a right to privacy. Stevens entertained the idea of defending the decision on the principle that women deserved equal protection of the law. The text of the Constitution provides the right of "equal protection of the laws." The Constitution does not state a right to privacy. Many liberal commentators agreed with conservatives that a right to privacy was porous bedrock on which to build pro-choice law. The equal protection doctrine, meaning that women should enjoy the same authority over their bodies as men, seemed constitutionally firmer.

"As I mentioned the other morning at breakfast, JPS is considering writing an opinion staking out the equal protection basis for the right to choose," Dangel advised Blackmun. "This is certainly a perfect case to do it, since the issues are raised by the spousal notification provision. Moreover, I think it's important to get this out there for the troika to think about over the summer before the court considers *Bray*. [*Bray v. Alexandria Clinic*, 1993, concerned unfettered access to abortion clinics by women seeking treatment or consultation]. Unfortunately, [Stevens's] clerk has indicated that the Justice is waffling on this idea, evidently because he feels it might tread on territory you plan to cover."[42]

Two days later, Dangel pushed her point: "[Stevens] could address this in his separate writing. Given his scholarly opinion in *Bray* explaining the opposition to the right to choose is discrimination against women, he would be the logical person to make this argument. You may want to mention this possibility to him to assure him that you have no objection to his 'going his own way.' . . . You probably should act surprised when he calls. I did want to give you fair warning."[43] Three days later Dangel reported her understanding that Stevens was not waffling: "GOOD NEWS. JPS's clerk informs me that the Justice has again changed his mind—he's writing a concurrence/dissent setting out the equal protection argument!"[44]

Dangel's hopes, if they were ever warranted, were dashed. Stevens may have preferred the equal protection theory. But, in the end, he apparently was not willing on his own to inject it into the *Planned Parenthood v. Casey* decision. Doing so would overshadow the work of the troika, which Stevens immediately had applauded as "impressive,"[45] and throw a monkey wrench in the delicate political dynamic at work. It would awkwardly set side by side the troika's position that *Roe v. Wade,* because of stare decisis, was the law of the land based on a right to privacy, and an entirely new rationale for abortion rights, based on the Constitution's equal protection clause.

In the end, the equal protection rationale found its way slightly into the troika's opinion as well as the separate writings of Stevens and Blackmun. O'Connor, Kennedy, and Souter inserted the concept obliquely to defend stare decisis: "For two decades of economic and social developments, people have organized intimate relationships and made choices that define their views of themselves and their places in society, in reliance on the availability of abortion in the event that contraception should fail. The ability of women to participate equally in the economic and social life of the Nation has been facilitated by their ability to control their reproductive lives."

Stevens agreed with the troika's approach but was a bit more assertive in championing the equal protection clause: "The societal costs of overruling *Roe* at this late date would be enormous. *Roe* is an integral part of a correct understanding of both the concept of liberty and the basic equality of men and women." Later in his concurrence, he used the terms "equal dignity" and "equal respect," implying but not stating government's obligation to provide "equal protection" to women who chose to have an abortion: "Part of the constitutional liberty to choose is the equal dignity to which each of us is entitled. A woman who decides to terminate her pregnancy is entitled to the same respect as a woman who decides to carry the fetus to term. The mandatory waiting period [in the Pennsylvania law under review] denies women that equal respect."

It was left to Blackmun, the justice most closely associated in the public mind with the abortion issue, to place the equal protection guarantee squarely into the record. In doing so, he ran the risk of admitting that he had been wrong in his initial *Roe v. Wade* reasoning. Three days before the results of the case were issued, an admittedly harried Stephanie Dangel ("end-of-term blues," she said[46]) expressed disappointment in Stevens, telling her boss (with information based entirely on the clerk grapevine), that Stevens "had reversed without explanation his position on some of the issues in this case."[47]

In a critique that blasted Stevens but also confirmed his rise above the lone dissenter reputation, Dangel wrote: "I can't help but think that JPS sees that there's power in the middle, and therefore that's where he's moving. In short, I think JPS is taking for granted that you will always be here to make the principled argument, so he's free to go off and build coalitions in the middle.

. . . We've already got plenty of Justices in this case willing to compromise and perpetuate myths. The people of America need someone to tell them the truth. And, as the author of *Roe,* I think you're the only person who can do it."[48]

What Dangel failed to recognize, however, was that if the rationale for *Roe v. Wade* was to be amended using the Constitution's equal protection guarantee, Blackmun was the one to do it. Blackmun's statement on this subject carried more weight than the same words from Stevens or any other justice. Blackmun went partway: "A State's restrictions on a woman's right to terminate her pregnancy also implicate constitutional guarantees of gender equality," he wrote in his concurrence. "By restricting the right to terminate pregnancies, the State conscripts women into its service. . . . This assumption—that women can simply be forced to accept the 'natural' status and incidents of motherhood—appears to rest upon a conception of women's role that has triggered the Equal Protection Clause." As an example of an unacceptable assumption about women, Blackmun cited *Craig v. Boren* from 1976, the case from Stevens's freshman term concerning different age rules for men and women in an Oklahoma law about purchasing beer. The Court ruled that the gender distinction in the law was unconstitutional under the equal protection clause. It was a potent choice of precedent by Blackmun in relation to Stevens. The opening sentences of Stevens's solo concurrence in *Craig v. Boren* first voiced two of the bedrock principles that guided much of his work throughout his tenure: "There is only one Equal Protection Clause. It requires every State to govern impartially." In these two simple sentences, Stevens revealed his consistent displeasure with dubious attempts by the Court toward parsing core constitutional principles instead of allowing judges to decide cases. In the context of the *Craig* ruling, and especially the Stevens concurrence, Blackmun placed a woman's right to choose more firmly under the Constitution's broad umbrella. Although the constitutional basis for abortion remained the right of privacy, liberals hailed the *Planned Parenthood v. Casey* decision in part for acknowledging the alternate and constitutionally stronger basis of equal protection for women. "This opinion makes sense and puts the right to abortion on a firmer jurisprudential ground than ever before," Professor Laurence H. Tribe of the Harvard Law School, a leading liberal scholar, told *The New York Times*.[49] The decision upholding *Roe* energized conservative voters, but nonetheless Democrat Bill Clinton, a pro-choice candidate, was elected president.

In a last-minute memo to Blackmun, Stevens urged his colleague to remove the final two paragraphs of his opinion, which threw the hard-fought politics inside the Court into the public domain. Blackmun refused. "In one sense, the Court's approach is worlds apart from that of the chief justice and Justice Scalia. And yet, in another sense, the distance between the two approaches is short— the distance is but a single vote," Blackmun wrote. "I am 83 years old. I cannot remain on this Court forever, and when I do step down, the confirmation process for my successor well may focus on the issue before us today. That, I regret, may be exactly where the choice between the two worlds will be made."

Of course, *Roe v. Wade*'s strongest critic also saw the debate extending beyond the Court. Setting aside his occasionally snarling tone, Scalia faced the five votes against him and concluded his dissent with eloquence: "By foreclosing all democratic outlet for the deep passions this issue arouses, by banning the issue from the political forum that gives all participants, even the losers, the satisfaction of a fair hearing and an honest fight, by continuing the imposition of a rigid national rule instead of allowing for regional differences, the Court merely prolongs and intensifies the anguish. We should get out of this area, where we have no right to be, and where we do neither ourselves nor the country any good by remaining."

Stevens's preference for working inside the Court's political process while remaining independent of politics outside the Court is evident in his reluctance to give speeches to general audiences beyond groups of lawyers and law students. As a result, Stevens usually stays above the fray. He broke that rule, inadvertently or not, in the summer of 1987 amid the controversy over President Reagan's nomination of Federal Circuit Judge Robert H. Bork to succeed Justice Powell. In what Stevens called a digression from his main topic, he informed the annual Eighth Circuit Judicial Conference that he had advised the American Bar Association that Bork was "a very well qualified candidate and one [who] will be a very welcome addition to the Court." He then read from opinions written by Bork to prove his point. It's likely that Stevens was aware that his endorsement would add fuel to pro- and anti-Bork fires raging at the time. He told his audience, "I see no reason why I shouldn't express [my opinion] publicly."[50]

But the most pointed criticism of Stevens came from University of Chicago law professor Philip B. Kurland, an authority on constitutional law who at the time was associated as "of counsel" to Stevens's former law firm, Rothschild, Barry and Myers. Kurland opposed Bork's nomination to the Court. He made his comment in a review of *The Supreme Court: How It Was, How It Is* by Chief Justice Rehnquist for *The New York Times*: "It may seem strange that today's Justices, who have inadequate time to write their own opinions, can nevertheless find time for these extrajudicial compositions. It is, however, probably getting more difficult for them to sit quietly in the face of the often jejune comments of law professors, law students, and those who were called by Justice Felix Frankfurter, 'newspaper columnists.' And the Justices' suffering becomes more acute as the Supreme Court becomes more politicized—to the point that a sitting Justice, John Paul Stevens, recently endorsed publicly the nomination to the Court of Judge Robert Bork."[51]

Another critic of Stevens's statement was Judge Bork, who had first met fellow circuit appeals court Judge Stevens in joint antitrust work as lawyers in Chicago. "I was surprised that he endorsed me and that he would do so publicly," he said. "Stevens had a reputation as a good moderate-to-conservative judge on the Seventh Circuit. When he came to the Court he became extremely liberal. I had told a friend he'll be sound and solid and won't innovate much. A year later the guy called me back and said, you got it all wrong."[52]

Stevens's Bork endorsement may be the exception that proves the rule regarding his strategy toward public exposure. On abortion, the hottest Court topic in at least two generations, he is rarely singled out but rather is identified with a wing of the Court that wants to preserve the essence of *Roe v. Wade*. But his alleged "hostility" to religion is one simplistic charge against him—an accusation with the intellectual feather's weight of a slogan or a one-liner on a bumper sticker—that has emerged in more than three decades of work for the Court. Like much of the debate about the intersection of religion and secular law, the charge against Stevens is full of confusion, irony, and hypocrisy. Its origin is obscure. It literally emerged from a law journal into public discourse over the last twenty years.

Despite an early reputation for belaboring his ideas, in his first term Stevens wrote just two sentences in dissenting from a majority opinion that endorsed state subsidies to sectarian organizations (*Roemer v. Maryland Public Works,* 1976): "I would add emphasis to the pernicious tendency of a state subsidy to tempt religious schools to compromise their religious mission without wholly abandoning it. The disease of entanglement may infect a law discouraging wholesome religious activity as well as a law encouraging the propagation of a given faith."

The Constitution's two-part pronouncement on religion is plain: "Congress shall make no law respecting the establishment of religion, or prohibiting the free exercise thereof." But the Establishment Clause and the Free Exercise Clause have been a source of intense debate and political strife since they were ratified. Like the Constitution's succinct religion clauses, Stevens's dissent in *Roemer* can be read in more than one way. To some, the dissent was a ringing endorsement of the sanctity of the "religious mission"; to others, it was a clever trick to deny taxpayer dollars to worthy organizations just because they have a religious component. But on its face, Stevens's dissent, like the First Amendment itself, does not indicate a bias for or against religion. Both speak to the Founding Fathers' desire not to have the government become entangled in religious disputes—what Thomas Jefferson called a wall of separation.

In twenty-two major decisions concerning religion in his first two decades on the Court, there is no evidence that "maverick" Stevens took extraordinary positions, according to analysis by Professor Robert S. Alley. Stevens agreed with the majority thirteen times and dissented eight times. In one case, he filed an opinion that was a concurrence-in-part and dissent-in-part.

In Alley's scorekeeping from the period 1976–1997, Stevens was nearly equal to Justice (later Chief Justice) Rehnquist, a hero of the religious right. Rehnquist agreed with the majority twelve times and dissented eight times. The only difference between the two men in this regard was that Rehnquist twice filed dissents-in-part and concurrences-in-part. To be sure, Rehnquist and Stevens agreed with each other only four times out of the twenty-two cases Alley tracked. But Stevens's slightly higher percentage of agreement with the Court hardly justifies accusations of anomalous bias beyond the Court consensus.[53]

Nonetheless, equanimity toward Stevens's votes on religion cases ended in 1989 when law professor Douglas Laycock of the University of Texas delivered a lecture at the Center for Church-State Studies at De Paul University Law School in Chicago. Laycock, a specialist on the religion clauses of the First Amendment, clerked at the Seventh Circuit U.S. Court of Appeals when Stevens worked there, and in 1975 he wrote a letter to President Ford in support of Stevens's nomination to the Supreme Court.

The title of Laycock's 1990 paper in the *DePaul Law Review*, "Formal, Substantive and Disaggregated Neutrality Toward Religion," based on his Center for Church-State Studies lecture, revealed the knotty problems he addressed and the likely small audience for his efforts.[54] In analyzing a selection of Supreme Court votes from 1972 through 1990, he classified ways in which justices responded to their duty to "make no law" respecting the establishment and free expression of religion. Laycock defined "hostility to religion" as a justice who votes against government benefits to religion, such as state aid to religious schools (*Aguilar v. Felton*, 1985), and also votes against exemptions from laws to preserve the exercise of religious beliefs that may otherwise conflict with government regulations, such as wearing a yarmulke with a U.S. Air Force uniform (*Goldman v. Weinberger*, 1986).

The conservatives—Chief Justice Rehnquist and Justices White, Scalia, and Kennedy—tended to favor government benefits for religion (state aid to religious schools) and, at the same time, vote to deny individuals freedom to express their religious traditions in conflict with broader government interests (the yarmulke),

Laycock found. The liberals—Justices Brennan, Marshall, and Blackmun—tended to favor religious exemptions for individual expressions but oppose government support for religious institutions. Justice O'Connor was a swing vote between the two positions, Laycock found.

"Justice Stevens is the exception," he wrote. Stevens tended to oppose government support for religion (state aid) *and* exemptions for individual exercise of religious beliefs (the yarmulke), he said. "The apparent explanation of his pattern is hostility to religion. Religion in his view is subject to all the burdens of government, but entitled to few of the benefits."

This pattern, to the extent it can be found in a fuller review of Stevens's votes on religious clause cases, may seem like simple consistency—keeping government and religion at arm's length across both of the First Amendment's religious clauses, like his brief dissent in *Roemer.* But for the religious right, Laycock's analysis and rhetoric presented fresh ammunition against the Supreme Court. The term *hostility* stuck to Stevens. On the other hand, another word, *indoctrination,* which Stevens has used to describe religious education, agitated religious conservatives.

In 2000, a dissent by Rehnquist denounced Stevens's six-to-three opinion against student-sponsored prayers at public high school football games (*Santa Fe Independent School District v. Doe*), saying it "bristles with hostility to all things religious in public life." Conservative leader Phyllis Schlafly, who rose to national prominence through her opposition to the proposed Equal Rights Amendment for women in the 1970s, said Stevens's remarks during oral argument in a First Amendment case (*Elk Grove United School District v. Newdow,* 2005) "showed his hostility to religion."[55]

Professor Robert F. Nagel of the University of Colorado School of Law declared in a 2003 *Chicago-Kent Law Review* article, "Stevens appears to be hostile to religious beliefs."[56] He extrapolated from that assertion to throw verbal flames on the fire, suggesting that Stevens is "intentionally dishonest, politically opportunistic, cruelly suppressive, and morally hypocritical," especially in cases concerning aggressive abortion protesters who claim religious inspiration.[57] Working the bellows, law professor Michael Stokes Paulsen of the

University of St. Thomas School of Law wrote that Stevens's opposition to prejudice against homosexuals by a Boy Scouts of America organization (*Boy Scouts of America v. Dale,* 2000) was "stunningly bigoted . . . one of the most intolerant-of-religion opinions ever to appear in the U.S. Reports [of Court opinions]."[58]

In a more restrained assessment, former Stevens clerk Eduardo Moises Penalver explored the phrase "hostility toward religion" in an analysis of Stevens's opinions and asserts that, "Stevens is not the antireligious crank that scholars sometimes make him out to be. A careful look at his voting in religion cases suggests that he has a healthy respect for religious thought, although this respect is tempered by a fear of the divisive power of religious disputes in public life." Stevens "appears to respect religion as a powerful motivator of human action that is largely protected by the political process." But he argued that Stevens needs to give more weight to "the unique value of religious belief systems in the lives of human beings."[59]

The rarity of the harsh language against Stevens invites further inspection. Professor Laycock remained troubled by Stevens's jurisprudence concerning religion but described his DePaul remarks as a "harsher description" than he would give then and one that was "written when I was younger."[60] In a 2004 *Harvard Law Review* article, he wrote, "Only Justice Stevens generally appears to vote against religion in the funding, speech, and regulation cases, and even he has found important exceptions."[61] He listed five cases, four of which were available to him for the *DePaul Law Review* article but not mentioned. In each case, Stevens was part of a unanimous Court upholding religious interests:

Church of Lukumi Babalu Aye v. City of Hialeleah (1993), in which the Court voided a city ordinance aimed at banning animal sacrifice performed by a religious group as part of its rituals.

Frazee v. Illinois Department of Employee Security (1989), in which the Court required Illinois to pay unemployment compensation to an individual who, citing his religious beliefs, refused to take a job that required him to work on Sunday.

Corporation of the Presiding Bishop of the Church of Jesus Christ of Latter-Day Saints v. Amos (1987), in which the Court upheld the right of the Mormon Church, under the 1964 Civil Rights Act, to discriminate in hiring workers for a public, not-for-profit agency it supported.

Witters v. Washington Department of Services for the Blind (1986), in which the Court endorsed the right of a visually impaired individual who was studying at a private Christian school to be a pastor, missionary, or youth director to receive state vocational rehabilitation aid, despite the religious purpose of his studies.

McDaniel v. Paty (1978), in which the Court invalidated a state law that barred ministers and priests from being members of the Tennessee state legislature and a state constitutional convention.

Other pieces of would-be tinder in Stevens's religious clauses woodpile demonstrate the over-reaction by conservative commentators. In the five-to-four Boy Scouts of America (BSA) case that unsettled Professors Paulsen and Nagel, Stevens based his dissent against homosexual discrimination on the civil rights law of New Jersey, where the case arose, and the following official words of the Boy Scouts of America, a nonprofit group that is federally chartered by Congress: "Scouting does not seek to impose its beliefs upon others who do not share them. Virtually every religion is represented in Scouting, and the BSA does not define or interpret God. That is the role of the Scout's family and religious advisors. Scouting respects those who do not share its beliefs and it would not ask others to alter their faith in any fashion in order to become Scouts. They too are free to follow their own beliefs. Rather, the BSA membership believes that the principles set forth in the Scout Oath and Law are central to the BSA goal of teaching the values of self-reliance, courage, integrity, and consideration to others."[62]

Phyllis Schlafly's concern about Stevens's oral argument colloquy in *Elk Grove United School District v. Newdow* is notable for several reasons. Michael A. Newdow, a brash medical doctor, lawyer, and atheist, sued to have the words "under God" stricken from the

Pledge of Allegiance, which his daughter was asked to recite daily in her elementary school. In a unanimous opinion written by Stevens, the Court threw out Newdow's case, saying he did not have proper standing to bring it. The Court refused to rise to Newdow's bait. Thanks to Stevens's unanimous opinion, Schlafly's side won, but she and her supporters remained dissatisfied.

Stevens barely participated in the *Newdow* oral argument, compared to swing voters O'Connor and Kennedy, who asked many questions. Much of the questioning by justices, including Stevens, concerned whether the "under God" phrase, inserted in the pledge during an American anti-communist mania in 1954, carried enough significance fifty years later to prompt a potentially explosive First Amendment adjudication under the religion clauses. "It's a very important question," Stevens said.[63]

In a classic Stevens rhetorical trap, he asked Terence J. Cassidy, the lawyer for the school district, to comment on the following sentence in a so-called friend-of-court brief: "If the religious portion of the pledge is not intended as a serious affirmation of faith, then every day government asks millions of school children to take the name of the Lord in vain."[64] Cassidy, speaking on behalf of a school district, not a religious sect, avoided the snare by maintaining that the pledge was not an endorsement of religion but merely one of many patriotic expressions that might be recited and studied in school. He said the provocative friend-of-court statement was irrelevant to the issue before the Court. Stevens agreed.

Michael Newdow "managed to wow the spectators, charm the press, and even—although they would never admit it—impress most of the justices," recalled Supreme Court reporter Dahlia Lithwick.[65] But Cassidy, in effect, insisted on a secular focus. As a result, Schlafly and her supporters, as well as Newdow, were marginalized.

Stevens's opinion for the Court, in which Justices Kennedy, Souter, Ginsburg, and Breyer joined and Justices Rehnquist, O'Connor, and Thomas filed concurrences, preserved the current pledge text without explicitly doing so. The opinion came down on Flag Day 2004 (June 14), fifty years to the day after Congress inserted "under God." But, in the spirit of the First Amendment, Stevens deftly separated religiosity from the issue. He gave the religious right its victory in the worst way possible—by minimizing their claims as well as Newdow's atheism. His low-temperature resolution of a hot-potato case, pegged to the judgment that Newdow was ineligible to bring the suit, stood in contrast to the performance of the only justice who did not participate—Justice Scalia.

Fifteen months before *Elk Grove v. Newdow* was argued in Washington, D.C., but while the case was percolating hotly in California on its way to the Supreme Court, Scalia told a general audience in Virginia, near his son Paul's assigned residence as a Catholic priest, "Government will not favor Catholics, Protestants, Muslims, Jews. But the tradition was never that the government had to be neutral between religiousness and nonreligiousness."[66] He said if Americans wanted to remove "under God" from the Pledge of Allegiance, they should do so at the ballot box or through the legislative process, not through acts of unelected judges.[67] But his remarks also were aimed expressly against litigant Michael Newdow's interests, although Scalia did not discuss specific cases. His speech came less than a month after the federal appeals court in California had restated its findings for *Newdow.* In a decision written by Nixon appointee Judge Alfred T. Goodwin, a unanimous three-judge Ninth Circuit appeals panel upheld Newdow's complaint that his daughter's school may not expose her every day to religious indoctrination against his teachings as an atheist.

Later that year, responding to a motion by Newdow, the Supreme Court announced that Scalia would not participate in *Elk Grove v. Newdow.* Scalia's zeal on behalf of traditional ideas and established institutions had carried him beyond his job description. In the justices' closed-door conference on the case, he did not debate or vote. "Justice Out of Case About Which He Cares," declared a *Washington Post* headline.

Stevens, on the other hand, remained at his post. He crafted for himself and his seven remaining colleagues a solution to Michael Newdow's well-articulated challenge. In doing so, Stevens returned to the public record a matter close to his heart. He read aloud in the courtroom the portion of his opinion that included words from the dissent that he had read aloud in *Texas v. Johnson* fifteen years earlier. In the interim his son, John, had died in a Florida hospice of a brain tumor. After his son's death in 1996, Stevens, without explanation, recused himself from several cases concerning the Agent Orange defoliant spread by American forces in Vietnam.

The nation's flag, he said in *Elk Grove v. Newdow,* was a symbol of its "proud traditions . . . of freedom, or equal opportunity, of religious tolerance and of good will for other peoples who share our aspirations." Recitation of the Pledge of Allegiance to the flag, before and after Congress inserted the "under God" phrase, "is a patriotic exercise designed to foster national unity and pride in those principles."

CHAPTER ELEVEN

The Independent Justice

"You should always—and by that I mean at least three times a week—engage in physical exercise," Justice Stevens told students at the new John Paul Stevens High School in San Antonio, the first institution named for him. "Whether you play competitive sports, do pushups, run-in-place, or flex your muscles if you are unable to do anything more vigorous, please exercise regularly. I have followed this rule all my life—I still manage to hold my own on the tennis court—and I have never regretted it."

At the school's dedication in September 2005, students gave him an *S* letter jacket displaying the school's mascot, the solitary, deadly falcon. He gave them three wishes: joy in learning, power to help friends and neighbors, and success "in securing the blessing of liberty." "It is this kind of joy, power and success that should characterize the graduates of John Paul Stevens High School," he said. "Go, falcons!" He also gave them a brief lecture, noting that San Antonio's Northside Independent School District had decided to name a number of high schools after U.S. Supreme Court justices: "By choosing to honor judges instead of popularly elected officials, your school district celebrates the principle that an independent judiciary administering neutral rule of law, rather than catering to popular opinion, is a matter of fundamental importance in a free society."[1]

When John and Maryan made the trip to Texas for the dedication ceremony, Stevens was acting chief justice of the United States. William Rehnquist had died earlier in the month, and a new chief,

John G. Roberts, Jr., was being confirmed by the Senate. Just after he returned to Washington, Stevens was called to a ceremony he would have preferred to avoid.

Like presidents before him, President George W. Bush arranged for the new justice to be sworn in in the East Room of the White House before live television and an audience of Washington officialdom. As acting chief, the job fell to Stevens. He was paired with the president behind Roberts and his wife, Jane, entering and leaving the ornate room. The Robertses walked side by side along a flag-festooned corridor; Bush and Stevens maintained a symbolic distance from one another. Bush "teared up momentarily" during the ceremony.[2] Stevens did not.

Several years earlier, Stevens had said, "I have refused to attend these [White House] events, because I believe symbols, like the flag, are important." He likewise did not join fellow justices in the House of Representatives for State of the Union addresses by presidents. "The political aspect of a federal judge's career should end when his or her nomination is confirmed. It is, in my judgment a serious matter to replace an important symbol of the independence of the federal judiciary with an event that tends to blur the critical distinction between political and judicial service. As is the case with a number of other important issues, I regret that my colleagues do not share my concern."[3]

An independent Supreme Court has several meanings. Amid his behind-the-scenes collaborations and strategizing, which grew more active with his seniority, Stevens has never abandoned his maverick streak. In *Scott v. Harris* (2007), a little noticed case, the longtime fan of the fictional lawyer/sleuth Perry Mason filed a lone dissent.

The case concerned a Coweta County, Georgia, deputy sheriff, Timothy Scott, who, during a high-speed chase, used his car's front bumper to bump the rear of Victor Harris's speeding car. The authorized police maneuver was designed to cause the fleeing car to spin, forcing the driver to stop. But Harris lost control, crashed, and was rendered a quadriplegic. A videotape camera mounted on Scott's patrol car captured the incident. Harris sued Scott and the county, saying his constitutional protection from unreasonable seizure was violated in the incident. At the Supreme Court, Deputy Scott was appealing decisions by district and appeals courts in Georgia that barred him from winning a summary judgment against Harris without a trial. The videotape had never been shown to a jury.

The Court rarely views original evidence. In a famous incident, the nine justices deliberating in *Jacobellis v. Ohio* (1964) watched a screening of a film titled *The Lovers* that contained explicit sexual content. Afterward they ruled that an exhibitor of the movie in Cleveland Heights, Ohio, had not engaged in "pornography" as the Court previously had defined the offence. "I know it when I see it, and the motion picture involved in this case is not that," wrote Justice Potter Stewart in his concurring opinion in *Jacobellis*.

In *Scott v. Harris* the Court decided to view the videotape to determine whether it should be seen by a jury to aid in evaluating Scott's and Harris's competing claims. The Court reversed the Georgia court rulings and found in Scott's favor. According to Justice Scalia's account for the eight-vote majority, "We see (Harris's) vehicle racing down narrow, two-lane roads in the dead of night at speeds that are shockingly fast. . . . We see it swerve around a dozen other cars, cross the double yellow line, and force other cars traveling in both directions to their respective shoulders to avoid being hit."

Stevens saw something quite different and concluded that a regular jury, not "eight of the jurors of this Court," should be allowed to hear and see the evidence to decide whether Scott's action violated Harris's constitutional rights. He noted that Harris used his turn signals to pass cars and slowed down when oncoming traffic prevented him from passing, contrary to Scalia's depiction of "a Hollywood-style car chase of the most frightening sort." Moreover, Stevens suggested that the presence of other cars on the shoulders of the road could have been the result of police car lights and sirens breaking the late night serenity of a rural area, not fear of Harris's vehicle. In a footnote, Stevens, then eighty-seven, hinted that his colleagues were less familiar than he was with the situation: "Had they learned to drive when most high-speed driving took place on two-lane roads rather than on superhighways—when split-second judgments about the risk of passing a slow-poke in the face of oncoming traffic were routine—they might well have reacted to the videotape more dispassionately."

Stevens seemed to take "an almost childlike—well, maybe that's too strong—pride in his interpretation of the car chase video, which is so contrary to how the majority viewed it," said Tony Mauro, Supreme Court reporter for *The National Law Journal.* "Stevens seems to be recalling the days when he learned to drive and how to drive on two-lane roads" near his family's summer home in Lakeside, Michigan, Mauro said.[4]

Examples abound, especially in the period beginning in the late 1990s, of Stevens playing the role of liberal iconoclast as well as liberal leader. But Stevens's independence from such labels has not disappeared. Women's advocate groups did not celebrate the Court's "senior liberal" after he joined conservative majorities in two cases of government-authorized gender discrimination, *Miller v. Albright* (1998) and *Nguyen v. Immigration and Naturalization Service* (2001). "The biological differences between single men and single women provide a relevant basis for differing rules governing their ability to confer citizenship on children born in foreign lands," Stevens wrote in *Miller v. Albright* in an opinion joined by Justice Rehnquist. Justice Ginsburg calls these the "Madame Butterfly" cases, because they relate to unequal treatment of U.S.–born fathers and Asian–born women who bear a child out of wedlock. She said Stevens lives in a time warp from World War II gender stereotypes on this issue because he favored a federal law that gives preference to the mother.[5] Commenting on the *Nguyen v. INS* case, Steven R. Shapiro, legal director of the American Civil Liberties Union, said: "The Court's decision cannot be explained except on the basis of the outmoded stereotype that mothers are more likely than fathers to develop a caring relationship with their children. By ignoring the facts in favor of stereotypes, today's decision represents a backwards step in the Court's effort to guarantee constitutional equality for men and women."[6]

Judicial independence can be as clear as Stevens's solo dissent in *Scott v. Harris* or his uncharacteristically conservative votes in the Madame Butterfly cases. But the concept of independence often is defined by noting its absence. In *The Responsible Judge: Readings in Judicial Ethics,* John T. Noonan, Jr., a senior judge on the Ninth Circuit U.S. Court of Appeals in San Francisco, and Kenneth I. Winston of the John F. Kennedy School of Government at Harvard University provide examples.[7]

In the late 1930s, federal appeals judge Martin T. Manton was considered a likely candidate for the U.S. Supreme Court until Thomas E. Dewey, the federal prosecutor in Manhattan, charged him with participation in a corruption scheme, whereby he used his office to solicit payments from parties in lawsuits.

In 1945, a congressional subcommittee chaired by Representative C. Estes Kefauver of Tennessee found that a federal district judge in Pennsylvania, Albert W. Johnson, had, for fifteen years, "notoriously engaged in the barter and sale of court offices," especially attorneys appointed in bankruptcy cases, and that "his decisions, decrees, orders, and rulings were commonly sold for all 'the traffic would bear.'"

The absence of independence, of course, entails more than bribe-taking.

• In 1978, the chief justice of the Superior Court of Massachusetts, Robert M. Bonin, resigned after disclosures that he had knowingly purchased tickets and attended a fund-raising event staged to support defendants in a case pending in his court.

• As Stevens had written in his constitutional law examination, Chief Justice Roger B. Taney chose to reach beyond the narrow issues in a case titled *Scott v. Sandford* to announce broad opinions about the rights of slaves and the ability of Congress to limit slavery. Historians have accused Taney of being in league with incoming president James Buchanan regarding the timing of the decision in the Dred Scott case.

• One of the Supreme Court's icons, Justice Felix Frankfurter, was criticized for improperly engaging in a scheme to postpone the Court's consideration of school desegregation until a unanimous vote of nine justices could be assured. Frankfurter's clerks recalled that he was worried about political and enforcement issues in the country if the integration, which he favored on the basis of law, was issued by a divided court.

•   In 1991, in a case concerning a warrantless search by police (*California v. Acevedo*), Justice Stevens accused the Court's majority of surrendering its independence from the executive branch of government. In a five-vote opinion written by Justice Blackmun, the Court strengthened the power of police to search an automobile, saying in part that previous Court rulings restricting warrantless searches of vehicles "impeded effective law enforcement." Stevens argued that the court should not empathize with police more than with an individual's constitutional right to privacy: "No impartial observer could criticize this Court for hindering progress in the war on drugs," he wrote in dissent. "On the contrary, decisions like the one the Court makes today will support the conclusion that this Court has become a loyal foot soldier in the Executive's fight against crime."

Steven's dedication to judicial independence is hardly exceptional or quixotic. State and federal judges throughout the country are working to expose and blunt the power of money and special interests in judicial selection. Still, a suit to correct the most egregious episode of money influence on a court in recent years—a West Virginia mine operator paid more than $3 million to elect a judge who would overturn a $50 million judgment against him—drew just five of nine votes on the Supreme Court in the spring of 2008 (*Caperton v. A.T. Massey Coal Co.*). The subject of judicial independence does not resonate in the public or press, which is more attracted to the debates and outcomes of judicial decisions than to the process. "Independent" is an even more abstract concept in the law than "liberal" or "conservative."

Nonetheless one of Stevens's best known opinions, in *Bush v. Gore* (2000), raised to the level of national discourse, however briefly and inadequately, the specter of a coerced judicial system—not the malfeasance of a particular judge but the undermining of the entire third branch. It was assumed by some that Republican appointee

Stevens had "gone Democratic," as his father might have said, when he issued a harsh dissent against the majority decision that put George W. Bush in the White House. The dissent made Stevens a celebrity of sorts. Shortly after the *Bush v. Gore* ruling, comedian Al Franken, elected a U.S. senator from Minnesota in 2008, wrote new lyrics for "Hang On, Sloopy," a popular 1965 song by the McCoys. Franken called his version "Hang on, Stevens:"

> Stevens might be eighty six years old.
> But I think he looks spry when he's wearing that robe.
> Stevens, I don't care if you lose your mind.
> Just wait until Bush leaves before you resign.[8]

Stevens, of course, did not take sides publicly in the 2000 election. He did, however, take sides in favor of Florida's right to complete its presidential vote count that year and the power of Florida judges to monitor the process without interference by the U.S. Supreme Court. The Bush forces, he wrote in conclusion, engaged in a "federal assault on the Florida election procedures," displaying

> an unstated lack of confidence in the impartiality and capacity of state judges who would make the critical decisions if the vote count were to proceed. . . . The endorsement of that position by the majority of this Court can only lend credence to the most cynical appraisal of the work of judges throughout the land. It is the confidence in the men and women who administer the judicial system that is the true backbone of the rule of law. Time one day will heal the wound to that confidence that will be inflicted by today's decision. One thing, however, is certain. Although we may never know with complete certainty the winner of this year's Presidential election, the identity of the loser is perfectly clear. It is the Nation's confidence in the judge as the impartial guardian of the rule of law. I respectfully dissent.

Stevens's dissent is notable for a reason beyond its memorable rhetoric. All four dissenters—Justices Stevens, David Souter, Stephen Breyer, and Ruth Ginsburg—filed opinions. These divided, hurriedly written responses (not all of the dissenters joined each other's opinions) reflected several disagreements with aspects of the majority view as well as disunity among the dissenters. The effect was to dilute what might have been a solid rebuttal to the possibility, however remote, of a political act by the Court's majority in favor of Bush. Political science professor Howard Gillman of the University of South California, in his analysis of *Bush v. Gore,* concluded that the threat to the independence of the Florida court system that so concerned Stevens paled in comparison to the lack of independence displayed by the *Bush v. Gore* majority on the U.S. Supreme Court: "As it turned out, the problem was not so much that the people would feel persuaded by the majority and thus lose confidence in state judges; it was clear that many people thought (rightly or wrongly) that the five conservatives on the U.S. Supreme Court—through their own actions—were the ones not acting as 'impartial guardians of the law.'"[9]

A unanimous dissent by Stevens, the senior member of the four, might have expressed a "glittering generality," though one worth having, about independence and restraint on the Supreme Court. Without impugning the motives of the majority, the dissenters could have presented a united front, enumerating the thin reeds of evidence and legal scholarship that the majority relied on in taking up the case and, ultimately, in installing Bush. The Court's self-inflicted wound might have been stanched somewhat by a four-vote countervailing force. Instead, the conclusion of Stevens's opinion became a new entry in the seventeenth edition of *Bartlett's Familiar Quotations,* but its impact on preserving judicial independence was not immediately apparent.

A Gallup Organization poll taken shortly after the *Bush v.Gore* decision found that an unusual gap had opened suddenly between Republican and Democratic support for the Court. Eighty percent of Republicans approved of the Court, up from 60 percent the previous August; 42 percent of Democrats approved, down from 70 percent.[10] The 38-point gap narrowed to nearly zero by the middle of 2003. But the post–*Bush v. Gore* divide in public sentiment was disturbing. "This high degree of politicization cannot be good for the institution," wrote Professor Steven G. Calabresi of the Northwestern University School of Law and a co-founder of the conservative

Federalist Society. "The nomination and confirmation process for future Supreme Court vacancies, already under tremendous strain, is now probably going to be incomparably more difficult."[11]

Calabresi's forecast became more probable on January 21, 2010, when the conservative majority on the Court wielded extraordinary power, summarily discarding a century of laws and judicial rulings that barred corporations and labor unions from spending money from their treasuries for or against candidates in federal elections. To accomplish this strike against legal tradition, the five-vote majority ruling in *Citizens United v. Federal Election Commission* reached well beyond the initial pleadings of the Citizens United, a not-for-profit issue-advocacy corporation that had produced a movie critical of Hillary Clinton when she was a candidate for the Democratic nomination for president in 2008.

Rather than strictly addressing *Citizens United*'s particular complaints under the federal campaign finance law known as the McCain–Feingold Act, Justice Kennedy overruled past Court decisions that barred electioneering expenditures by all corporations and unions for any reason. "Our Nation's speech dynamic is changing," Kennedy, one of the Court's leading free speech advocates, wrote, "and informative voices should not have to circumvent onerous restrictions to exercise their First Amendment Rights. . . . Corporations, like individuals, do not have monolithic views. On certain topics corporations may possess valuable expertise, leaving them the best to point our errors or fallacies in speech of all sorts, including the speech of candidates and elected officials."

This time, Stevens corralled the Court's three other liberals, including newcomer Justice Sotomayor, in a ninety-page joint dissent that he wrote and read haltingly for twenty minutes from the bench when the decision was announced. "At bottom, the Court's opinion is . . . a rejection of the common sense of the American people, who have recognized the need to prevent corporations from undermining self-government since the founding [of the nation] and who have fought against the distinctive corruption potential of corporate electioneering since the days of [President] Theodore Roosevelt. It is a strange time to repudiate that common sense. While American democracy is imperfect, few outside the majority of this Court would have thought its flaws included a dearth of corporate money in politics."

Stevens's skepticism toward direct electioneering by corporations and unions was, until the majority ruling in *Citizens United,* traditionally accepted wisdom among liberals and conservatives alike. Indeed, his dissent, like his dissent in *Bush v. Gore,* is best read as an impassioned defense of deliberate lawmaking and judicial interpretation by a jurist who has witnessed firsthand the evolution of law and judging for more than fifty years. As in *Bush v. Gore,* the Court's conservatives could not pretend to stand apart from the charge of judicial activism or even radicalism.

Stevens, in essence, warned that the majority opinion was a historic self-inflicted wound that could erode confidence in the Court: "The Court's ruling threatens to undermine the integrity of elected institutions across the Nation. The path it has taken to reach its outcome will, I fear, do damage to this institution. . . . The majority decides this case on a basis relinquished [in the district court proceedings], not included in the questions presented to us by the litigants, and argued here only in response to the Court's invitation. This procedure is unusual and inadvisable for a court. . . . There are principled, narrower paths that a Court that was serious about judicial restraint could have taken."

But the Stevens dissent was not limited to concerns about the integrity of lawmaking and judicial review. He answered Kennedy's contention that the technologies and substance of modern political speech demand greater participation by corporations and unions. "When citizens turn on their televisions and radios before an election and hear only corporate electioneering," Stevens wrote, "they may lose faith in their capacity, as citizens, to influence public policy. A Government captured by corporate interests, they may come to believe, will neither be responsive to their needs nor willing to give their views a fair hearing. . . .To the extent that corporations are allowed to exert undue influence in electoral races, the speech of the eventual winners of those races may also be chilled. Politicians who fear that a certain corporation can make or break their reelection chances may be cowed into silence about that corporation. . . . The marketplace of ideas is not actually a place where items—or laws—are meant to be bought and sold."

Stevens's reverence for an independent judiciary as a check on undue power requires that courtrooms not be hijacked by activist judges or radical litigants unwilling to play the rules as he sees them. In *Citizens United,* Stevens literally sat next to the insurgents. Another needling challenge to judicial independence in Stevens's experience dates back to the Conspiracy Seven trial. As Frank Greenberg of the Chicago Bar Association alleged at the time, political dissenters may have schemed to use Judge Julius Hoffman's courtroom as a stage for expressing their views with shock and awe. When the judicial process becomes an unwilling host to players in a drama outside the stated claims in a lawsuit, the independence of the third branch erodes.

In theory, courtrooms can be captured by such squatters in many ways. For example, business organizations frequently deride what they call a "strike" suit, which is defined as a lawsuit filed as a means of simple extortion against a deep-pocketed corporate defendant. In this concept, the plaintiffs hope never to have to win their case on its merits in court but rather to squeeze a large cash settlement from the strike target on the strength of negative publicity and the likely cost of a defense.

In the world of politics, a similar conspiracy theory centers on power, not money. For example, in the 1997 case of *Clinton v. Jones,* Democrats accused the Supreme Court of enabling a political version of a strike suit by conservatives against President Bill Clinton. Two days before the statute of limitations ran out on her in 1994, a former Arkansas state employee, Paula Corbin Jones, filed a federal suit against Clinton, formerly governor of Arkansas, charging Clinton with, among other things, sexual harassment while he was governor. The terms of Jones's complaint seemed straightforward and fairly routine in a legal sense. But political observers immediately sensed that forces behind Jones were not seeking a remedy for her but a judicial stage for harassing Clinton through depositions, motions, and other legal maneuvers, even if no trial ever took place. As procedural litigation in the case approached the Supreme Court, Clinton argued that a trial and its preliminaries should be postponed because of his job as president.

Justice Stevens, writing for a unanimous Court, ruled against Clinton. The notion of immunity for public officials from the judicial process is anathema to Stevens. In 1987, he issued a stern dissent against the Court's decision to void a white-collar prosecution technique that had been used to imprison his former Seventh Circuit colleague and former Illinois governor Otto Kerner (*McNally v. U.S.*). "In the long run, it is not clear how grave the ramifications of today's decision will be," he wrote, in a tone similar to his conclusion in the *Bush v. Gore* opinion. "Congress can, of course, negate it by amending the statute. . . . The possibilities that the decision's impact will be mitigated do not moderate my conviction that the Court has made a serious mistake. Nor do they erase my lingering questions about why a Court that has not been particularly receptive to the rights of criminal defendants in recent years has acted so dramatically to protect the elite class of powerful individuals who will benefit from this decision."

Not until near the end of his opinion in *Clinton v. Jones* did Stevens address the point of concern to Democrats—"the risk that our decision will generate a large volume of politically motivated harassing and frivolous litigation, and the danger that national security concerns might prevent the President from explaining a legitimate need for a continuance." Stevens was not convinced. "We are not persuaded that either of these risks is serious. Most frivolous and vexatious litigation is terminated at the pleading stage or on summary judgment, with little if any personal involvement by the defendant. Moreover, the availability of sanctions provides a significant deterrent to litigation directed at the President in his unofficial capacity for purposes of political gain or harassment. History indicates that the likelihood that a significant number of such cases will be filed is remote."

It's unlikely that the Supreme Court, under its rules, could have set aside the stated particulars of *Clinton v. Jones* while justices investigated ulterior motives of certain parties behind the scenes. But, as in the case of vexatious strike suits in the private sector, an independent judiciary must be wary of being compromised. "Stevens did not deal with the level of venality that was going on" said National Public Radio's Nina Totenberg. "He had no concept of what politics had become. He came from an era when crooked politics meant money, not ideological power."[12]

In their 2008 book *Making Your Case: The Art of Persuading Judges,* Justice Scalia and legal writing expert Bryan A. Garner offered fellow lawyers 115 precise suggestions for success in appearing before judges. After first advising lawyers to be sure that they are in the appropriate courtroom, one that has jurisdiction to decide their client's case, their second tip is, "Know Your Audience."

There are three steps, Scalia and Garner say, to knowing a judge: First, read what the judge has written and said in opinions, articles, and published speeches that might reveal all or part of his or her judicial philosophy—"what it is that leads this particular judge to draw conclusions"; second, inquire about the judge's courtroom demeanor, "how the judge runs the courtroom"; and "finally, learn as much as you can about the judge's background." Details of personal background, in addition to providing lawyers with practical material for courtroom sociability and tactics, "will humanize the judge for you, so that you will be arguing to a human being instead of a chair."[13]

Many nonlawyers, from well-known political figures to persons in the street, argue about legal controversies and what judges, especially Supreme Court justices with lifetime appointments, do. Scalia and Garner's advice seems to apply to any informed citizen. Debates about interpretations of law would be more productive if more was known about the interpreters of law. In turn, judges known to the public as individuals beyond politically inspired sound bites can achieve greater confidence in being independent.

The process of selecting judges would be more democratic and satisfactory if ordinary people recognized characteristics of good judges and bad judges. Yet public inquiry in recent years begins and ends with "liberal" or "conservative" labels plus references to *Roe v. Wade* and maybe one or two other decided cases. Most analyses of would-be justices fail to inform in the manner preferred by dispassionate lawyers and recommended by Scalia and Garner. In that spirit, Scalia and Garner's three-step analysis can be employed to take a citizen's look at one judge, John Paul Stevens, near the end of his career. Several guidelines for appointing judges emerge from his story:

Past is prologue.—An individual who uses whatever brilliance he or she possesses in unconventional but productive ways is more likely to withstand pressures to conform to political and legal doctrines. Make inquiries on this point. American society today is an assembly line for many talented individuals, starting with preschool and ending with employment at large corporations or professional organizations. This gilded cookie-cutter process could lead to the selection of judges who are ill-equipped to address novel issues that don't fit easily in the boxes of conventional legal theory and precedent, even as the people and controversies coming to the Court become ever more diverse and unpredictable.

Mentors shape lives.—The egos of persons considered for judicial appointment may be large and self-defining. But studying those who influenced the candidate professionally and otherwise can be illuminating. If the candidate cannot name several mentors and explain their influence beyond platitudes, find another candidate.

How did you get here?—One of the familiar quotations from the Mayor Richard J. Daley era in Chicago is "We don't want nobody nobody sent."[14] In choosing independent judges, the opposite rule should apply: "We don't want nobody *somebody* sent." Despite all the talk about merit selection of federal judges, every individual put forward for such a high public office has backers. The public deserves to know who they are and what their stake is in the candidate. Stevens had no political sponsorship. When he first joined the federal bench, his name surfaced through his work in the small community of nationally recognized antitrust lawyers. He never did them any favors, before or after putting on his robe.

Test for political naiveté.—Inside the Marble Palace, justices amuse themselves by placing small wagers on the outcome of national elections. Off the bench, some immerse themselves in the political/social maw of Washington. That's not necessarily detrimental. Ignorance of or aloofness toward politics is a handicap for a judge. Stevens is not a Washington gadabout, but he is an astute political observer dating back to his days as a spectator of Chicago politics.

Ask about the "political questions."—Since its founding, the Court has wrestled with cases raising essentially political questions that might best be decided by an electorate or a legislative body. As Stevens noted in his constitutional law examination, part of the legacy of judicial restraint in this area came from the historically vilified Chief Justice Roger B. Taney, of Dred Scott infamy. The Taney Court's decision in *Luther v. Borden* (1849) is a landmark in separating the three branches of government. Strict adherence to this principle—that the Court should stay out of politics—would have saved it from most of its self-inflicted wounds, including the *Bush v. Gore* judgment. The so-called political questions doctrine—questions that should be off-limits to the Court—should be fair game at any judicial confirmation hearing.

Good writers are good thinkers.—Any appellate court judge who lets his or her clerks write opinions should automatically be disqualified for higher judicial office. Obtain testimony on this point. As Stevens told his law clerk Lawrence Rosenthal, "I'll do all the first drafts. Sometimes you can be totally unsure how a case is supposed to come out until you sit down and write."[15] Roger J. Traynor, former chief of the California Supreme Court, put it this way: "I have not found a better test for the solution to a case than its articulation in writing, which is thinking at its hardest. A judge . . . often discovers his tentative views will not jell in the writing."[16]

Verify work habits.—Good writing may take time. But every case coming before the Supreme Court has its own momentum. A judge who agonizes too long over a written opinion or a response to the work of colleagues stands to become irrelevant. Justice Ginsburg said that a secret to Justice Stevens's power in shaping the court is the speed at which he provides useful written feedback to the work of fellow justices.[17] If the candidate is already a judge, evidence of work efficiency is easy to obtain statistically and anecdotally. If not, demand examples of work habits and interview associates. If the record of collegiality is weak, find someone else.

Judges make law.—Because their opinions are used as precedent, every appellate court, especially the Supreme Court, adds to the body of law each time it renders an opinion. Even lone dissents and concurrences advance law. The idea that an appellate judge can interpret law without making law is nonsense. Ignoring that fact by accepting the cartoonish view of a judge as a baseball umpire inhibits proper questioning of would-be judges. Ask the candidate to discuss, with specificity, examples of good lawmaking on the one hand and incidents when the Court committed a self-inflicted wound on the other. The best case study of recent vintage for this purpose is *Bush v. Gore*. Without asking a candidate how he or she would have ruled, a questioner could ask, "Should the Supreme Court have taken this case? Why or why not?" The answer might tell much about the candidate's understanding of the Court's role as the third branch of government.

In the same vein, pragmatism and principles need not conflict.— Oliver Wendell Holmes said law is an experiment. After more than three decades on the Court, Stevens continues to characterize his career as a work in progress. Critics often confuse pragmatism, which means experimentation toward constant improvement, with expediency. A judicial candidate who says he or she knows what the law requires either is not telling the truth or is unqualified for the job.

Finally, inquire about the candidate's health in a holistic way, not just the last medical checkup.—The evolution of a responsible judicial philosophy never ends, nor does the development of political skills needed inside the Court to make an impact on the law. A candidate for a lifetime appointment to a largely sedentary job who is not proactive about fitness should be barred from the team. At the other end of the line, Stevens several times has floated the idea of allowing older justices voluntarily to take senior status but still join the Court on occasion for cases when an active justice is not sitting for some reason. This step might help prevent old age and stubborn entrenchment from impairing the work of the Court and quicken the pace of Court turnover, making more seats available over time for fresh, independent voices.

In a landmark affirmative action case, *Regents of the University of California v. Bakke* (1977), Justice Stevens in his second full term established himself as a model of judicial restraint. When the case made headlines, other justices, experts in the civil rights movement, and many interested individuals debated strenuously the conflict between a state's desire to promote racial diversity to repair past discrimination and strengthen an equitable society on the one hand, and the guarantee of equal protection of the law in the Constitution and the Civil Rights Act of 1964 on the other. Allan Bakke, a white applicant to the University of California Medical School, claimed he was denied admittance because of special consideration being given to racial and ethnic minority applicants. A sharply divided Court ruled that he was harmed and should be admitted. Guiding that conclusion was Stevens's simple logic, as he wrote in one of six opinions filed in the case:

"It is . . . perfectly clear that the question whether race can ever be used as a factor in an admissions decision is not an issue in this case, and that discussion of that issue is inappropriate. . . . In unmistakable terms the [Civil Rights] Act [of 1964] prohibits the exclusion of individuals from federally funded programs because of their race. . . . The University's special admissions program violated Title VI of the Civil Rights Act of 1964 by excluding Bakke from the Medical School because of his race. It is therefore our duty to affirm the judgment ordering Bakke admitted to the University."

Anyone who concluded from this narrow reasoning, which merely cited the plain text of the Civil Rights Act, that Stevens was against affirmative action would have been mistaken. Over his tenure, Stevens has become more vocal in asserting the value of racial and ethnic diversity in certain settings. In no other area of law has Stevens been more forthright about his own development as a judicial pragmatist. He explained his growth in remarks to the 2005 Fordham (University) Law School Symposium on the Jurisprudence of Justice Stevens:

"During my early tenure on the Court, I thought it perfectly clear that the Civil Rights Act of 1964 prohibited discrimination against whites as well as blacks, even though Congress was principally concerned with discrimination against minorities. . . . With respect to the constitutionality of affirmative action, we have learned that justifications based on past sins may be less persuasive than those predicated on anticipated future benefits."[18]

In a 2004 speech to the annual judicial conference of the U.S. Sixth Circuit in Lexington, Kentucky, Stevens elaborated on the roots of his affirmative action activism. He was addressing the

Court's ruling in favor of an affirmative action program in student admissions at the University of Michigan Law School (*Grutter v. Bollinger*, 2003). He had assigned the opinion of the Court to Justice Sandra O'Connor and had not written separately. But in his Lexington remarks, Stevens was candid: "These cases, as you know, are particularly difficult in the affirmative action area. I have sometimes been on one side and sometimes on another. But I have often thought that there is a big difference between a case involving construction workers, because it doesn't seem to me that the race of the construction worker has much to do with the quality of the concrete that they put in the highway. But in the education field, there is a strong argument that the diversity of the study body may have an impact on the quality of the education that the students receive."[19]

Here is a judge judging, resolving an apparent conflict between the text of a law and the overarching aspiration of the Constitution. But to those less versed in the distinctions between statutory law and constitutional purposes, what are the rules? This question properly arises in considering the independence of a judge like Stevens.

In remarks to the Fordham symposium, Professor Andrew M. Siegel of the University of South Carolina School of Law, who clerked for Justice Stevens in the term of the *Bush v. Gore* decision, spoke of the risks he and other scholars see in judicial independence. Without clear rules to "mediate" between a judge's proclivities and the law, judges could be fickle and unaccountable, according to this viewpoint:

> If the Supreme Court's project is not only to decide cases correctly but also to provide citizens, politicians and lower courts with the tools to transform constitutional aspirations into lived reality, then unmediated interpretation is, at a minimum, disquieting. A Supreme Court that declines to provide more detailed guidance for adhering to, understanding, and embracing the Constitution but instead insists that the answer to every constitutional question can be achieved only through the nuanced application of judgment to texts is committing itself to serve as the ultimate arbiter of every close constitutional question and relegating the public, the other branches, and the lower courts to the role of specta-

tors. . . . Justice Stevens has proven time and again that wisdom and justice often flow from the application of judicial judgment to difficult and contentious issues. In the equal protection context in particular, his reluctance to adopt constraining doctrine has enabled him to write with enviable moral insight. However, even in a world where all judges were graced with his skill and humanity, leaving the interpretation of the Equal Protection Clause to the unmediated judgment of the Supreme Court would not be costless. In a world where we can safely assume that not every judge is a Justice Stevens, it may well be that those costs remain worth absorbing, but that conclusion is not self-evident.[20]

The enormous power of the Supreme Court and each member to apply personal judgment to evolving social concerns and thereby alter the lives of Americans deserves public attention, as Siegel suggests. But making things simpler by etching rules for judging on a tablet somewhere in order to "mediate" the creative mind of a judge is a fool's errand. As Stevens wrote in an unpublished draft to his *Texas v. Johnson* flag-burning dissent, "If judges had the souls of computers, this might therefore be a less difficult case."

Conservative judges who bill themselves as "strict constructionist," "textualist," or "originalist" claim they meet the test, but they frequently stray from their own purported rules to advance their aims. The majority opinion in *Bush v. Gore* is the best recent example. On the other hand, legendary liberals, including Justice Thurgood Marshall, occasionally relied on the literal, strictly construed text of a law in making their arguments. In *U.S. v. Locke* (1985), in an opinion joined by conservative Justices Warren Burger and Rehnquist, Marshall demanded that certain miners on federal lands obey a deadline imposed by Congress for making their annual claims "prior to Dec. 31" of each year, as the statute specifically provided, not on Dec. 31. He also made clear in his opinion that he was not enamored with the mining practices on federal lands under review in the case. Stevens—joined by Marshall's liberal colleague, Justice William Brennan—dissented, saying Marshall's textual literalism was an unreasonable burden on the miners.

Who would write the recipes for the nine cooks who will be working at the Supreme Court on cases and controversies as yet unimagined? Whose financial and political interests would prevail in the rules for "mediated" judging that Siegel and others desire? Who, on the other hand, would be relegated to the role of spectators in the process of rule-making for judges?

Constraining judicial independence, as formalized "mediation" rules do, is dangerous for two reasons: First, it violates the objective of an independent judiciary that the Founding Fathers drew from their faith in Americans to make decisions, then and in the future. Second, the essence of law is not a roadmap for drivers but an opportunity to drive. The Court's *Plessy v. Ferguson* (1896) ruling, which authorized states to discriminate against blacks under the rule of "separate but equal," was hardly the end of the story. The decision helped create the opportunity for the *Brown v. Board of Education* opinion of 1954, which overruled *Plessy*, as American society moved forward. Likewise, relying on external guidance for judging today would derail the opportunity for better judging tomorrow.

The answer to the problem posed by critics of judicial independence lies in the opposite direction from theirs. Rather than limiting independence by artificially defining the job of judging, the story of Justice Stevens demonstrates the value of selecting the most independent-minded men and women to wear the robes, roll up their sleeves, decide cases, and learn on the job. This solution has an enormous advantage over any exogenous judicial rulebook, no matter how carefully it might be vetted by law scholars. No one in a democracy needs be a spectator in the task of selecting judges.

Notes

Published case opinions are identified by name and year. Quotations from published cases readily available online are cited by title and year in the text and are noted separately.

ABBREVIATIONS

Individuals

Wiley B. Rutledge (WBR); John Paul Stevens (JPS)

Document Collections

Harry A. Blackmun Papers, Library of Congress, Washington, D.C. (HABP); Thurgood Marshall Papers, Library of Congress (TMP); Wiley B. Rutledge Papers, Library of Congress (WBRP); Everett M. Dirksen Papers, Dirksen Congressional Center, Pekin, IL (EMDP); Charles H. Percy Senatorial Papers, 1966–1985, Chicago History Museum, Chicago, IL (CHPSP); Charles H. Percy Papers, before 1966, Chicago History Museum (CHPP); Ernest J. Stevens Papers, Chicago History Museum (EJSP); Gerald R. Ford Presidential Library, Grand Rapids, MI (GRFPL); Richard Nixon Presidential Library of the National Archives and Records Administraion, College Park, MD (RNPL).

INTRODUCTION

1. David J. Barron, remarks at Symposium on the Jurisprudence of Justice Stevens, Fordham (University) School of Law, New York, NY, Oct. 1, 2005.

2. Elizabeth J. Sesemann, interview with authors, March 24, 2003.

3. Jeffrey A. Segal and Harold J. Spaeth, *The Supreme Court and the Attitudinal Model Revisited* (New York: Cambridge University Press, 2002), pp. 394–403.

4. Justice Ruth Bader Ginsburg, interview with authors, May 28, 2009.

5. Gregory Lee Johnson, interview with Barnhart, Nov. 8, 2005.

6. *Texas v. Johnson Files. 1989*, conference notes and memoranda, HABP and TMP.

7. *Texas v. Johnson*, oral argument, March 21, 1989, audio and text, Oyez Project <http:oyezproject.org>.

8. Kathi A. Drew, "A Supreme Court Experience: Personal Reflections on the 'Flagburning' Case," Skill Sheet for Home Educators, courtesy of Ms. Drew.

9. Patrick Quinn, e-mail to Barnhart, Feb. 9, 2007.

10. Christopher L. Eisgruber, "John Paul Stevens and the Manners of Judging," *Annual Survey of American Law*, New York University, 1992–1993, p. xxx.

11. Albert E. Jenner, quoted in "Craftsman for the Court," *Time*, Vol. 106, No. 23, Dec. 8, 1975, p. 58; Justice William A. Brennan, Jr., "Tribute to Justice Stevens," *Annual Survey of American Law*, New York University, 1992–1993, p.

xxi; Edward I. Rothschild, interview with authors, Feb. 7, 2003; Charles H. Percy, "A Man in the Middle," *Newsweek*, Dec. 8, 1975, p 23. Justice Ruth Bader Ginsburg, interview with authors, May 28, 2009.

12. Jeffrey Toobin, *The Nine: Inside the Secret World of the Supreme Court* (New York: Doubleday, 2007), p. 6.

13. Finley Peter Dunne, *Mr. Dooley's Opinions (*New York: R.H. Russell Publisher, 1901; facsimile printing by Kessinger Publishers, Whitefish, MT, 2004), p. 26.

14. Christopher L. Eisgruber, *The Next Justice: Repairing the Supreme Court Appointment Process* (Princeton: Princeton University Press, 2007), pp. 67, 74.

15. John Marshall, quoted in John Edward Oster, *The Political and Economic Doctrines of John Marshall* (New York: The Neal Publishing Co., 1914), p. 282.

16. Jack N. Rakove, *Original Meanings: Politics and Ideas in the Making of the Constitution* (New York: Alfred A. Knopf, 1997), pp. 298–300.

17. Earl Warren, *The Memoirs of Earl Warren* (New York: Doubleday, 1977), p. 5.

18. Gregory P. Margarian, remarks at symposium, "The Jurisprudence of Justice Stevens," Fordham (University) School of Law, Oct. 1, 2006, p. 1559.

19. Jeffrey Cole and Elaine E. Bucklo, "A Life Well Lived: An Interview with Justice John Paul Stevens," *Litigation*, Vol. 32, No. 2, Spring 2006, p. 9.

20. *Texas v. Johnson,* 1989, oral argument, audio and transcript, Oyez Project <http:oyezproject.org>.

21. Katherine Alyce Drew, interview with Barnhart, Oct. 28, 2004.

22. Edward Lazarus, *Closed Chambers: The Rise, Fall, and Future of the Modern Supreme Court* (New York: Penguin Books, 1999), pp. 35–36.

23. Nellie A. Pitts, interview with authors, Sept. 15, 2004.

24. Lawrence C. Marshall, interview with authors, June 20, 2003.

25. *Texas v. Johnson*, draft dissent, *Texas v. Johnson* File, TMP.

26. JPS, speech to Chicago Bar Association and Chicago Bar Foundation, Sept. 14, 2006, courtesy of Justice Stevens's chambers.

27. JPS, remarks at Ninth Circuit Judicial Conference, July 19, 2007, C-Span.

28. Harold J. Spaeth Supreme Court Database <www.cas.sc.edu/poli/juri/>, named after political science professor Harold J. Spaeth of Michigan State University and available through the University of South Carolina's Judicial Research Initiative. Data retrieval and analysis courtesy of Hemant Kumer Sharma of the University of Tennessee Political Science Department. Abner J. Mikva, interview with Barnhart, Feb. 23, 2009.

29. Abner J. Mikva, interview with Barnhart, Feb. 23, 2009.

1—THE FAMILY

1. *The Correlator*, 1937, University High School, Chicago, IL, p. 149.

2. George Bogert, interview with Barnhart, March 20, 2004.

3. Ernest J. Stevens, letter to J.S. and Helen Sheafe, Aug. 20, 1920, EJSP.

4. Edward Siskel, "The Business of Reflection," *University of Chicago Magazine*, Vol. 94, No. 6, August 2002, p. 29.

5. William J. Stevens, interview with authors, March 24, 2006.

6. June Moon, "Multum in Parvo: A History of Colchester, Illinois," second edition revised, pamphlet, McDonough County Genealogical Society, 1957, p. 56.

7. *People v. Stevens*, trial transcript, Criminal Court of Cook County, October 1933, p. 422, EJSP.

8. William K. Stevens, interview with authors, Sept. 23, 2005.

9. JPS speech, "The Meaning of Judicial Activism," Chicago Bar Association, Sept. 16, 1998, *Chicago Bar Association Record*, October 1998, p. 40.

10. John Dewey, *The School and Society*, ed. by Jo Ann Boydston (Carbondale: Southern Illinois University Press, 1980), p. 29.

11. George G. Rinder, interview with authors, Nov. 8, 2003.

12. Ernest J. Stevens, letter to Ben I. Greenbaum, Jr., March 2, 1928, EJSP.

13. William J. Glick, e-mail to Barnhart, June 23, 2003.

14. Cynthia Jo Rich, "Charlottean Recalls Days With Judge," *Charlotte Observer*, Nov. 29, 1975, pp. 1A, 6A.

15. Sam Hair, *Castle Park* (Berkeley: Creative Arts Book Co., 2000), p. 45.

16. Unsigned letter to Elizabeth S. Stevens by one of her grandchildren, Feb. 15, 1972, EJSP.

17. JPS, "Charlie's Rule," speech to State Bar Association of Michigan, *Michigan Bar Journal*, December 1999, p. 1402.

18. James Weber Linn, "Hosts of Chicago: An Account of Certain Innkeepers of the Public Houses," *The Chicagoan*, April 13, 1929, EJSP.

19. "Ernest J. Stevens Arrested in $1,000,000 Conspiracy," *Chicago Herald and Examiner*, Jan. 28, 1933, p. 1.

20. Ernest J. Stevens, letter to "Fuller," Feb. 2, 1933, EJSP.

21. "E.J. Stevens Leaves Home After Gang Raid: Bandits Seek Hidden $1,000,000, Get $1,372," *Chicago Daily Times*, Feb. 15, 1933, p. 1.

22. "Gunmen Rob Stevens Home: Pose as Police, Threaten to Seize Children," *Chicago Daily Tribune*, Feb. 15, 1933, p. 1.

23. William K. Stevens, interview with authors, July 1, 2003.

24. "E.J. Stevens Found Guilty," *Chicago Herald and Examiner*, Oct. 15, 1933, p. 1.

25. "E.J. Stevens Guilty," *Chicago Sunday Times*, Oct. 15, 1933, p. 1.

26. George Bogert, interview with Barnhart, March 20, 2004.

27. William K. Stevens, interview with authors, Sept. 23, 2005.

28. *People v. Stevens*, Supreme Court of Illinois, Oct. 22, 1934, 193 *North Eastern Reporter*, p. 160, EJSP.

29. Helen B. Barnett, letter to Elizabeth Stevens, April 29, 1933, EJSP.

30. W.T. Harsha, M.D., letter to E.J. Stevens, Jan. 14, 1935, EJSP.

31. Richard J. Stevens, "J.W.'s Pride," unpublished play, courtesy of William J. Stevens.

32. JPS, "Dedication Address," speech at Chicago-Kent College of Law, Sept. 11, 1992, *Chicago-Kent Law Review*, Vol. 68, No. 5, 1992, p. 5.

33. JPS, speech at Northwestern University School of Law, Aug. 4, 1984, GRFPL.

2—THE WAR

1. Ernest S. Stevens, letter to Ernest J. Stevens, Oct. 23, 1940, EJSP.

2. Charles H. Percy, oral history interview with Charles Stuart Kennedy, Association for Diplomatic Studies and Training, Foreign Affairs Oral History Project, June 11, 1998.

3. Mary Ann Dzuback, *Robert M. Hutchins: Portrait of an Educator* (Chicago: University of Chicago Press, 1991), pp. 102–3.

4. William H. McNeill, *Hutchins University: A Memoir of the University of Chicago*, 1929–1950 (Chicago: University of Chicago Press, 1991), p. 36.

5. *The Daily Maroon*, University of Chicago, Oct. 1, 1940, p. 1.

6. *The Daily Maroon*, University of Chicago, June 6, 1941, p. 2.

7. Perez Zagorin, interview with Barnhart, Dec. 23, 2005.

8. Norman F. Maclean, interview with Kay Bonetti, audiocassette tape, The American Audio Prose Library, May 1985.

9. Norman F. Maclean, "This Quarter I'm Taking McKeon: A Few Remarks on the Art of Teaching," *The University of Chicago Magazine*, Vol. 66, January/February 1974, pp. 8–12; reprinted in *Norman Maclean: American Authors Series* (Lewiston, ID: Confluence Press, 1988), p. 63.

10. George McElroy, "By Degrees," *The Daily Maroon*, University of Chicago, Oct. 3, 1941, p. 4.

11. JPS, interview with authors, May 28, 2009.

12. "Stevens Visits Campus, Plays Tennis," *The Chicago Maroon*, Oct. 23, 1979, pp. 1, 5.

13. Norman F. Maclean, interview with Kay Bonetti, audiocassette tape, The American Audio Prose Library, May 1985.

14. Norman F. Maclean, "Teaching and Storytelling," speech at University of Chicago, Feb. 19, 1978, reprinted in *Norman Maclean: American Authors Series*, p. 89.

15. Ernest S. Leiser, "A Change of Policy," *The Daily Maroon*, University of Chicago, Jan. 1, 1941, p. 2.

16. "Adler Opposes Hutchins on War," *The Daily Maroon*, University of Chicago, Jan. 27, 1941, p. 1.

17. "America and the War," *The Daily Maroon*, University of Chicago, Jan. 28, 1941, p. 2, and Jan. 31, 1941, p.2.

18. George McElroy, "By Degrees," *The Daily Maroon*, University of Chicago, Oct. 3, 1941, p. 4.

19. JPS, interview with authors, Oct. 6, 2003.

20. Leon P. Smith, Jr., "A Newly Discovered Manuscript Fragment of the Old French 'Partonopeus de Blois,'" *Modern Philology*, August 1961, p. 49.

21. "Smith Explains Best Counter Spy Training," *The Daily Maroon*, University of Chicago, Jan. 18, 1941, p. 1.

22. David A. Hatch, e-mail to Barnhart, April 5, 2006. The authors wish to thank Mr. Hatch of the National Security Agency and David Kahn, author of *The Codebreakers*, for helping explain the intricacies of World War II navy communications intelligence work and terminology.

23. JPS, speech, "COMINT Memories of a U.S. Supreme Court Justice,"

June 17, 1983, U.S. Cryptologic Veterans Association newsletter (Paducah, KY: Turner Publishing Co., 1996), p. 61.

24. Ibid.

25. Ernest S. Stevens, letter to Ernest J. Stevens, Dec. 17, 1941, EJSP.

26. JPS, letter to Ernest J. Stevens, Aug. 12, 1942, EJSP.

27. JPS, letter to Ernest J. Stevens, July 4, 1942, EJSP.

28. "Radio Deception," War Department Technical Bulletin, TB Sig 65, Feb. 9, 1945, Records of the Office of the Chief of Naval Operations, Records of the Naval Security Group, Inactive Stations, p. 6., National Archives and Records Administration, College Park, MD.

29. JPS, letter to Ernest J. Stevens, July 4, 1942, EJSP.

30. JPS, letter to Ernest J. Stevens, July 15, 1942, EJSP.

31. JPS, "COMINT Memories," June 17, 1983, U.S. Cryptologic Veterans Association newsletter (Paducah, KY: Turner Publishing Co., 1996), p. 61.

32. Edwin T. Layton, *"And I Was There": Pearl Harbor and Midway—Breaking the Secrets* (New York: William Morrow and Co., 1985), p. 467.

33. W. J. Holmes, *Double-Edged Secrets: U.S. Naval Intelligence Operations in the Pacific During World War II* (Annapolis: Naval Institute Press, 1979), p. 116.

34. JPS, interview with authors, May 28, 2009.

35. Layton, *"And I Was There,"* p. 25.

36. Robert W. Turner, letter to authors, June 27, 2003.

37. Robert W. Turner, interview with Barnhart, June 16, 2003.

38. JPS, "COMINT Memories," June 17, 1983, U.S. Cryptologic Veterans Association newsletter (Paducah, KY: Turner Publishing Co., 1996), p. 61, National Cryptologic Museum Library, Ft. Meade, MD.

39. Stanley Moe, e-mail to Barnhart, Jan. 12, 2006.

40. JPS, "COMINT Memories," p. 61.

41. JPS, interview with authors, May 28, 2009.

42. JPS, "COMINT Memories," p. 61.

43. Layton, *"And I Was There,"* p. 475.

44. JPS, "COMINT Memories," p. 61.

45. "Awards of Meritorious Service in the Case of Certain Communications Intelligence Personnel—Recommendations for," Oct. 23, 1945, p. 14, Records of the Office of the Chief of Naval Operations, Record Group 38, Box 4–1650–1, Com Nav Sec Gru, National Archives and Records Administration, College Park, MD.

46. JPS, "COMINT Memories," pp. 61–62.

3—THE SCHOOL

1. JPS, speech to Chicago Bar Association and Chicago Bar Foundation, Oct. 16, 2001, courtesy of Justice Stevens's chambers.

2. Leon Green, "Reconversion in Legal Education," *Illinois Law Review*, Vol. 40, No. 4, March–April 1946, p. 450.

3. Robert M. Hutchins, "The Threat to American Education," *Collier's*, Vol. 114, No. 27, Dec. 30, 1944, pp. 20–21.

4. Robert W. Turner, interview with Barnhart, June 16, 2003.

5. JPS, speech to the University of Arizona College of Law, Sept. 8, 1979, courtesy of Justice Stevens's chambers.

6. Robert W. Turner, letter to authors, June 27, 2003.

7. Arthur R. Seder, interview with authors, May 23, 2005.

8. JPS, interview with authors, May 28, 2009.

9. JPS, "Legal Questions in Perspective," address to Florida State University College of Law, Jan. 26, 1985, *Florida State University Law Review*, Vol. 13, No. 1, Spring 1985, pp. 1–7.

10. JPS, "Introductory Comment," *Northwestern University Law Review*, Vol. 75, No. 6, February 1981, p. 977.

11. JPS, "Comments: Price Fixing in the Motion Picture Industry," *Illinois Law Review*, Vol. 41, No. 5, January–February 1947, p. 645.

12. Ibid., p. 646.

13. Daniel Bertrand, W. Duane Evans, and Edna E.L. Blanchard, "The Motion Picture Industry—A Pattern of Control," Monograph 43, Temporary National Economic Committee, 1941, quoted at ibid, p. 646.

14. JPS, "Judicial Restraint," speech to the University of San Diego Law School, Oct. 10, 1984, *San Diego Law Review*, Vol. 22, 1985, pp. 440–41.

15. Constitutional Law examination question and Stevens's handwritten exam answers, 1947, Nathaniel L. Nathanson Papers, Northwestern University Library.

16. Arthur R. Seder, interview with authors, May 23, 2005.

17. Ibid.

18. Ibid.

19. Laura Krugman Ray, "Clerk and Justice: The Ties That Bind John Paul Stevens and Wiley B. Rutledge," *Connecticut Law Review*, Vol. 41, No. 1, November 2008, p. 230.

20. W. Willard Wirtz, letter to WBR, May 23, 1947, WBRP.

21. W. Willard Wirtz, interview with authors, Sept. 14, 2004.

4—THE GREAT WRIT

1. "James Laughlin, Trial Lawyer, Dies," *Washington Post*, March 21, 1976, p. C4.

2. *Ahrens v. Clark*, 1948, memoranda, conference notes, opinion drafts from papers of Justices Harold H. Burton, William O. Douglas, Robert H. Jackson, and Wiley B. Rutledge, Library of Congress, Washington, D.C.

3. William M. Wiecek, *The Birth of the Modern Constitution: The United States Supreme Court, 1941–1953* (New York: Cambridge University Press, 2006), p. 400.

4. Arthur M. Schlesinger, Jr., "The Supreme Court: 1947," *Fortune*, Vol. XXXV, No. 1, January 1947, pp. 73, 201, 212.

5. John P. Frank, "The United States Supreme Court: 1947–1948," *The University of Chicago Law Review*, Vol. 16, No. 1, Autumn 1948, pp. 1, 55.

6. Robert von Mehren, interview with Barnhart, Dec. 7, 2006.

7. Stanley L. Temko, interview with authors, Sept. 17, 2004.

8. Ibid.

9. Ibid.

10. W. Willard Wirtz, interview with authors, Sept. 14, 2004.

11. Dennis J. Hutchinson, "The Black-Jackson Feud," *Supreme Court Review*, Vol. 1988 (Chicago: University of Chicago Press, 1988), p. 207.

12. William O. Douglas, interview with Walter F. Murphy, Tape 9, Side A&B, Seeley G. Mudd Manuscript Library, Princeton University.

13. WBR, *A Declaration of Legal Faith* (Clark, NJ: The Lawbook Exchange Ltd., 2004, reprint; originally published by University of Kansas Press, 1947), pp. 6, 11.

14. Joseph P. Lash, ed., *From the Diaries of Felix Frankfurter* (New York: W.W. Norton & Co., 1975), p. 205.

15. Ibid.

16. Stanley L. Temko, interview with authors, Sept. 17, 2004.

17. John B. Spitzer, interview with Barnhart, Jan. 17, 2007.

18. JPS, "Mr. Justice Rutledge," in *Mr. Justice*, ed. by Allison Dunham and Philip B. Kurland (Chicago: University of Chicago Press, 1956), p. 321.

19. John B. Spitzer, interview with Barnhart, Jan. 17, 2007.

20. Thurgood Marshall, brief, *Sipuel v. Board of Regents of the University of Oklahoma*, 1948, quoted in Richard Kluger, *Simple Justice: The History of Brown v. Board of Education and Black America's Struggle for Equality* (New York: Vintage Books, 2004), p. 258.

21. JPS, memorandum to WBR, *Fisher v. Justices of Oklahoma Supreme Court*, 1948, WBRP.

22. WBR, dissent draft, *Fisher v. Hurst*, 1948, WBRP.

23. JPS, "Mr. Justice Rutledge," p. 322.

24. Ibid., p. 333.

25. *Ahrens v. Clark Files*, 1948, memoranda, conference notes, opinion drafts from papers of Justices Harold H. Burton, William O. Douglas, Robert H. Jackson, and Wiley B. Rutledge, Library of Congress, Washington, D.C.

26. Ibid.

27. Ibid.

28. Ibid.

29. Ibid.

30. Ibid.

31. "Recent Cases," *University of Chicago Law Review*, Vol. 16, 1948–1949, pp. 337, 340.

32. John P. Frank, "The United States Supreme Court: 1947–1948," *The University of Chicago Law Review*, Vol. 16, No. 1, Autumn 1948, pp. 1, 55.

33. JPS, letter to WBR, July 24, 1947, WBRP.

34. Robert von Mehren, interview with Barnhart, Dec. 7, 2006.

35. *Rasul v. Bush*, April 20, 2004, oral argument audio and text transcript, Oyez Project <http://oyezproject.org>.

36. Joseph Thai, "The Law Clerk Who Wrote *Rasul v. Bush*: John Paul Stevens's Influence From World War II to the War on Terror," *Virginia Law Review*, Vol. 92, 2006, p. 529.

5—THE CLIENT

1. JPS, letter to WBR, Jan. 22, 1949, WBRP.
2. JPS, letter to WBR, Sept. 4, 1948, WBRP.
3. JPS, "Filling a Supreme Court Vacancy," speech to Gerald R. Ford Museum, Sept. 16, 1999, courtesy of Justice Stevens's chambers.
4. JPS, letter to WBR, Jan. 22, 1949, WBRP.
5. JPS, letter to WBR, Sept. 4, 1948, WBPR.
6. JPS, letter to WBR, Jan. 22, 1949, WBPR.
7. Jerold S. Solovy, interview with Barnhart, April 10, 2003; Edward I. Rothschild, interview with authors, Feb. 17, 2003.
8. JPS, letter to WBR, July 11, 1949. In this letter, Stevens voiced his opinion of the spectacular trial of former State Department official and accused spy Alger Hiss, a story that dominated newspapers at the time. "For the past few weeks I have been deeply troubled by the Hiss trial. . . . Through the early stages of the trial, and through most of Hiss' testimony, I had not the slightest doubt of his innocence and was indignant at the prosecution. But then Hiss failed, in my mind, to explain away the typewriter evidence. I could have accepted an explanation that he took some documents home with him, was in violation of security rules, and abstracted them at home, but I find it almost impossible to believe his defense that his typewriter was used but not by him or Mrs. Hiss. . . . Of course the most shocking turn of events came with the announcement—I believe by the F.B.I.—that the F.B.I. would investigate the four jurors who voted for acquittal. If the government resorts to that kind of pressure, the possibility of a fair trial of any case with political implications would seem to be precluded. Either vote for the Gov't or have the F.B.I. investigate you!"
9. Edward R. Johnston, *Some Recollections on My More Than Seventy Years at the Illinois Bar* (Chicago: Jenner & Block, 1981), pp. 44, 45, 47.
10. JPS, letter to WBR, Jan. 22, 1949, WBRP.
11. Edward R. Johnston and John Paul Stevens, "Monopoly of Monopolization—A Reply to Professor Rostow," *Illinois Law Review*, Vol. 44, No. 3, July–August 1949, pp. 274, 275.
12. Ronald Reagan, "Business Ballots and Bureaus," speech to Seraphics Society of New York City, May 15, 1959, CHPP.
13. JPS, letter to WBR, July 11, 1949, WBRP.
14. Richard A. Posner, e-mail to Barnhart, April 10, 2006.
15. WBR, testimony to U.S. Senate Committee on Banking and Commerce, June 9, 1933, quoted in John M. Ferren, *Salt of the Earth, Conscience of the Court: The Story of Justice Wiley Rutledge* (Chapel Hill: University of North Carolina Press, 2004), p. 93.
16. WBR, *A Declaration of Legal Faith*, pp. 25, 27.
17. JBS, "Judicial Predilections," speech to Clark County (Nevada) Bar Association, Aug. 18, 2005, courtesy of Justice Stevens's chambers.
18. Ibid.
19. Stephen Rothman, "Lawyer Suing Sanitary District is a Controversial Figure," *Chicago Sun-Times*, Nov. 18, 1963, p. 12.
20. JPS, interview with authors, May 28, 2009.

21. Leah Nathanson, interview with Barnhart, Feb. 21, 2007.

22. Biographical file, Harry R. Booth, *Chicago Tribune*, Dec. 2, 1959.

23. Edward I. Rothschild, interview with authors, Feb. 17, 2003.

24. Emanuel Celler, quoted in Roger I. Abrams, *Legal Bases: Baseball and the Law* (Philadelphia: Temple University Press, 1998), p. 61.

25. Bowie Kuhn, interview with Barnhart, Sept. 16, 2003.

26. JPS, "Memorandum for Members," July 25, 1951, Records of U.S. House of Representatives, Committee on the Judiciary, Records Group 233, National Archives and Records Administration (NARA), Washington, D.C..

27. *Hearings Before the Subcommittee on the Study of Monopoly Power of the Committee of the Judiciary, House of Representatives, Serial No. 1, Part 6, Organized Baseball,* 1951 (Washington: Government Printing Office), Records Group 233, NARA, p. 23.

28. Ibid., p. 747.

29. "Baseball's Reserve Clause Gets OK," *Chicago Daily Tribune*, May 23, 1952, p. B1.

30. JPS, letter to E. Ernest Goldstein, Dec. 4, 1951, Records of U.S. House of Representatives, Committee on the Judiciary, Records Group 233, NARA.

31. Unsigned letter to JPS, Sept. 19, 1952, Records of U.S. House of Representatives, Committee on the Judiciary, Records Group 233, NARA.

32. Bowie Kuhn, interview with Barnhart, Sept. 16, 2003.

33. Marvin Miller, interview with Barnhart, Aug. 29, 2003.

34. Alan L. Unikel, interview with authors, Dec. 12, 2003.

35. William G. Myers, interview with authors, Aug. 15, 2003.

36. JPS, "Random Recollections," speech to University of San Diego School of Law, April 7, 2004.

37. Quoted in James R. Williamson, *Federal Antitrust Policy During the Kennedy-Johnson Years* (Westport, CT: Greenwood Press, 1995), p. 57.

38. Ken Harrelson, interview with Barnhart, Sept. 5, 2003.

39. JPS, quoted in Herbert Michelson, *Charlie O: Charles Oscar Finley vs. the Baseball Establishment* (Indianapolis: Bobbs-Merrill Co., 1975), p. 69.

40. Quoted in Herbert Michelson, *Charlie O: Charles Oscar Finley vs. the Baseball Establishment* (Indianapolis: Bobbs-Merrill Co., 1975), p. 81.

41. Bowie Kuhn, interview with Barnhart, Sept. 16, 2003.

42. William Cunningham, interview with Barnhart, Aug. 28, 2003.

43. JPS, interview with authors, Oct. 6, 2003.

44. William Cunningham, interview with Barnhart, Aug. 28, 2003.

45. JPS, speech to Rotary Club of Chicago, Oct. 6, 1973. Subject File: Supreme Court Appointments, GRFPL.

6—THE SENATOR

1. JPS, "Picasso's Contribution," letter to the editor, *Chicago Tribune*, Aug. 21, 1967, p. 20.

2. JPS, "Dedication Address," speech at Chicago-Kent College of Law, Sept. 11, 1992, *Chicago-Kent Law Review*, Vol. 68, No. 5, 1992, p. 7.

3. See Michael Powell, "Anatomy of a Counter-Bar Association: The

Chicago Council of Lawyers," *American Bar Foundation Research Journal*, 1979, pp. 504–5.

4. Charles H. Percy, letter to Independent Voters of Illinois, Oct. 3, 1964, CHPSP.

5. "2 Wards Take Opposite Sides in G.O.P. Race," *Chicago Tribune*, April 4, 1954, p. 6.

6. Abner J. Mikva, interview with Barnhart, Feb. 23, 2009.

7. JPS, "Opening Assembly Address," speech to American Bar Association Annual Meeting, Orlando, FL, Aug. 3, 1996, reprinted in *St. John's Journal of Legal Commentary*, Vol. 12, Fall, 1996, pp. 21–32.

8. Gerald R. Ford, letter to William Michael Treanor, Sept. 21, 2005, quoted in William Michael Treanor, "Introduction: Symposium, The Jurisprudence of Justice Stevens," *Fordham Law Review*, Vol. LXXIV, No. 4, March 2006, p. 1559.

9. Herman Kogan, *The First Century: The Chicago Bar Association, 1897– 1974* (Chicago: Rand McNally & Co., 1974), p. 252.

10. Harold E. Rainville, memo to Everett M. Dirksen, Dec. 18, 1968, EMDP.

11. Ibid.

12. Rainville, memo to Everett M. Dirksen, Jan. 18, 1969, EMDP.

13. George M. Burditt, interview with authors, Jan. 14, 2005.

14. Rainville, memo to Everett M. Dirksen, Jan. 18, 1969, EMDP.

15. Rainville, memo to Everett M. Dirksen, Dec. 18, 1968, EMDP.

16. Everett M. Dirksen, letter to Richard G. Kleindienst, March 3, 1969, EMDP.

17. Frank J. McGarr, interview with Barnhart, Jan. 19, 2006.

18. Susan R. Mullen, interview with authors, Oct. 7, 2003.

19. John J. Coffey III, interview with Barnhart, Oct. 28, 2005.

20. Susan R. Mullen, interview with authors, Oct. 7, 2003.

21. Elizabeth J. Sesemann, interview with authors, March 24, 2003.

22. Carol LaBarge, interview with Barnhart, Oct. 29, 2004.

23. Nancy Barker, interview with authors, Jan. 8, 2004.

24. Elizabeth J. Sesemann, interview with authors, March 24, 2003.

25. William J. Bauer, interview with authors, Nov. 12, 2004.

26. JPS, foreword to Kenneth A. Manaster, *Illinois Justice: The Scandal of 1969 and the Rise of John Paul Stevens* (Chicago: University of Chicago Press, 2001), p. xi.

27. Milton I. Shadur, interview with authors, Sept. 5, 2003.

28. Howard J. Trienens, interview with authors, April 22, 2005.

29. Milton I. Shadur, interview with authors, Sept. 5, 2003.

30. Joseph G. Coughlin, interview with authors, Feb. 18, 2005.

31. Bob Seltzner, "Dateline: Calumet," *The Daily Calumet*, Dec. 2, 1975, p. 4.

32. Nathaniel Sack, interview with authors, Feb. 25, 2005.

33. "Report of Special Commission of the Supreme Court of Illinois in Relation to No. 39797, *People of the State of Illinois v. Theodore J. Isaacs*," State of Illinois Archives, pp. 53, 61.

34. Tom Merritt, letter to Everett M. Dirksen, March 29, 1969, EMDP.

35. Everett M. Dirksen, letter to Tom Merritt, April 7, 1969, EMDP.

36. Charles H. Percy, letter to Everett M. Dirksen, March 7, 1969, EMDP.

37. Dirksen, letter to Kleindienst, March 3, 1969, EMDP.

38. Mike Royko, "Bane target of bias charge," *Chicago Daily News*, May 28, 1969, p. 3.

39. Jacob M. Braude, letter to Charles H. Percy, April 17, 1969, EMDP.

40. Mike Royko, "Bane target of bias charge," *Chicago Daily News*, May 28, 1969, p. 3.

41. Bud Krogh, memo to Tod Hullin, July 28, 1969, White House Central Files, RNPL.

42. Bud Krogh, memo to Bill Hopkins, July 28, 1969, White House Central Files, RNPL.

43. William J. Bauer, interview with authors, Nov. 12, 2004.

44. Joseph A. Farrell, memo to Charles H. Percy, Oct. 27, 1969, CHPSP.

45. Robert S. Ingersoll, letter to Charles H. Percy, Oct. 6, 1969, Papers of Justin A. Stanley, Dartmouth College.

46. "Law Firm" contact list, 1962, CHPSP.

47. Justin A. Stanley, letter to Charles H. Percy, Dec. 3, 1969, Papers of Justin A. Stanley, Dartmouth College.

48. Ibid.

49. Justin A. Stanley, oral history interview with Philip N. Cronenwett, Papers of Justin A. Stanley, Dartmouth College, Sept. 20, 1990, p. 35.

50. Joseph A. Farrell, memo to Charles H. Percy, March 17, 1970, CHPSP.

51. Sara Evans Barker, interview with authors, May 24, 2006.

52. Edgar D. Jannotta, letter to Charles H. Percy, Feb. 14, 1969, CHPSP.

53. Charles H. Percy, letter to John Mitchell, Sept. 22, 1969, Papers of Ralph Tyler Smith, Abraham Lincoln Presidential Library.

54. Joseph A. Farrell, memo to Charles H. Percy, January 26, 1970, CHPSP.

55. Jack E. Walker, letter to Ralph T. Smith, Jan. 21, 1970, Papers of Ralph Tyler Smith, Abraham Lincoln Presidential Library.

56. Joseph A. Farrell, memo to Charles H. Percy, Feb. 3, 1970, CHPSP.

57. Ibid.

58. Edward I. Rothschild, interview with authors, Feb. 17, 2003.

59. Joseph A. Farrell, memo to Charles H. Percy, Feb. 3, 1970, CHPSP.

60. Robert E. Riggs and L. Cordell McCarrey, "Justice Stevens and the Law of Antitrust," *University of Pittsburgh Law Review*, Vol. 43, 1982, p. 651.

61. Charles H. Percy, oral history interview with Charles Stuart Kennedy, Association for Diplomatic Studies and Training, Foreign Affairs Oral History Project, June 11, 1998.

62. Manaster, *Illinois Justice*, p. 265.

63. Milton I. Shadur, interview with authors, Sept. 5, 2003.

64. Jeffrey Cole and Elaine E. Bucklo, "A Life Well Lived: An Interview with Justice John Paul Stevens," *Litigation*, Vol. 32, No. 3, Spring 2006, p. 11.

65. Charles H. Percy, oral history interview with Charles Stuart Kennedy, Association for Diplomatic Studies and Training, Foreign Affairs Oral History Project, June 11, 1998.

66. Robert Judd Sickels, *John Paul Stevens and the Constitution: The Search for Balance* (University Park, PA: Pennsylvania State University Press, 1988), p. 35.

67. Charles H. Percy, oral history interview with Charles Stuart Kennedy,

Association for Diplomatic Studies and Training, Foreign Affairs Oral History Project, June 11, 1998.

68. Manaster, *Illinois Justice,* p. 266.

69. John N. Mitchell, letter to Franklin B. Lincoln, March 27, 1970, White House Central Files, RNPL.

70. Thomas P. Ford, letter to Peter M. Flanigan, May 11, 1970, White House Central File, RNPL.

71. Peter M. Flanigan, letter to Thomas P. Ford, May 27, 1970, White House Central File, RNPL.

72. Charles H. Percy, letter to John N. Mitchell, June 23, 1970, White House Central Files, RNPL.

73. Judson H. Miner, interview with Barnhart, Jan. 27, 2006.

74. Ibid.

75. "Report of Proceedings: Hearing Held Before Subcommittee on Nominations of the Committee on the Judiciary, U.S. Senate," Oct. 1, 1970, White House Subject File, Supreme Court Appointments, GRFPL.

76. Joseph A. Farrell, memo to Charles H. Percy, April 20, 1970, CHPSP.

7—THE BENCH

1. JPS, speech to Rotary Club of Chicago, Oct. 6, 1973, Subject File: Supreme Court Appointments, GRFPL.

2. "The Oral History of Judge Luther M. Swygert as Told to Collins T. Fitzpatrick, Circuit Executive, and Ray Solomon, Director of the Court History Project, United States Court of Appeals for the Seventh Circuit," June 19, 1985, Tape 7, pp. 15–18. Courtesy of Collins T. Fitzpatrick.

3. Richard Phillips, e-mail to Barnhart, Feb. 2, 2007.

4. JPS, "The Education of a Judge," speech to Northwestern University School of Law, 1973, Subject File: Supreme Court Appointments, GRFPL.

5. JPS, memo to judges of U.S. Court of Appeals for the Seventh Circuit, Nov. 18, 1970, Thomas E. Fairchild Papers, archives of the Wisconsin Historical Society, Madison, WI.

6. Julius J. Hoffman, "Whom Are We Protecting? Some Thoughts on the Fifth Amendment," *American Bar Journal,* Vol. 40, July 1954, p. 584.

7. "Probe is Asked on Disruption in Courtroom," *Chicago Tribune,* Nov. 6, 1969, p. 2.

8. JPS, interview with Barnhart, March 6, 2007.

9. Ibid.

10. JPS, memo to Seventh Circuit judges, Fairchild Papers, Nov. 18, 1970, Thomas E. Fairchild Papers, archives of the Wisconsin Historical Society, Madison, WI.

11. JPS, speech at memorial ceremony for Luther M. Swygert, May 6, 1988, courtesy of Justice Stevens's chambers.

12. Collins T. Fitzpatrick, interview with Barnhart, March 2, 2007.

13. Abner J. Mikva, interview with Barnhart, Feb. 23, 2009.

14. Michael L. Shakman, transcript of oral history interview with Mark DePue, Feb. 14, 2008, Abraham Lincoln Presidential Library, Springfield, IL, p. 18.

15. Henry L. Pitts, letter to Kenneth A. Manaster, Aug. 13, 1999, quoted in Manaster, *Illinois Justice,* p. 27.

16. Ibid., p. 48.

17. Ibid.

18. Ibid.

19. Walter V. Schaefer, "Deposition in the Matter of Special Commission in Relation to No. 39797," June 25, 1969, pp. 96–97, 99. Courtesy of Kenneth A. Manaster.

20. Ibid., pp. 94–95.

21. "Report of Special Commission of the Supreme Court of Illinois in Relation to No. 39797, *People of the State of Illinois v. Theodore J. Isaacs,*" State of Illinois Archives, p. 16.

22. JPS, "Foreword," *Illinois Justice,* p. xii.

23. Gregory A. Adamski and Stephen B. Engelman, "Civil Rights and Civil Liberties," *Chicago-Kent Law Review*, Vol. 52, No. 2, 1975, p. 246.

24. Nixon White House Tapes, May 28, 1971, Conversation 506–3, Oval Office, RNPL.

25. Lesley Oelsner, "Opinions by Stevens Hint Attitudes of Nominee to Court," *The New York Times*, Dec. 8, 1975, p. 37.

26. JPS, "The Education of a Judge," speech to Northwestern University School of Law, 1973, Subject File: Supreme Court Appointments, GRFPL.

27. Ibid.

28. Frank. M. Coffin, *The Ways of a Judge: Reflections from the Federal Appellate Bench* (Boston: Houghton Mifflin Co., 1980), p. 59.

29. James S. Whitehead, interview with authors, Oct. 18, 2002.

30. Robert A. Garrett, interview with authors, Oct. 8, 2003.

31. H. Douglas Laycock, letter to Gerald R. Ford, Nov. 17, 1975, Subject File: Supreme Court Appointments, GRFPL.

32. Gary Senner, interview with authors, May 6, 2003.

33. Robert A. Garrett, interview with authors, Oct. 8, 2003.

34. Coffin, *The Ways of a Judge,* p. 196.

35. Gary Senner, interview with authors, May 6, 2003.

36. "Annotated News Summary," President's Office Files, October 1969, RNPL.

37. JPS, untitled speech to Chicago Bar Association and Chicago Bar Foundation, Oct. 16, 2001, courtesy of Justice Stevens's chambers.

38. JPS, interview with authors, Oct. 6, 2003.

39. JPS, letter to Wilbur F. Pell, June 28, 1978, Wilbur F. Pell, Jr., Collection, Law Library, Indiana University Maurer School of Law, Bloomington, IN.

40. JPS, letter to Daniel J. Boorstin, Nov. 2, 1979, Wilbur F. Pell, Jr., Collection, Law Library, Indiana University Maurer School of Law, Bloomington, IN.

41. Gary Senner, interview with authors, May 6, 2003.

42. JPS, speech to Chicago Bar Association and Chicago Bar Foundation, Oct. 16, 2001, courtesy of Justice Stevens's chambers.

43. Lawrence Rosenthal, interview with authors, April 18, 2003.

44. Brandon Becker and Michael F. Walsh, "The Interpenetration of Narrow Construction and Policy: Mr. Justice Stevens' Circuit Court Opinions," *San Diego Law Review*, Vol. 13, 1976, pp. 899–930.

45. Ibid., p. 904.

46. Ibid., pp. 923–24.

47. Audrey Colom and Lee Novick, letter to James O. Eastland, Dec. 8, 1975, Congressional Relations Office Files, Presidential Appointments, GRFPL.

48. James S. Whitehead, interview with authors, Oct. 18, 2002.

49. *Fitzgerald v. Porter Memorial Hospital*, 1975, Sprecher dissent draft, Robert A. Sprecher Papers, Northwestern University Library, Evanston, IL.

50. Marcia K. Sowles, interview with Barnhart, Feb. 9, 2007.

51. Linda A.M. Georgeson, interview with Barnhart, Feb. 12, 2007.

52. Kenneth Harmon, Barbara Moss, et al., "Special Project, The One Hundredth and First Justice: An Analysis of the Opinions of Justice John Paul Stevens, Sitting as a Judge on the Seventh Circuit Court of Appeals," *Vanderbilt Law Review*, Vol. 29, 1976, p. 145.

53. Brandon Becker and Michael F. Walsh, "The Interpenetration of Narrow Construction and Policy: Mr. Justice Stevens' Circuit Court Opinions," *San Diego Law Review*, Vol. 13, 1976, p. 928n171.

54. "Nomination of John Paul Stevens to be a Justice of the Supreme Court: Hearings Before the Committee of the Judiciary, United States Senate," Dec. 8, 9, 10, 1975, U.S. Government Printing Office, p. 34.

55. Ibid., p. 57.

56. Ibid.

57. "Biography of Justice John Paul Stevens," NARAL Pro-Choice America <http://www.ProChoiceAmerica.org>.

8—THE PRESIDENT

1. John Anthony Maltese, *The Selling of Supreme Court Nominees* (Baltimore: Johns Hopkins University Press, 1995), pp. 90–91.

2. "Nomination of John Paul Stevens to be a Justice of the Supreme Court: Hearings Before the Committee of the Judiciary, United States Senate," Dec. 8, 9, 10, 1975, U.S. Government Printing Office, p. 78.

3. Gerald R. Ford, interview with authors, Sept. 10, 2003.

4. Donald H. Rumsfeld, letter to authors, Oct. 26, 2004.

5. Gerald R. Ford, interview with authors, Sept. 10, 2003.

6. William E. Farrell, "For Top Legal Post: Edward Hirsch Levi," *The New York Times*, Jan. 15, 1975, p. 14.

7. Robert H. Bork, "Edward Levi," in *Remembering the University of Chicago: Teachers, Scientists and Scholars*, ed. by Edward Shils (Chicago: University of Chicago Press, 1991), p. 291.

8. Charles H. Percy, handwritten note, Feb. 3, 1969, CHPSP.

9. Donald H. Rumsfeld, speech at tribute to Milton Friedman, May 9, 2002, U.S. Department of Defense, public affairs.

10. Edward H. Levi, remarks at swearing-in ceremony, Feb. 7, 1975, *Congressional Record*, Senate.

11. Jack Fuller, interview with Barnhart, Dec. 2, 2003.

12. Jack Fuller, e-mail to Barnhart, April 12, 2009.

13. Ibid.

14. Warren E. Burger, letter to Gerald R. Ford, Nov. 10, 1975, Philip W. Buchen Files, GRFPL.

15. Edward H. Levi, memo to Gerald R. Ford, Nov. 10, 1975, Richard B. Cheney Files, GRFPL.

16. Douglas P. Bennett, memo to Richard B. Cheney, Nov. 17, 1975, Philip W. Buchen Files, GRFPL.

17. Victor H. Kramer, memo on interview with Edward H. Levi, May 24, 1989, Composite Oral History, GRFPL.

18. Levi memo to Ford, Nov. 10, 1975, Richard B. Cheney Files, GRFPL.

19. Victor H. Kramer, memo on interview with Edward H. Levi, May 24, 1989, Composite Oral History, GRFPL.

20. Victor H. Kramer, "The Case of Justice Stevens: How to Select, Nominate and Confirm a Justice of the United States Supreme Court," *Constitutional Commentary*, Vol. 7, 1990, p. 332.

21. Gerald R. Ford, handwritten notes, undated, Presidential Handwriting File, GRFPL.

22. Gerald R. Ford, interview with authors, Sept. 10, 2003.

23. Nicholas M. Horrock, "Ford Considers Woman for the Supreme Court," *The New York Times*, Nov. 13, 1975, p. 60.

24. Edward H. Levi, memo to Ford, Nov. 10, 1975, Richard B. Cheney Files, GRFPL.

25. Ibid.

26. Nixon White House Tapes, Oct. 25, 1971, Conversation 304–7, Oval Office, RNPL.

27. Arlin Adams, Legal Oral History Project, Biddle Law Library, University of Pennsylvania Law School, Philadelphia, PA, July 1, 1999, transcript, pp. 7, 10.

28. Victor H. Kramer, "Second Telephone Call from Edward Levi," Nov. 1, 1989, Composite Oral History, GRFPL.

29. Tom Mathews, "A Man in the Middle," *Newsweek*, Dec. 8, 1975, p. 23.

30. Charles H. Percy, *Congressional Record*, Senate, April 22, 1975, CHPSP.

31. Edward H. Levi, letter to Lewis F. Powell, Feb. 12, 1980, Edward H. Levi Papers, University of Chicago Library Special Collections.

32. Betty Ford, with Chris Chase, *The Times of My Life* (New York: Harper & Row, 1978), p. 232.

33. JPS, "Filling a Supreme Court Vacancy," speech to Gerald R. Ford Museum, Sept. 16, 1999, courtesy of Justice Stevens's chambers.

34. Edward C. Schmults, memo, "John Paul Stevens," Nov. 28, 1975, Kenneth Lazarus Files, GRFPL.

35. Sharon Baldwin, interview with authors, June 6, 2003.

36. JPS, "Filling a Supreme Court Vacancy," speech to Gerald R. Ford Museum, Sept. 16, 1999, courtesy of Justice Stevens's chambers.

37. Ibid.

38. "Checklist," Congressional Relations Office Files, GRFPL.

39. Max L. Friedersdorf, "Judge John Paul Stevens/Congressional Reaction," memo to Gerald R. Ford, Congressional Relations Office Files, GRFPL.

40. News Conference at the White House with Ron Nessen, Nov. 28, 1975, Office of the Counsel to the President Files, GRFPL.

41. William F. Buckley, "Ford's Nominee," *National Review*, Vol. XXVII, No. 49, Dec. 19, 1975, p. 1458.

42. George F. Will, "Hemmed In," *National Review*, Vol. XXVII, No. 49, Dec. 19, 1975, p. 1464.

43. "Good Choice for a Change," *The Nation*, Vol. 221, No. 20, Dec. 13, 1975, pp. 612–13.

44. Rowland Evans and Robert Novak, "The Reasoning Behind Stevens' Nomination," *The Washington Post*, Dec. 4, 1975, p. 19.

45. *Face the Nation*, CBS, Dec. 12, 1975, transcript, Edward H. Levi Papers, University of Chicago Library Special Collections.

46. "Conversation with the President by Selected Newsmen," Dec. 31, 1975, Office of the White House Press Secretary, transcript, Edward H. Levi Papers, University of Chicago Library Special Collections.

47. Gerald R. Ford, Reading Copies, Presidential Speeches, GRFPL.

48. Warren E. Burger, memo to Gerald R. Ford, Jan. 8, 1975, Presidential Handwriting File, GRFPL.

49. JPS, "Filling a Supreme Court Vacancy," speech to Gerald R. Ford Museum, Sept. 16, 1999, courtesy of Justice Stevens's chambers.

9—THE NEWCOMER

1. George A. Rutherglen, interview with Barnhart, April 21, 2009.

2. JPS, speech to Rotary Club of Chicago, Oct. 6, 1973, Subject File: Supreme Court Appointments, GRFPL.

3. Nellie A. Pitts, interview with authors, Sept. 15, 2004.

4. George A. Rutherglen, interview with Barnhart, April 21, 2009.

5. "An Interview with Supreme Court Justice John Paul Stevens," *The Third Branch*, Administrative Office of the U.S. Courts Office of Public Affairs, Vol. 39, No. 4, April 2007.

6. George A. Rutherglen, interview with Barnhart, April 21, 2009.

7. Nina Totenberg, interview with authors, Oct. 8, 2003.

8. "Gadfly to the Brethren," *Time*, July 21, 1980.

9. Dennis J. Hutchinson, interview with Barnhart, Jan. 26, 2004.

10. Bradley C. Canon, "Justice John Paul Stevens: The One Ranger in a Black Robe," Charles M. Lamb and Stephen C. Halpern, eds., *The Burger Court: Political and Judicial Profiles* (Urbana: University of Illinois Press, 1991), p. 346.

11. Ibid.; see JPS, "Some Thoughts on Judicial Restraint," speech to American Judicature Society, Aug. 6, 1982, *Judicature*, Vol. 66, No. 5, November 1982, pp. 177–83, and JPS, "Deciding When to Decide: The Docket and the Rule of Four," David M. O'Brien, *Judges on Judging: Views from the Bench*, second edition (Washington, D.C.: CQ Press, 2004), pp. 96–103.

12. JPS, remarks to attendees of dinner sponsored by the Illinois Special Events Commission, videotape by Illinois Information Service, 1976, Charles H. Percy Collection, Chicago History Museum.

13. JPS, speech to Illinois State Bar Association, Jan. 22, 1977, *Illinois Bar Journal*, April 1977, p. 508.

14. Kenneth A. Lazarus, letter to JPS, June 2, 1976; Betty Southard Murphy, letter to JPS, June 2, 1976; Charles H. Percy, letter to JPS, June 17, 1976, CHPSP.

15. Jonathan C. Carlson and Alan D. Smith, "The Emerging Constitutional Jurisprudence of Justice Stevens," *The University of Chicago Law Review*, Vol. 46, 1978, p. 206.

16. Russell W. Galloway, Jr., "The First Decade of the Burger Court: Conservative Dominance," *Santa Clara Law Review*, Vol. 21, 1981, pp. 916, 919.

17. William D. Popkin, "A Common Law Lawyer on the Supreme Court: The Opinions of Justice Stevens," *Duke Law Journal*, Vol. 1989, No. 5, November 1989, pp. 1088–89.

18. Leslie Bender, "The Powell-Stevens Debate on Federalism and Separation of Powers," *Hastings Constitutional Law Quarterly*, Vol. 15, Summer 1988, p. 585.

19. Justice Ruth Bader Ginsburg, interview with authors, May 28, 2999.

20. The Oyez Project, *Califano v. Goldfarb*, 1977, oral argument available at <http://oyez.org>.

21. John P. Wagner, "Justice Stevens and the Emerging Law of Sex Discrimination,"*Pepperdine Law Review*, Vol. 9, 1982, pp. 422, 424.

22. Ibid., p. 425.

23. Ibid., p. 386.

24. Carlson and Smith, "The Emerging Constitutional Jurisprudence of Justice Stevens," *The University of Chicago Law Review*, Vol. 46, 1978, p. 235.

25. Douglas William Ey, Jr., Charles C. Lamb III, Charles L. Schlumberger, D.J. Simonetti, James D. Spratt, Jr., and Joel Randall Tew, "Special Project: Justice Stevens, the First Three Terms," *Vanderbilt* [University] *Law Review*, Vol. 32, 1979, pp. 671–72.

26. *Planned Parenthood of Central Missouri v. Danforth* (1976) File, HABP.

27. *Thornburg v. American College of Obstetricians and Gynecologists* (1986) File, HABP.

28. Ibid.

29. Warren E. Burger, memo to "The Conference," May 4, 1976, *Gregg v. Georgia* File, Oct. 1975 Term, HABP.

30. John M. Ferren, *Salt of the Earth, Conscience of the Court: The Story of Wiley Rutledge* (Chapel Hill: University of North Carolina Press, 2004), p. 351.

31. JPS, memo to Wiley B. Rutledge, *Fook v. United States*, February 1948, WBRP.

32. JPS, "Filling a Supreme Court Vacancy," speech to Gerald R. Ford Museum, Sept. 16, 1999, courtesy of Justice Stevens's chambers.

33. "Nomination of John Paul Stevens to be a Justice of the Supreme Court: Hearings Before the Committee of the Judiciary, United States Senate," Dec. 8, 9, 10, 1975, U.S. Government Printing Office, pp. 26–28.

34. John C. Jefferies, Jr., *Justice Lewis F. Powell, Jr.: A Biography* (New York: Fordham University Press, 2001), pp. 426–27.

35. Ellen S. Kreitzberg, interview with authors, June 2, 2003.

36. James S. Liebman and Lawrence C. Marshall, "Less is Better: Justice Stevens and the Narrowed Death Penalty," *Fordham Law Review*, Vol. LXXIV, No. 4, March 2006, p. 1633.

37. *Report of the Commission on Capital Punishment,* April 2002, State of Illinois, p. 105.

38. Liebman and Marshall, "Less is Better: Justice Stevens and the Narrowed Death Penalty," *Fordham Law Review,* Vol. LXXIV, No. 4, March 2006, p. 1618.

39. Linda Greenhouse, "Justice Stevens Renounces Capital Punishment," *The New York Times,* April 18, 2008, p. A22.

10—THE JUSTICE

1. Katherine S. Jedlicka, interview with authors, March 24, 2003.

2. Susan R. Mullen, interview with authors, Oct. 7, 2003.

3. JPS, "Memorandum to the Conference," Nov. 14, 1979, HABP. 1979 Term, TMP.

4. "Milestones," *Time,* April 28, 1980.

5. Stanley L. Temko, interview with authors, Sept. 17, 2004.

6. Ibid.

7. Thomas E. Fairchild, memo "To All Members of the Court," Jan. 25, 1980, Robert A. Sprecher Papers, Northwestern University Library, Evanston, IL.

8. Wilbur F. Pell, Jr., letter to JPS, March 14, 1980, Wilbur F. Pell, Jr., Collection, Law Library, Indiana University Maurer School of Law, Bloomington, IN.

9. Terry Stephan, "A Justice for All," *Northwestern,* Vol. 11, No. 3, Spring 2009, p. 15.

10. Laura Krugman Ray, "Clerk and Justice: The Ties That Bind John Paul Stevens and Wiley B. Rutledge," *Connecticut Law Review,* Vol. 41, No. 1, November 2008, pp. 250, 251–52.

11. JPS, "Learning on the Job," *Fordham Law Review,* Vol. LXXIV, No. 4, March 2006, p. 1567.

12. The Green Bag <http://www.greenbag.org/bobbleheads/stevens>. Thanks to Dennis J. Hutchinson for donating one of the bobbleheads.

13. Harold J. Spaeth Supreme Court Database <www.cas.sc.edu/poli/juri/>, named after political science professor Harold J. Spaeth of Michigan State University and available through the University of South Carolina's Judicial Research Initiative. Data retrieval and analysis courtesy of Hemant Kumer Sharma of the University of Tennessee Political Science Department.

14. Nina Totenberg, interview with Barnhart, Aug. 19, 2003.

15. Theodore B. Olson. "Supreme Court Roundup, October 2003 Term," speech to the Federal Society, July 9, 2004, Washington, D.C.

16. Vincent Blasi, ed., *The Burger Court: The Counter-Revolution That Wasn't* (New Haven: Yale University Press, 1983), p. 252.

17. Nina Totenberg, interview with Barnhart, Aug. 13, 2003.

18. "The Statistics," *Harvard Law Review,* Vol. 122, No. 1, November 2008, pp. 516–29.

19. Ginsburg, interview with authors, May 28, 2009.

20. Ibid.

21. Edward Siskel, interview with authors, Oct. 8, 2007.

22. Kathy Moriarity, memo to Stephanie Dangel, Jan. 9, 1992, *Burson v. Freeman* File, HABP.

23. Linda Greenhouse, "Slim Margin: Moderates on Court Defy Predictions," *The New York Times*, July 5, 1992, Section 4, p. 1.

24. Linda Greenhouse, *Washington Week,* Public Broadcasting System, March 5, 2004.

25. JPS, "Memorandum to the Conference," Feb. 24, 1992, John Paul Stevens Files, HABP.

26. Lewis F. Powell, Jr., letter to JPS, Feb. 25, 1991, Lewis F. Powell, Jr., Papers, Washington and Lee School of Law, Lexington, VA.

27. Conference Notes, *Burson v. Freeman*, HABP.

28. Stephanie Dangel, memo to Harry A. Blackmun, March 24, 1992, *Burson v. Freeman* File, HABP.

29. Dangel, memo to Blackmun, April 29, 1992, *Burson v. Freeman* File, HABP.

30. Dangel, memo to Blackmun, Feb. 4, 1992; Dangel, memo to Blackmun, *Burson v. Freeman* File, April 16, 1992, HABP.

31. Dangel, memo to Blackmun, April 29, 1992, *Burson v. Freeman* File, HABP.

32. Dangel, memo to Blackmun, March 25, 1992, *Burson v. Freeman* File, HABP.

33. Blackmun, memo to JPS, Feb. 7, 1992, *Burson v. Freeman* File, HABP.

34. Blackmun, memo to Scalia, May 4, 1992, *Burson v. Freeman* File, HABP.

35. JPS, memo to Blackmun, March 25, 1992, *Burson v. Freeman* File, HABP.

36. Molly McCusic, memo to Harry A. Blackmun, Jan. 4, 1992, *Planned Parenthood v. Casey* File, HABP.

37. Ibid.

38. Tinsley E. Yarbrough, *David Hackett Souter: Traditional Republican on the Rehnquist Court* (New York: Oxford University Press, 2005), p. 258.

39. Dangel, memo to Harry A. Blackmun, June 16, 1992, *Planned Parenthood of Pennsylvania v. Casey* File, HABP.

40. Ibid.

41. Dangel, memo to Blackmun, June 8, 1992, *Planned Parenthood of Pennsylvania v. Casey* File, HABP.

42. Dangel, memo to Blackmun, June 16, 1992, *Planned Parenthood of Pennsylvania v. Casey* File, HABP.

43. Dangel, memo to Blackmun, June 21, 1992, *Planned Parenthood of Pennsylvania v. Casey* File, HABP.

44. Dangel, memo to Blackmun, June 18, 1992, *Planned Parenthood of Pennsylvania v. Casey* File, HABP.

45. JPS, memo to O'Connor, Kennedy, and Souter, June 3, 1992, *Planned Parenthood of Pennsylvania v. Casey* File, HABP.

46. Dangel, memo to Blackmun, July 1, 1992, *Planned Parenthood of Pennsylvania v. Casey* File, HABP.

47. Dangel, memo to Blackmun, June 26, 1992, *Planned Parenthood of Pennsylvania v. Casey* File, HABP.

48. Ibid.

49. Linda Greenhouse, "A Telling Court Opinion: The Ruling's Words Are About Abortion, But They Reveal Much About the Authors," *The New York Times*, July 1, 1992, Section A, p. 1.

50. *Legal Times*, Aug. 10, 1987 p. 15.

51. Philip B. Kurland, "Making and Remaking the Law of the Land," *The New York Times*, Sept. 20, 1987, Section 7, p. 3.

52. Robert H. Bork, interview with authors, Oct. 9, 2003.

53. Robert S. Alley, ed., *The Constitution and Religion: Leading Supreme Court Cases on Church and State* (Amherst, NY: Prometheus Books, 1999), p. 37.

54. Douglas Laycock, "Formal, Substantive and Disaggregated Neutrality Toward Religion," *DePaul Law Review*, Vol. 39, 1990, p. 1010.

55. Phyllis Schlafly, *The Supremacists: The Tyranny of Judges and How to Stop It* (Dallas: Spence Publishing Co., 2004), p. 22.

56. Robert F. Nagel, "Six Opinions by Mr. Justice Stevens: A New Methodology for Constitutional Cases?" *Chicago-Kent Law Review*, Vol. 78, No. 2, 2003, p. 528n87.

57. Ibid., p. 516.

58. Michael Stokes Paulsen, "Scouts, Families, and Schools," *Minnesota Law Review*, Vol. 85, 2001, p. 1917, quoted in Nagel, "Six Opinions by Mr. Justice Stevens: A New Methodology for Constitutional Cases?" *Chicago-Kent Law Review*, Vol. 78, No. 2, 2003.

59. Eduardo Moises Penalver, "Treating Religion as Speech: Justice Stevens's Religion Clause Jurisprudence," *Fordham Law Review*, Vol. LXXIV, No. 4, pp. 2241, 2256–57.

60. Douglas Laycock, e-mail to Barnhart, Oct. 22, 2005.

61. Douglas Laycock, "Theological Scholarships, The Pledge of Allegiance, and Religious Liberty: Avoiding the Extremes But Missing the Liberty," *Harvard Law Review*, Vol. 118, 2004, p. 202.

62. "Reaffirmation of the Position of the Boy Scouts of America on Duty to God," Boy Scouts of America National Executive Board, June 1991.

63. *Elk Grove Unified School District v. Newdow*, oral argument, March 24, 2004, Oyez Project <http://oyez.org>.

64. Ibid.

65. Timothy R. Johnson and Jerry Goldman, eds., *A Good Quarrel: America's Top Legal Reporters Share Stories from Inside the Supreme Court* (Ann Arbor: University of Michigan Press, 2009), p. 13.

66. Jacqueline L. Salmon, "Scalia Defends Public Expression of Faith; Recent Rulings Have Gone Too Far, Justice Says During Tribune to Va. Gathering," *The Washington Post*, Jan. 13, 2003, p. B3.

67. "Scalia Attacks Church-State Court Rulings," *The New York Times*, Jan. 13, 2003, Section A, p. 19.

11—THE INDEPENDENT JUSTICE

1. JPS, remarks at dedication ceremony for John Paul Stevens High School, San Antonio, TX, Sept. 27, 2005.

2. Sheryl Gay Stolberg and Elisabeth Bumiller, "Senate Confirms Roberts

as 17th Chief Justice," *The New York Times*, Sept. 30, 2005, p. 1.

3. JPS, "Filling a Supreme Court Vacancy," speech to Gerald R. Ford Museum, Sept. 16, 1999, courtesy of Justice Stevens's chambers.

4. Tony Mauro, interview with authors, May 29, 2009.

5. Ruth Bader Ginsburg, interview with authors, May 28, 2009. Emily Bazelon, "The Place of Women in the Court," *The New York Times*, July 7, 2009, Section MM, p. 22.

6. Steven R. Shapiro, quoted in "Supreme Court Citizenship Decision OKs Gender Discrimination, ACLU Says," June 11, 2001, ACLU press release <www.aclu.org>.

7. John T. Noonan, Jr., and Kenneth I. Winston, eds., *The Responsible Judge: Readings in Judicial Ethics* (Westport, CT: Praeger Publishers, 1993).

8. Courtesy of Senator Al Franken. Used by permission.

9. Howard Gillman, *The Votes That Counted: How the Court Decided the 2000 Presidential Election* (Chicago: University of Chicago Press, 2001), p. 150.

10. Jeffrey M. Jones, "Public Gives Supreme Court Passing Grade," Oct. 3, 2008 <http://www.gallup.com/poll>.

11. Steven G. Calabresi, "A Political Question," in Bruce Ackerman, ed., *Bush v. Gore: The Question of Legitimacy* (New Haven: Yale University Press, 2002), p. 143.

12. Nina Totenberg, interview with authors, Oct. 8, 2003.

13. Antonin Scalia and Bryan A. Garner, *Making Your Case: The Art of Persuading Judges* (St. Paul: Thomson/West, 2008), pp. 5–6.

14. Milton L. Rakove, *We Don't Want Nobody Nobody Sent: An Oral History of the Daley Years* (Bloomington: Indiana University Press, 1979), p. 318.

15. Lawrence Rosenthal, interview with authors, April 18, 2003.

16. Roger J. Traynor, quoted in Noonan and Winston, *The Responsible Judge,* p. 175.

17. Ruth Bader Ginsburg, interview with authors, May 28, 2009.

18. JPS, "Learning on the Job," *Fordham Law Review*, Vol. LXXIV, No. 4, March 2006, p. 1565.

19. JPS, speech to Sixth Circuit Judicial Conference, Lexington, KY, May 7, 2004.

20. Andrew M. Siegel, "Equal Protection Unmodified: Justice John Paul Stevens and the Case for Unmediated Constitutional Interpretation," *Fordham Law Review,* Vol. LXXIV, No. 4, March 2006, p. 2368.

Selected Bibliography

Abraham, Henry J. *The Judicial Process: An Introductory Analysis of the Courts of the United States, England, and France,* Seventh Edition. New York: Oxford University Press, 1998.

———. *Justices, Presidents and Senators: A History of the U.S. Supreme Court Appointments from Washington to Clinton.* Lanham, MD: Rowman & Littlefield Publishers, Inc., 1999.

Abrams, Roger I. *Legal Bases: Baseball and the Law.* Philadelphia: Temple University Press, 1998.

Ackerman, Bruce, ed. *Bush v. Gore: The Question of Legitimacy.* New Haven: Yale University Press, 2002.

Allegrini, Robert V., and Geraldine Hempel Davis. *Chicago's Grand Hotel: A History of the Hilton Chicago.* Lafayette, CO: Moonlight Publishing, 2002.

Alley, Robert S., ed. *The Constitution and Religion: Leading Supreme Court Cases on Church and State.* Amherst, NY: Prometheus Books, 1999.

Bickel, Alexander M. *The Least Dangerous Branch: The Supreme Court and the Bar of Politics,* Second Edition. New Haven: Yale University Press, 1962.

Biskupic, Joan. *Sandra Day O'Connor: How the First Woman on the Supreme Court Became Its Most Influential Justice.* New York: HarperCollins Publishers, 2005.

Blasi, Vincent, ed. *The Burger Court: The Counter-Revolution That Wasn't.* New Haven: Yale University Press, 1983.

Brisbin, Jr., Richard A. *Justice Antonin Scalia and the Conservative Revival.* Baltimore: Johns Hopkins University Press, 1997.

Carter, Linda E., Ellen S. Kreitzberg, and Scott H. Howe. *Understanding Capital Punishment Law,* Second Edition. Newark, NJ: Matthew Bender & Co./The LexisNexis Group, 2008.

Coffin, Frank M. *The Ways of a Judge: Reflections from the Federal Appellate Bench.* Boston: Houghton Mifflin Co., 1980.

Cohan, William D. *The Last Tycoons: The Secret History of Lazard Frères & Co.* New York: Doubleday, 2007.

Danelski, David J. *A Supreme Court Justice Is Appointed.* New York: Random House, 1964.

Dewey, John. *The School and Society,* edited by Jo Ann Boydston. Carbondale: Southern Illinois University Press, 1980.

Dunham, Allison, and Philip B. Kurland. *Mr. Justice.* Chicago: University of Chicago Press, 1956.

Dunne, Finley Peter. *Mr. Dooley's Opinions.* New York: R.H. Russell Publisher, 1901 (Kessinger Publishing reprint, 2004).

Dworkin, Ronald. *Law's Empire.* Portland, OR: Hart Publishing, 2007.

Dzuback, Mary Ann. *Robert M. Hutchins: Portrait of an Educator.* Chicago: University of Chicago Press, 1991.

Eisgruber, Christopher L. *The Next Justice: Repairing the Supreme Court Appointments Process*. Princeton, NJ: Princeton University Press, 2007.

Ferren, John M. *Salt of the Earth, Conscience of the Court: The Story of Justice Wiley Rutledge*. Chapel Hill: University of North Carolina Press, 2004.

Firestone, Bernard J., and Alexej Ugrinsky, eds. *Gerald R. Ford and the Politics of Post-Watergate America,* Volumes I and II. Westport, CT: Greenwood Press, 1993.

Ford, Gerald R. *A Time to Heal: The Autobiography of Gerald R. Ford*. New York: Harper & Row Publishers, 1979.

Gallagher, Elizabeth F., ed. "Symposium, The Jurisprudence of Justice Stevens," *Fordham Law Review* ,Vol. LXXIV, No. 4, March 2006, pp. 1557–2369.

Gillman, Howard. *The Votes That Counted: How the Court Decided the 2000 Presidential Election*. Chicago: University of Chicago Press, 2001.

Goldman, Sheldon. *Picking Federal Judges: Lower Court Selection from Roosevelt Through Reagan*. New Haven: Yale University Press, 1997.

Goldstein, Robert Justin. *Burning the Flag: The Great 1989–1990 American Flag Desecration Controversy*. Kent, OH: Kent State University Press, 1996.

Greenhouse, Linda. *Becoming Justice Blackmun: Harry Blackmun's Supreme Court Journey*. New York: Times Books, 2005.

Hair, Sam. *Castle Park*. Berkeley, CA: Creative Arts Book Co., 2000.

Hall, Kermit L., James W. Ely, Jr., and Joel B. Grossman, eds. *The Oxford Companion to the Supreme Court of the United States,* Second Edition. New York: Oxford University Press, 2005.

Hallwas, John E. *The Bootlegger: A Story of Small-Town America*. Urbana: University of Illinois Press, 1998.

Harms, William, and Ida DePencier, *Experiencing Education: 100 years of Learning at the University of Chicago Laboratory Schools*. The University of Chicago Laboratory Schools, 1996.

Hartley, Robert E. *Charles H. Percy: A Political Perspective*. Chicago: Rand McNally & Co., 1975.

Holmes, W.J. *Double-Edged Secrets: U.S. Naval Operations in the Pacific During World War II*. Annapolis: Naval Institute Press, 1979.

Hopkins, Mark E., ed. "Symposium: Perspectives on Justice John Paul Sevens," *Rutgers Law Journal*, Vol. 27, No. 3, Spring 1996, pp. 521–661.

Hutchinson, Dennis J. *The Man Who Once was Whizzer White: A Portrait of Justice Byron R. White*. New York: The Free Press, 1998.

Jacobsohn, Gary J. *Pragmatism, Statesmanship, and the Supreme Court*. Ithaca, NY: Cornell University Press, 1977.

Jeffries, Jr., John C. *Justice Lewis F. Powell, Jr.: A Biography*. New York: Fordham University Press, 2001.

Johnson, Timothy R., and Jerry Goldman, eds. *A Good Quarrel: America's Top Legal Reporters Share Stories from Inside the Supreme Court*. Ann Arbor: University of Michigan Press, 2009.

Johnston, Edward R. *Some Recollections of My More Than Seventy Years at the Illinois Bar*. Chicago: Jenner & Block, 1981.

Kahn, David, *The Codebreakers: The Comprehensive History of Secret Communications from Ancient Times to the Internet*. New York: Scribner, 1996.

Kallina, Jr., Edmund F. *Courthouse Over White House: Chicago and the Presidential Election of 1960*. Orlando: University Press of Florida, 1988.

Klarman, Michael J. *From Jim Crow to Civil Rights: The Supreme Court and the Struggle for Racial Equality*. New York: Oxford University Press, 2004.

Kluger, Richard. *Simple Justice: The History of Brown v. Board of Education and Black America's Struggle for Equality*. New York: Vintage Books, 2004.

Kogan, Herman. *The First Century: The Chicago Bar Association, 1874–1974*. Chicago: Rand McNally & Co., 1974.

Kovaleff, Theodore Philip. *Business and Government During the Eisenhower Administration: A Study of the Antitrust Policy of the Antitrust Division of the Justice Department*. Athens, OH: Ohio University Press, 1980.

Kuhn, Bowie. *Hardball: The Education of a Baseball Commissioner*. Lincoln, NE: University of Nebraska Press, 1987.

Lamb, Charles M., and Stephen C. Halpern, eds. *The Burger Court: Political and Judicial Profiles*. Urbana: University of Illinois Press, 1991.

Lash, Joseph P., ed. *From the Diaries of Felix Frankfurter*. New York: W.W. Norton & Co., Inc., 1975.

Layton, Edwin T. *"And I Was There": Pearl Harbor and Midway—Breaking the Secrets*. New York: William Morrow and Company, Inc., 1985.

Lazarus, Edward. *Closed Chambers: The Rise, Fall, and Future of the Modern Supreme Court*. New York: Penguin Books, 1999.

Levi, Edward H. *An Introduction to Legal Reasoning*. Chicago: University of Chicago Press, 1949.

Levy, Leonard W. *The Establishment Clause: Religion and the First Amendment, Second Edition, Revised*. Chapel Hill: University of North Carolina Press, 1994.

MacNeil, Neil. *Dirksen: Portrait of a Public Man*. New York: World Publishing Co., 1970.

Maltese, John Anthony. *The Selling of Supreme Court Nominees*. Baltimore: Johns Hopkins University Press, 1995.

Maltz, Earl M., ed. *Rehnquist Justice: Understanding the Court Dynamic*. Lawrence: University Press of Kansas, 2003.

Manaster, Kenneth A. *Illinois Justice: The Scandal of 1969 and the Rise of John Paul Stevens*. Chicago: University of Chicago Press, 2001.

Martin, Jay. *The Education of John Dewey: A Biography*. New York: Columbia University Press, 2002.

Martin, John Barlow. *Adlai Stevenson of Illinois*. New York: Doubleday & Co., 1976.

Masters, Edgar Lee. *Spoon River Anthology*. New York: The MacMillan Co., 1914.

McFarland, Ron, and Hugh Nichols. *Norman Maclean*. Lewiston, ID: Confluence Press, Inc., 1988.

McNeill, William H. *Hutchins University: A Memoir of the University of Chicago, 1929–1950*. Chicago: University of Chicago Press, 1991.

Menand, Louis. *The Metaphysical Club: A Story of Ideas in America*. New York: Farrar, Straus and Giroux, 2001.

Mettler, Suzanne. *Soldiers & Citizens: The G.I. Bill and the Making of the Greatest Generation*. New York: Oxford University Press, 2005.

Michelson, Herbert. *Charlie O: Charles Oscar Finley vs. the Baseball Establishment.* Indianapolis: Bobbs-Merrill Company, Inc., 1975.

Miller, Marvin. *A Whole Different Ball Game: The Inside Story of Baseball's New Deal.* New York: Simon & Schuster, A Fireside Book, 1991.

Murray, David. *Charles Percy of Illinois.* New York: Harper & Row Publishers, 1968.

Noonan, John T., Jr., and Kenneth I. Winston, eds. *The Responsible Judge: Readings in Judicial Ethics.* Westport, CT: Praeger Publishers, 1993.

O'Brien, David M., *Constitutional Law and Politics, Volume Two: Civil Rights and Civil Liberties,* Fourth Edition. New York: W.W. Norton & Co., 2000.

———. *Storm Center: The Supreme Court in American Politics*, Sixth Edition. New York: W.W. Norton & Co., 2003.

Palmer, Jan. *The Vinson Court Era: The Supreme Court's Conference Votes, Data and Analysis.* New York: AMS Press, 1990.

Perry, Barbara A. *The Priestly Tribe: The Supreme Court's Image in the American Mind.* Westport, CT: Praeger Publishers, 1999.

Persily, Nathanial, Jack Critin, and Patrick J. Egan, eds., *Public Opinion and Constitutional Controversy.* New York: Oxford University Press, 2008.

Rahl, James A., and Kurt Schwerin. *Northwestern University School of Law: A Short History.* Chicago: Northwestern University School of Law, 1960.

Ring, Kevin A., ed. *Scalia Dissents: Writings of the Supreme Court's Wittiest, Most Outspoken Justice.* Washington, D.C.: Regnery Publishing Inc., 2004.

Rutledge, Wiley B. *A Declaration of Legal Faith.* Clark, NJ: The Lawbook Exchange Ltd., 2004, reprint; originally published by University of Kansas Press, 1947.

Ryden, David K., ed. *The U.S. Supreme Court and the Electoral Process.* Washington, D.C.: Georgetown University Press, 2000.

Savage, David G. *Turning Right: The Making of the Rehnquist Supreme Court.* New York: John Wiley & Sons, Inc., 1992.

Scalia, Antonin, and Bryan A. Garner. *Making Your Case: The Art of Persuading Judges.* St. Paul: Thomson/West, 2008.

Schlafly, Phyllis. *The Supremacists: The Tyranny of Judges and How to Stop It.* Dallas: Spence Publishing Co., 2004.

Schwartz, Bernard. *The Ascent of Pragmatism: The Burger Court in Action.* Reading, MA: Addison-Wesley Publishing Co., 1990.

———. *Decision: How the Supreme Court Decides Cases.* New York: Oxford University Press, 1996.

———. *A History of the Supreme Court.* New York: Oxford University Press, 1993.

Segal, Jeffrey A., and Harold J. Spaeth. *The Supreme Court and the Attitudinal Model Revisited.* Cambridge: Cambridge University Press, 2002.

Sickels, Robert Judd. *John Paul Stevens and the Constitution: The Search for Balance.* University Park, PA: Pennsylvania State University Press, 1988.

Simon, James F. *The Center Holds: The Power Struggle Inside the Rehnquist Court.* New York: Simon & Schuster, 1995.

Solomon, Rayman L. *History of the Seventh Circuit, 1891–1941.* Washington, D.C.: U.S. Government Printing Office, 1981.

Toobin, Jeffrey. *The Nine: Inside the Secret World of the Supreme Court.* New York: Doubleday, 2007.

——. *Too Close to Call: The Thirty-Six-Day Battle to Decide the 2000 Election*. New York: Random House, 2002.

Tribe, Laurence H. *American Constitutional Law*, Third Edition, Volume One. New York: Foundation Press, 2000.

——. *God Save This Honorable Court: How the Choices of Supreme Court Justices Shape Our History*. New York: Random House, 1985.

Uroksky, Melvin I. *Division and Discord: The Supreme Court Under Stone and Vinson, 1941–1953*. Columbia, SC: University of South Carolina Press, 1997.

Vinson, Fred M., et al. "A Symposium to the Memory of Wiley B. Rutledge," *Iowa Law Review*, Vol. 35, No. 4, Summer 1950, pp. 541–699.

Warren, Earl. *The Memoirs of Earl Warren*. New York: Doubleday, 1977.

Watters, Mary. *Illinois in the Second World War: Volume II, The Production Front*. Springfield, IL: Illinois State Historical Society, 1952.

Wiecek, William M. *The Birth of the Modern Constitution: The United States Supreme Court, 1941–1953*. New York: Cambridge University Press, 2006.

Williams, Juan. *Thurgood Marshall: American Revolutionary*. New York: Three Rivers Press, 1998

Williamson, James R. *Federal Antitrust Policy During the Kennedy-Johnson Years*. Westport, CT: Greenwood Press, 1995.

Woodward, Bob, and Scott Armstrong. *The Brethren: Inside the Supreme Court*. New York: Avon Books, 1979.

Yalof, David Allistair. *Pursuit of Justices: Presidential Politics and the Selection of Supreme Court Nominees*. Chicago: University of Chicago Press, 1999.

Yarbrough, Tinsley E. *David Hackett Souter: Traditional Republican on the Rehnquist Court*. New York: Oxford University Press, 2005.

——. *Harry A. Blackmun: The Outsider Justice*. New York: Oxford University Press, 2008.

Index of Selected Cases

General Index

Walker, Jack E., 152
Warren, Earl, 13, 65, 227; Warren
  Court, 158, 198
Washington Post, The, 64, 69, 251
White, Byron R.: appointment to
  the Supreme Court, 163; capital
  punishment cases, 212, 218–19;
  Court alignment, 232, 238;
  Navy association with Stevens,
  96; photo, *122*; political speech
  case (*Burson v. Freeman*), 234,
  237; region cases, 246; Robert
  F. Kennedy's deputy attorney

general, 96; *Texas v. Johnson,* 16,
  19; Warren Court, 198
Whitehead, James S., 169, 177
Will, George, 195
Wirtz, W. Willard, 62–63, 68
Wrigley, Philip K., 92, 142, 143

Yale University, 7, 23, 37, 79; Law
  School, 38, 79
Yamamoto, Isoroku, 50

Zagorin, Perez, 39